Taming the Tourists

How Cardiff beat the All Blacks, Springboks and Wallabies

Alan Evans

Vertical Editions

First published in the United Kingdom in 2003 by Vertical Editions, 18-20 Blackwood Hall Lane, Luddendenfoot, Halifax HX2 6HD

Editor, Valerie Rice

ISBN 1-904091-06-7

Jacket design and typeset by HBA, York

Printed and bound by Biddles, Guildford

Contents

To my wife, Lyn, and children, Jonathan and Laura.
All of them, sooner or later, became rugby fans.

Acknowledgements

My first and biggest thanks must be extended to all the hundreds of players who have over the years established the enviable reputation of the Cardiff Rugby Football Club in the world of rugby. In particular, the series of matches with the All Blacks, Springboks and Wallabies have carried the club's name to the other side of the globe and, whatever the future holds, the residue of goodwill emanating from these will survive for many years yet.

This book has been the vehicle to put some structure into my previously fragmented knowledge and understanding of early matches in the series. For the immediate post-war years I am indebted to the help of Dr Jack Matthews and Bleddyn Williams who, as always, were generous with their time to share reminiscences and to point me in the direction of others among their contemporaries. As a result, it was fascinating to hear for the first time the views of people such as Billy Cleaver and the Irish international, Des O'Brien.

It is no coincidence in terms of the success of the club between, for instance, 1950 and 1990 that so many former players gave their service unstintingly to honorary committee work at the Arms Park. From many of them has come further fascinating anecdotes – some, admittedly, unprintable, but nevertheless enjoyable! Much of the tactical insights in the book have come from respected blue and blacks such as Dr CD Williams, Alun Priday, Howard Norris, Colin Howe, Lloyd Williams, John Evans and David Hayward.

The All Blacks' match of 1953 has thrown up a wealth of archive material which, I hope, has been put to good use in the pages that follow. A long afternoon spent with Geoff Beckingham gave me even more information on the personalities involved and the nuances of the team during that era. This was also an opportunity to consult again some notes I had taken when interviewing two other members of the 1953 team,

Rex Willis and John Nelson, in 1999. Sadly both of these fine men have passed away since then. My thanks go, too, to Mrs Jean Llewellyn, widow of the full back in 1953, John.

Several players from the 1970s and 1980s have helped with information and no research would have been complete without a consultation with the four-time club captain, John Scott. As anticipated, it was time well spent.

Three great matches were played between 1905 and 1908 and my analysis of the contribution of Percy Bush to them could not have been completed without the invaluable assistance of Ken Poole. Ken, a Cardiff player himself in the 1970s, has compiled an incredible archive of the life and times of Bush and one day, hopefully, his own biography of the great fly-half will appear.

For those pioneering days, I have also referred to several books. The club's first historian, C S Arthur, published *History and Statistics* in 1907 and it is far more than a dry tome of facts and figures having marvellous cameos on the players of the time. Further afield, the works of Gallaher and Stead for the 1905 All Blacks, Paddy Carolin (1907 Springboks) and Ivor Difford (1912 Springboks) were consulted. Peter Sharpham's recent volume, *The First Wallabies,* was another helpful source.

In the inter-war years the tours of the Second and Third All Blacks were well covered in the published diaries of Read Masters (1924) and Oliver and Tindill (1935) respectively. There was also good reason to turn to the post-war works of the Kiwi broadcaster, Winston McCarthy, and the ultimate wordsmith, Terry McLean. Overseeing the entire span of the matches were two histories by *The Western Mail's* former sports editor, John Billot – namely, *All Blacks in Wales* and its companion, *Springboks in Wales.*

I am indebted to the Huw Evans Picture Agency, the Western Mail and Echo and Ifor Davies of Print Partnership, Cardiff for supplying several of the photographs used in this book.

My particular thanks are extended to Karl Waddicor of Vertical Editions, who first approached me with the bones of a project that he felt should be 'something big on Cardiff Rugby Club'. It was my good fortune that his overture coincided with the eve of the fiftieth anniversary of the great match of 1953. The rest, as they say, is history.

Alan Evans, Cardiff, August 2003

Foreword by
Bleddyn Williams

The year 2003 is a special one for many people in Welsh rugby marking as it does the fiftieth anniversary year of when Cardiff and Wales beat that other great rugby nation, New Zealand. It was my great privilege to share in both those historic occasions and to be chosen as captain of my club and my country was a special honour that I will always treasure.

During every November since then, the players in the Cardiff team have gathered together for a quiet celebration to mark what was regarded as one of the greatest days in the club's proud history. On several occasions we have been joined by players from the All Blacks' team of 1953 and their presence has served as a reminder of the camaraderie that invariably flourishes through the great sport of rugby. The real story of the 1953 match and the others we played against overseas' teams is how new friends were made for life and that is what sport is all about. Sadly as the years have gone by our numbers have dwindled. At the present time seven of the Cardiff team survive but the contribution of our other eight team mates lives on in our conversation and reminiscences.

Beating the All Blacks was a real milestone for the Cardiff club because generations of fine players ever since the first match in 1905 had been endeavouring to beat the great sides they sent over to Wales. On a personal note, I have always had the highest respect for their players and traditions after first encountering them in the Kiwis' team that toured Britain in 1945. Then I saw what rugby meant to them at first hand when I toured as a British Lion in 1950. We never won a test match out there and I missed the first test that ended in a draw. So to play against them again at Cardiff Arms Park and beat them was something special.

The victory over the All Blacks was, however, only the latest in a series of famous triumphs over the formidable rugby countries from the southern hemisphere. The Springboks succumbed to the brilliance of Percy Bush's Cardiff team in 1907 and, the following year, Bush and his comrades repeated the feat against the Wallabies. That was a great era for the Cardiff club. After the Second World War we again had a succession of strong Cardiff teams. I relished the prospect of playing against the Wallaby and Springboks' teams of that period and again they were great occasions for the club. Whether playing in these matches or watching from the terraces and grandstands, every person involved in Cardiff Rugby Football Club had no doubt that the visit of the touring teams was a red letter day.

I am delighted that this book sets out to trace the long history of sporting contact between Cardiff and our counterparts from New Zealand, Australia and South Africa. It is a history that needs to be recorded and it does so very comprehensively. In reading it we are reminded not only of the matches but also of the many fine players and, indeed, good men who have helped to make Cardiff Rugby Football Club synonymous with all that is best in the world of rugby. One day, hopefully, the men in black, green or gold will play the blue and blacks again at Cardiff Arms Park. If not, the achievements of the past will live on. No one can take them away.

Bleddyn Williams
President, Cardiff Athletic Club
August 2003

Introduction

'We have got to try things…if we fail, we fail,
but we have got to be different.'

Bleddyn Williams' final words of advice before his Cardiff team left
the dressing room tucked away underneath the old north grandstand
of Cardiff Arms Park on 21 November 1953 had a resonance all of
their own. Less than an hour and a half later the same 15 players
returned exhausted to the same cramped room with their job done
and their place in the history of the club and the wider rugby world
beyond assured. They had indeed tried things, they had been
different – and they certainly hadn't failed. They had beaten the All
Blacks of New Zealand by eight points to three. For the next half-
century they would meet annually to spend quiet evenings reflecting
on the events of that grey winter's afternoon. They would invariably
toast absent friends who, as is the way with these things, gradually
outnumbered those still alive and in attendance as the years went by.
But they would never beat their chests in triumph at their famous
win. That was not their way of doing things. As Williams is the first to
admit himself, 'It was a great performance by the players involved in
the match and it was a famous win, but what was more important was
that it again confirmed the Cardiff club's place at the top table of the
game.'

Bleddyn Williams' philosophical, if not matter-of-fact, assessment
of the significance of the day is important. Even by 1953 the club had
already played the All Blacks, Springboks and Wallabies ten times
stretching back to the start of the century and these fixtures had
rarely had the billing of David versus Goliath encounters. Far from it.
Long before the heroics of Williams' team the mighty touring sides
from Australia and South Africa had been comprehensively beaten by
various generations of blue and black – but the wearers of the silver
fern were a bit different. The Springboks had power, the Wallabies

guile and the All Blacks a combination of both together with a lot more. As one or other of them arrived every three or four years they would test and invariably triumph, with rare slip-ups, against the greatest teams in the British Isles. Their visits to the local towns were occasions in themselves, especially for midweek games that were played in the afternoons and when schools and factories closed so that everyone could come to watch and admire these strangers from far-off lands.

The All Blacks had a special, almost indefinable aura about them. Though they had struggled in mighty test series against the frighteningly focused Springboks, they had the Indian sign over British teams. At home they had seen off successive Lions' teams, losing only once in 12 internationals in the process. When they came to Europe they were equally difficult to beat. When they weren't totally overwhelming their opponents they had a knack of always being able in the final analysis to wriggle out of the tightest of corners and escape with the most unlikely – and sometimes undeserved – of victories. As well as the internationals they had played 85 games against clubs, counties and regional sides the length and breadth of the British Isles and France and had been beaten only once, by Swansea in 1935. Cardiff, on the other hand, had played and lost three times against the All Blacks, the only consolation being a solitary success against some of their countrymen.

In the dim and distant past, there had been the forerunners of the All Blacks, the New Zealand Native Team, or Maoris, of 1888-89. In an incredible six-month odyssey that criss-crossed the British Isles several times they played 74 matches, including five in 10 days in South Wales over the Christmas period. They were by no means unbeatable, losing 20 of their matches, but that was hardly surprising as they sometimes played matches on three consecutive days. They arrived at Cardiff Arms Park on 29 December, barely 72 hours after they had comprehensively beaten Newport, then the power base of the Welsh clubs, by three tries to nil. Cardiff, however, was a club quickly establishing a reputation of its own. In the previous three seasons it had lost only eight games of the 82 played and now it would record a triumph over overseas visitors at the first attempt. In front of 12,000 spectators, a crowd big enough to pack the terraces of the emerging Arms Park, the club won the match by a goal and a try to a try. At the time a try was worth one point and a goal three, so the unfamiliar score-line read four points to one in favour of Cardiff.

Any false sense of achievement would be put in a different context 17 years later when for the first time a full New Zealand side arrived in Britain, again with a demanding itinerary of 35 matches. Dave Gallaher's legendary team were to lose just once, to Wales. The Cardiff club was in the midst of a golden era of its own. Yet even with great names like E Gwyn Nicholls, Rhys Gabe and Bert Winfield in its ranks and led by Percy Bush, it was to feel the full force and frustration of having victory snatched away from them by the New Zealanders. The pattern was set. Twice more, in 1924 and 1935, the All Blacks would play Cardiff and, in all truth, won the games with increasing ease.

Meanwhile, the Springboks and Wallabies sent their strongest teams to these shores. Unlike what was to emerge in the 1970s and 1980s, when they arrived with increasing and unnecessary regularity, and a degree of mystery and magic was forfeited, these tours were few and far between and as such eagerly anticipated as major events on the sporting calendar. The visits invariably meant 30 or more matches and, like the All Blacks, the Springboks were particularly hard to beat – they lost only seven times in 113 games between 1907 and 1952, but one of those defeats was at the Arms Park against Cardiff. And the club had been even more successful against the Wallabies, with a 100 per cent record in the two matches played by 1953 – and further success was to follow.

A second Golden Era was to develop in the seasons after the Second World War. Young men deprived of official matches for half-a-dozen years, which in many cases coincided with a period when they were probably in their prime, seized the belated opportunity to play first-class rugby – and a degree of excellence often followed. Nowhere was this more evident than at Cardiff Arms Park.

Cardiff's first post-war captain in 1945 was Dr Jack Matthews, and he was succeeded in turn by Haydn Tanner, Bleddyn Williams, Bill Tamplin, Rex Willis and Sid Judd, all international players in their own right. The teams they led over the years contained many other great names like Billy Cleaver, Frank Trott, Cliff Davies, Les Manfield, Gwyn Evans, Cliff Morgan, Gareth Griffiths and countless more. These were men of ability and of ambition. And one ambition shone above all others. Imbued with a sense of history (and of the club's history in particular) that was typical of their generation, they desperately wanted to continue a great tradition and play against and hopefully beat an international touring team from the southern hemisphere. As luck would have it, between 1947 and 1953 all three major powers from the other side of the world toured the British Isles – and their fixtures against the club team of Cardiff were universally regarded as the keynote games outside the test matches. They attracted massive coverage in the national as well as local newspapers of the pre-television age.

Each game, against the Wallabies in 1947, the Springboks four years later and the All Blacks of 1953 was important in its own right. What had gone before, and the several other great days that would follow when the club would take the field against the touring teams, must not be forgotten. The benchmark match, however, was that of 1953 – and the build-up to that arguably began way back in 1905.

PART ONE

NEW ZEALAND

1

Percy Bush and the Rampageous Aggressors

The Cardiff club first locked horns with the full might of a New Zealand rugby team on Boxing Day, 1905, and the match could not have been staged at a better time. The original All Blacks were the stuff of legend, a mighty team led by a strict disciplinarian, Dave Gallaher. They had recorded 27 straight victories – and 22 of their opponents had failed to score any points at all against them – before they had gone down to a famous defeat by Wales through Teddy Morgan's historic try. Now, 10 days later, they were returning to Cardiff Arms Park to play a club side that was itself developing a formidable reputation in the British game. Cardiff were unbeaten in 12 matches so far that season but this was only the beginning of what was to become the first Golden Era in the club's history. Over the course of 125 matches between September 1905 and April 1909 the team would lose only 11 times, a formidable achievement by any standard. The fixture list in these years was the strongest imaginable, with Newport and Swansea, already powers in the land, played four times a season. The Barbarians came twice every year at Easter and Christmas while the English rugby strongholds of Leicester, Blackheath, Bristol, Gloucester and the universities of Oxford and Cambridge comprised more than half the opposition in any one season. In 1905, however, it was clear that the real yardstick to the club's true position in the rugby hierarchy would be a match against the All Blacks.

It was a challenge that the club must have relished. Within the team of that era there were charismatic personalities and great players in abundance. Five of them had already played for Wales and another five would follow them in the next two or three years. Two of the already established stars, Gwyn Nicholls and Bert Winfield, had led the side in six of the previous seven seasons and in September 1905 the role had been taken over by Percy Bush. Here was the archetypal Welsh fly-half, mercurial and unpredictable, but always a potential match-winner. Years later one of the first historians of the game, WJ Townsend Collins, concluded, 'Percy Bush was a most daring and elusive runner, a wonderful kick, a little over-confident, a little variable, but on his day second to none.'

In some quarters Bush's appointment in succession to Cecil Biggs, one of a family of six brothers that served the club well over a period of 10 years, may have raised a few eyebrows, but he had served a long, and indeed unusual, apprenticeship. Bush, too, had family connections with the club. His brother Fred had fleetingly played at Cardiff at the turn of the century. Percy had made his first-class debut at the Arms Park at the age of 20, playing on the wing against Newport on 25 November 1899. He made a good enough impression to play a dozen times that season but over the next couple of years his appearances in blue and black were infrequent, merely 10 games between September 1900 and April 1902. This was partly due to an injury that sidelined him for the second half of the 1901-02 season but he was also training to be a schoolteacher and there seems every likelihood that he played at least occasionally for University College, Cardiff. What is more certain is that he followed Fred up to Penygraig, a hotbed of competitive rugby in the valleys at the time.

This was in no way surprising for the matches in the Glamorgan League were as keenly fought as any involving the big towns like Cardiff, Swansea, Llanelli and Newport against their rivals from across the Severn. The valley clubs also produced a galaxy of international players: the back row of the Wales pack that comprehensively beat Ireland at Lansdowne Road, Dublin in 1902 was made up of Harry Jones of Penygraig, Will Osborne of Mountain Ash, and Treherbert's Dai 'Tarw' Jones. So for a couple of years the Bush brothers played alongside each other in the Penygraig back division where they needed all their wiles to break down the opposition markers of teams such as Treherbert and Llwynypia. The star man in the latter club was undoubtedly Willie Llewellyn, the lightning-fast wing who marked his international debut against England in 1899 with four tries. The clubs were not confined to intense, tribal contests as the local newspaper, *The Rhondda Leader*, notes that Penygraig opened their 1900-01 season with a visit from the Dublin club, Old Wesley.

By the autumn of 1902, however, Percy Bush had returned to Cardiff to play and work. He was teaching at a local school and he cemented his place at the rugby club with 11 tries in 20 appearances. At this stage he was still being picked to play in the three-quarters, usually out on the wing, rather than his favoured pivot position. This would have been no great hardship for the back line alongside him included, as well as Nicholls, another star, 22-year-old Rhys Gabe. The centre combination of these two came to be regarded as nothing short of brilliant while behind them in the last line of defence Bert Winfield was a great full back. Townsend Collins also paid tribute to 'The most scientific kicker Wales ever had at full back.' Even Willie Llewellyn played one game for the club in the away match at Oxford University. It was not unusual for even the top players to make 'guest' appearances. Gabe is another example, dividing his playing time in some seasons between Cardiff and Llanelli.

Yet it was still a stuttering season for the club, losing 12 of the 32 matches played and giving little indication of the great days that lay just around the corner. The turning point for both the team and several individuals within it came midway through the following year. The omens had not been auspicious with the side losing three of the first 11 games and Bush did not appear at all until the Christmas period. But when he did – on Christmas Eve 1903 against London Welsh at the Arms Park – it was to be a key moment in his career. At last he was chosen in the outside-half position and his partner at half-back was the young window cleaner from Canton, Dickie David. Cardiff won the game 23-5, with Bush scoring a try and dropping a goal. It was a notable win but there was even better to follow 48 hours later against the Barbarians. The club fielded the same back division – Winfield at full back, Nicholls and Gabe at centre, Cecil Biggs and the Scottish international, Dr Alec Timms, on the wings, and Bush alongside David at half-back. The previous Easter the Baa-Baas had won by 10 points to 4; this time they were overwhelmed by 41 points to 3. Bush and Gabe both scored a brace of tries but Nicholls went one better with a hat-trick. It was arguably the day when the club's Golden Era began. It was certainly the moment when some notable careers took shape.

Dickie David was to play in all remaining 18 fixtures of the season and Bush missed only three of them. It was a pattern repeated over the next four years with David, remarkably, being virtually ever-present – in 1904-05 he played in 29 of the 30 fixtures – and Bush's contribution only interrupted by his many other commitments. As with all distinguished half-back pairings in the Principality their strengths and weaknesses were endlessly debated. When Bush eventually won his first caps for Wales David was left to kick his heels in club rugby as the national berth had long since been claimed by Swansea's Dicky Owen. The latter's 35 internationals were to put him at the top of the all-time cap-winner's list for the next 50 years but his partnership with Bush did not receive universal approval.

No less an authority than Gwyn Nicholls had strong views on the subject. Writing in his mainly instructional book, *The Modern Rugby Game – and how to play it,* in 1908, Nicholls could hardly be accused of sitting on the fence:

'I may quote the conjunction of [Dickie] Owen with Bush of Cardiff. These two, in their respective positions, are absolutely unequalled at the present time, and yet when paired are, comparatively speaking mind, dire failures. Comparatively speaking mind, only – the men being so exceptionally good in themselves that they could not by any possibility be *actually* dire failures in conjunction.

Somehow or other they do not seem to fit. Owen's style of passing does not suit Bush's style of taking the ball, and the former fails to accurately anticipate the position which Bush instinctively takes up. Their telepathic communication, in short, is somewhat defective.

On the other hand, if [Dickie] David and Bush are put together behind the scrum, what better arrangement could be desired? Both work together like parts of a machine, and each anticipates the other's movements to a nicety.'

Nicholls was well placed to reach these conclusions. Steadily, if that is the right word, through the second half of the 1903-04 club season the Bush-David influence grew. Though mighty Swansea were still too strong for Nicholls' developing team, and two matches with Newport were drawn, there were notable wins over the Barbarians again and there was a rare double over Llanelli. The club's first historian was Charley Arthur. A considerable player himself, he had won three caps for Wales, captained the club and was its long-serving honorary secretary. He witnessed the 8-5 victory at Stradey Park in January 1904 when Cardiff played half the game without the injured Nicholls and was suitably impressed:

> 'Our chance of ultimate success was not bright, and as the second half progressed Llanelli played with irresistible dash, and obtained the lead by one goal to one try. This lead they looked like adding to as they made continuous onslaughts on our line; but about three or four minutes before the call of time we got a little over half-way, when Percy Bush got hold of the ball and made a wonderfully clever run, dodging several Llanelli men in extraordinary fashion and scoring a try wide out which Winfield converted into a goal. There never was a match which was pulled out of the fire with more dramatic suddenness, as all the Cardiff supporters had abandoned any hope of winning the game.'

Clearly the form of Percy Bush was making critics sit up and take notice and further plaudits came his way over the Easter period. Cardiff beat the Barbarians on the Saturday and four days later one of the highlights of the domestic season was the East v West match at the Arms Park. A crowd of 20,000 saw Bush, Gabe and Nicholls, who was again to leave the field injured, steer their side to a big win. But the representative spotlight was to beam even brighter on Bush and Gabe in the weeks ahead. A British Isles rugby team was about to tour Australia and, for the first time, the eyes of New Zealand and the eyes of the selectors were drawn towards the resurgence of the game in Wales. When an earlier squad had toured Australia in 1899 Gwyn Nicholls had been the sole Welsh representative – although the Cardiff-based doctor, Alec Timms, had also won selection. It was no better four years later when Newport's Reg Skrimshire was the only player from west of the Severn. By 1904, however, the dominating influences of British rugby were shifting. Wales were unbeaten in seven games against England and their back play was the envy of the home nations. Nicholls, due to his burgeoning business activities, declared himself unavailable for a second trip to the Antipodes – but there were plenty of other Welsh backs ready to fill the void.

As it happens the international matches of 1904 had not been particularly successful for Wales. A draw against England at Leicester was followed by a big win over the eventual champions Scotland at Swansea and then a 12-14 defeat in Belfast. But it was a time in which selection for a British tour depended on availability as much as ability. The Welsh stars, particularly the backs, were generally professional men who could afford to be away for up to six months. Thus, Rhys Gabe, Willie Llewellyn, Dr Teddy Morgan and Swansea's Fred Jowett qualified for the tour on both counts. The incumbent half-backs in the Wales team, on the other hand, simply could not afford to be away from their jobs for any length of time: Dicky Owen was a steelworker and his Swansea clubmate, Dick Jones, was a stonemason. But the British selectors stayed in Wales for their replacements. Newport's Tommy Vile was given the nod at scrum-half – and Percy Bush filled the void at fly-half. Both had yet to play for their country but, particularly in Bush's case, it was to prove an inspired choice.

For Bush the tour was a triumph from first to last. Off the field he was the life and soul of the party; on it he was the spark that lit a brilliant back division. A personal contribution of a record-breaking 100 points tells only half the story. The British team won all 14 matches on the Australian leg of the tour and Bush dominated the three test matches. In the first at Sydney Cricket Ground the match was a stalemate until well into the second half. Then Bush combined with Rhys Gabe to score a try and moments later dropped a goal, then worth four points. That opened the floodgates and Willie Llewellyn added two late tries for a 17-0 win. The second test in Brisbane three weeks later followed a similar pattern and Australia was leading into the second period. Cue for the brilliance of Bush, as noted in *Wallaby Gold*, a volume celebrating 100 years of Australian test rugby:

'… the second half, with British five-eighth Bush dominating, was a repeat of the first test. Bush, from Cardiff, dashed to the blind-side from a scrum, beat Redwood and Verge, and touched down to level the scores. Almost from the resumption,

Bush landed a towering field [drop] goal from near halfway. He added a further four points when Morgan marked from a kick and handed it to the Welshman for an attempt at goal, as the laws of the day allowed.'

Another victory in the third test back in Sydney was a formality but the story was very different when the side moved on to New Zealand. Only two of the four warm-up matches were won and the test match in Wellington was lost 3-9. Yet Bush still made his mark. His elusive skills worried the New Zealanders and were to be a factor when Wales plotted the epic victory over the All Blacks the following year. An eye witness in Wellington reported in *The New Zealand Times:*

'It was a struggle between the New Zealand forwards … and tricky British backs and one man stood out in strong relief – the little Welshman, P Bush. Whenever the ball reached him in the second spell there would be a rush of New Zealand forwards to fall upon him lest he might, by his lightning drop-kicks, turn his side's probable defeat into victory.'

So Percy Bush and his team mates had seen at first hand the power of the All Blacks. A little over a year later the All Blacks would arrive in Cardiff for the ultimate test of his club's strength. It was Rhys Gabe who reflected on what the great tour of 1905-06 would mean for the game in the British Isles:

'People in this country could have no conception of the expertness, the artistry and the enthusiasm of this 1905 side before they arrived; but we who had the experience of playing against these well-trained and rampageous aggressors, knew full well what to expect.'

The Cardiff team, at least, would be more aware than most of what lay ahead. As well as their British team tourists, Bush and Gabe, others had some experience of playing against the visitors. Johnnie Williams, Reggie Gibbs, and the forwards Jack Powell and Dai Westacott had played for a Glamorgan County side against the All Blacks at Swansea five days earlier. In addition, of course, Bert

Winfield, Nicholls, Gabe and Bush had all been part of the star-studded Wales team that had secured the historic victory on 16 December. Their presence, in itself, would only serve to make the All Blacks hungry for revenge.

Cardiff's hand was further strengthened by the settled nature of the side. There had been some uncertainty about Nicholls' intentions. He was now 31 years of age, newly married and continuing to build a successful business with Winfield: the Victoria Hygienic Laundry. But it was not unusual for the great centre to flirt with retirement. In the previous season he had not played rugby until the turn of the year and thereafter appeared only six times in club colours. The pattern was to some degree repeated in this great campaign of 1905-06. His first appearance came against Blackheath on 9 December, suitably marking the occasion by scoring one of Cardiff's six tries, but his form and his reputation were good enough to guarantee an immediate summons to the national cause. His appetite was now whetted for his club to emulate the achievement of his country against the world champions.

Around him were men of experience. His business partner Bert Winfield had himself led the club for two years between 1901 and 1903 and had already won the first five of his 15 international caps. Tragically, the full back, who was also qualified to play for England, was killed in 1919 when the motor bike he was riding hit a farm gate that was obstructing a country lane. In the three-quarter line Nicholls was joined by Rhys Gabe and the wings, Johnnie Williams and Ralph Thomas. Gabe was one of the most gifted sportsmen of his generation for as well as his 24 caps for Wales and four tests for the 1904 British team, he was a considerable cricketer, racing cyclist and water polo player. He scored 12 tries in international rugby and 51 in 115 games for Cardiff but this impressive strike rate paled into insignificance alongside the prolific Williams.

John Lewis Williams, a native of Whitchurch in the city, was only 23 at the time of the All Blacks match and did not win his first international cap until the following season. When he did, however, he was a roaring success, scoring 17 tries in 17 matches, including two hat-tricks, and toured New Zealand with the 1908 British team. Like Winfield he was to die tragically young, killed in the Battle of the Somme at the age of 33.

Bush and David, of course, were the half-backs but that did not complete the line-up behind the pack. Cardiff selected an extra back, or 'rover', to counteract a controversial tactic employed by the All Blacks throughout their tour. This was the role adopted by their captain, Dave Gallaher. Originally a front row forward for his province, Auckland, he had developed the idea of a 'wing forward' for his side, literally someone who was only loosely part of the pack and would fly around the field in pursuit of the ball. That was fine as far as it went – but there was an added advantage to his side. By also feeding the ball into the scrummages and then letting the official scrum-half pick up the quick heel at the back he was proving to be a very effective obstacle to any opponent wishing to get near to the ball. Basically it meant that his team had two scrum-halves. This was also at a time when there was often no specialisation among the forwards in rugby union, regardless of whether there were seven or eight of them in a pack. As the individuals arrived at scrums or line-outs they merely formed up and waited for the ball to be either fed into a scrum or thrown into a line-out.

British players had first encountered Gallaher's strategy on the tour to New Zealand in 1904 and now it was continued by the visiting All Blacks. This had caused great consternation during the early matches of the tour. Rhys Gabe had seen the opening fixture against Devon in Exeter and he reported:

'The forward formation of 2-3-2 in itself was surprising enough, but when the front two took up position on each side of the flank forward of Devon's front rank, the home forwards were absolutely nonplussed with this frustration. The ball, put in the scrum by Gallaher, the wing forward, was out to Roberts [the scrum-half] before the home forwards had been able to form up.'

The British critics soon concluded that Gallaher was an arch-obstructionist but the referees failed to come to any firm decision or interpretation as to the legality of Gallaher's contribution. Ironically, only in one game on the English leg of the tour, against Surrey at Richmond, did a referee penalise the ploy – and Gallaher wasn't playing, his place being taken by George Gillett. That Gillett was normally a full-back – and, indeed, played in that position in three of the five test matches – is further proof of the lack of positional specialisation. When Gallaher combined with his fellow All Black, Billy Stead, to write their seminal work, *The Complete Rugby Footballer*, at the end of the tour, his blood was obviously still boiling. They observed:

'… the referee completely upset all our plans by penalising us every time we hooked the ball. The result was that we had to let our opponents have it so we might play the forward game against them and in this way we won by 11 points to nil … Six free kicks were awarded to Surrey in the first 20 minutes, and the explanation which the referee is alleged to have given – that we were not playing the game, and that our hookers were handling the ball out of the scrum, screened by their bent knees – was preposterous.'

Clearly scrum skulduggery was in its infancy – Cardiff's own Geoff Beckingham was to offer a far more sophisticated trick against a future generation of All Blacks half a century later – but the reference to *hookers* rather than a hooker is interesting. The full England side when they played the international against New Zealand at Crystal Palace did at least attempt to employ an extra back opposite Gallaher but the tactic was unfamiliar and, inevitably, unsuccessful against a player so well versed in the art. It would be a different story when the All Blacks reached Wales for the final four matches of the tour. The match programme for the international match at Cardiff Arms Park noted of Gallaher:

'The wing forward whose methods have caused so much heated discussion in the rugby world. A powerful forward, and the best winger in the team [sic]; a fiery free-lance, whose dart on to the opposing half-back is sudden and unerring, and whose grip is uncertain.'

Wales' answer was to select Pontypool's Cliff Pritchard as the 'extra back', not only as a counter-balance to Gallaher but also as a perfect decoy to the wiles of Percy Bush. The tactic worked famously in the build-up to Teddy Morgan's match-winning and legend-launching try that won the game. Next up for the tourists was the match with Glamorgan at Swansea – and the selectors turned to Cardiff's Reggie Gibbs to take up where Pritchard had left off. There was no repeat victory but Glamorgan's backs, with Johnnie Williams also in their number, embarrassed the All Blacks several times before the match was lost. Cardiff had seen enough to repeat the experiment with Reggie Gibbs when the great day dawned on 26 December, 1905.

Reggie Gibbs was another of the club's stars in the making. He had made his first team debut in September 1901 at the tender age of 19 but had hardly been seen for the next four years. Another all-rounder, he had also played county cricket for Glamorgan, was a dab hand at billiards and in his working life established a prosperous position as a ship owner. For him the 1905-06 rugby season was to be a portent of even greater things to come. During the campaign he scored 10 tries in only 12 games, was awarded his club cap for his efforts, and on 3 February 1906 he played his first international for Wales against Scotland at Cardiff Arms Park. Like his club colleague Johnnie Williams, Gibbs was a prolific try-scorer with 17 in 16 games for Wales and 90 in 130 club matches for Cardiff. He had played brilliantly in the Glamorgan match and now would be a valuable weapon in the club's armoury as the preparations for the All Blacks match proceeded.

The plans were upset in one sense when one of the cornerstones of the pack, Dai Westacott, was declared unfit to play. He had already locked horns with the All Blacks in the Glamorgan match but had injured his shoulder 48 hours later in a club game against London Welsh – there was never any question of players being 'rested' in 1905. So the onus up front fell on the sole international player left, Billy Neill, and six others.

Neill was a fascinating character. Though born and bred in Cardiff, where he was a crane driver in the docks, he was of Irish extraction and the family name was 'O'Neill'. Thinking that his Irish surname would not help his cause with the Welsh selectors, the young Billy anglicised it – and he went on to win 11 caps. Before arriving at the Arms Park he had given great service to the local St Peter's club. Eventually, like so many of his unskilled contemporaries, he signed professional forms for Warrington from where he also won international rugby league caps.

Neill was the ideal hard man to face up to the All Blacks and with him in the pack were two coal-trimmers, John Alf Brown and Jack Powell, the experienced vice-captain, George Northmore, the policeman Fred Smith, and, at the back, Llew George and Ernie Rumbelow. They were under no illusions that, if the gifted backs were to stretch the tourists, they simply had to deliver the ball to them.

The build-up to the big game went as well as could be expected. Despite the early season worries of Charley Arthur – '... at the beginning the three-quarter line was somewhat unsettled ... and the opening matches did not give promise of the best season on record being in store for our club' – the team had remained unbeaten. The return to regular action of Gwyn Nicholls had also been a huge fillip. Among the scalps before Christmas were Newport, beaten home and away, and more significantly Swansea, a club that Cardiff had beaten only once in the previous 19 meetings.

As Boxing Day dawned the showdown with the All Blacks attracted a terrific level of interest. Arthur reported:

> 'A far greater number of persons witnessed the match than has ever before been drawn to see a club game in Wales, and the gate [money] came to £1,862 odd. This one gate alone was more than the total gate receipts of any season prior to 1892-93, and it is worthy of record that all our members, ground and workmen's ticket holders, entered free of charge, and that the whole of the grandstand was reserved free of charge to our members and lady's ticket holders; for no other match has the grandstand been reserved for members, and they have had to take their chance of a seat with the paying public.'

The match was obviously a special occasion and the chief rugby reporter of the age, WJ Hoare of *The Western Mail*, who always wrote under the by-line of 'Old Stager', began his eye-witness account by noting that the 'excitement [was] so intense that one imagined it was the international battle all over again'.

The teams had taken the field to the strains of *Men of Harlech* played by the Tongwynlais Brass Band and Hoare continued his report in a way that just about managed to balance admiration for his countrymen with a veiled criticism of the opposition:

> 'Gallaher, far from being made the subject of hostile applause and 'barracking' as some of the London specials inaccurately announced in the Welsh match, was cheered as he led his men on. A Welsh football crowd is in the main composed of men able to follow every phase of skilled play in the game, and while it is able to recognise offences against the laws by the New Zealand captain, it is none the less appreciative of the skill of the wing forward when he confines himself to legitimate play.'

Talk about a barbed compliment! So the game was underway from George Northmore's kick-off – and kicking of the ball was the order of the day in the early stages as both sides settled. Gallaher was penalised for offside at the first scrum and that must have given the All Blacks food for thought. The referee, Gil Evans, was one of their favoured officials. They wrongly thought he was English, as he lived in Birmingham. In fact he was from Swansea originally, though that in no way suggests he was anything other than impartial. The tour management had unsuccessfully attempted to have Mr Evans, who had refereed the international game with England, brought in for the Glamorgan match at Swansea in preference to the named Welsh-based official. Whatever their reasons for making an issue of the appointment they could at least not complain that the final three games of the tour against the clubs of Newport, Cardiff and Swansea were all in the capable hands of Mr Evans.

The first running break, appropriately, came from Percy Bush as he burst down the blind-side only for his link with Johnnie Williams to falter at the last minute. Cardiff's next scoring opportunity, and it must have been an ambitious one, was an attempted drop goal from halfway by the wing, Ralph Thomas. Drop goals, realistic or not, were a feature of the age and soon Billy Wallace was equally unsuccessful for the All Blacks. One way or another the surfeit of kicking, whether punts, drop-shots or foot rushes continued but there was undeniably a great pace to the play by both sides. Problems were also continuing at the set pieces as instanced by this marvellous piece of Hoare reportage:

'Then Cardiff had a penalty for an informality in the scrummage – it looked like a case of hands – but no great advantage accrued.'

Away from the forwards Cardiff were also gaining the upper hand and Bush was testing and teasing the opposing defence:

'The Cardiff captain shone effulgently, David had given him a very good pass, and 'the Prince of Dodgers' artfully brought the defence around him and then threw to Nicholls and a mighty groan of disappointment arose when it was seen that the ball had canted off his knees, the Welsh captain having come up at too great a pace, otherwise a try was a certainty...as Wallace would have needed to be as fast again as a ten seconds man to have got within yards of him.'

New Zealand were being thrown out of their stride with penalties continuing at the scrums and misunderstandings in midfield both in attack and defence – but still Cardiff hadn't put any points on the board. Then the great backs made their mark:

'Play was proceeding just inside the Colonials' 25, when Northmore got the ball after play from a scrummage, wound up with JL Williams making a clear feint and then kicking for his forwards. The real attack baffled the Colonials, as Northmore passed with great judgement to Neil, who equalled the vice-captain's skill in throwing the ball wide to Gabe, The left centre, divining the moment, ran to meet the ball, and continuing his run made one of the unbeatable long swerves for which he is famous, and passing to Nicholls placed the line at the mercy of the Welsh captain – indeed if Nicholls had been covered RC Thomas was on the wing absolutely unmarked. Nicholls gained the try which was worthy of the best of Welsh play.'

Bert Winfield's conversion hit an upright before going over the bar to ensure the full five points. For the first time in 31 matches on tour a club side had taken the lead against the All Blacks with an opening try. The visitors received another setback when forward Jim

O'Sullivan was stretchered off with a broken collar bone. The response from Gallaher's men was predictable. After some further speculative kicking the ball was at last kept in hand and Hunter, Deans and 'Mona' Thompson linked for the latter to race along the wing for the equalising try a few minutes before the interval. Wallace converted magnificently from the edge of touch and the sides were locked at 5-5 at the interval.

W J Hoare's half-time summary was encouraging:

'Territorially, Cardiff had much the better of the game, and as their forwards had been much better helped by their backs, and the strain upon the latter had been less than upon the Colonials', there were hopes that the Citizens would stay the course.'

That confidence was well founded because for the next half-hour there was no further scoring. With his side reduced to 14 men because of O'Sullivan's injury, Gallaher was forced to abandon his rover role and play among the forwards. With no wing forward to get among them, Cardiff's backs saw the chance to move the ball wide and both Williams and Gabe came close to adding a second try. Winfield failed with three kicks at goal and Cardiff's frustration was growing. Then came the fateful moment that was to haunt Percy Bush for the rest of his career.

An innocuous kick by the All Black forward 'Tiger' Seeling bounced harmlessly over the home goal-line and was well-covered by the club captain. Bush decided to wait for a few All Blacks to waste their energy pointlessly chasing the ball before he would touch down for the 'minor' and subsequent drop-out on the 25. What happened next could be attributed to one of the tenets of All Black play: never give up anything as a lost cause. In *The Complete Rugby Footballer* Gallaher and Stead wrote:

'When a kick has been made [upfield] the whole team go rushing up and in such circumstances there is a considerable chance of the taker being so hustled or hurried that he may misfield the ball'.

Indeed there was – as the unfortunate Bush was to discover – though, perversely, reports suggest there was only a lone All Black harrying him as he dallied with the bouncing ball within his own in-goal area. The chaser was George Nicholson and he must have been as amazed as anyone as the legendary Bush hesitated and allowed the ball to bounce away from him. The All Black pounced and the try was awarded with a simple conversion from Wallace to follow. WJ Hoare felt that Bush had "lost his head" but the player himself eventually offered a different explanation:

> 'When that long kick went rolling over our goal-line, I saw this New Zealand forward chasing it. He had a long way to go and there was no danger for us. I let him come; it would waste his energy, not mine. As he came near I stooped to pick up the ball but just then it bounced awkwardly off one of its points. It rolled out of my reach and I tried to kick it, but missed. Before I had the chance to recover the New Zealander had scored'.

Suddenly Cardiff was five points behind with very little time left. Momentarily, Hoare noted that the home side were at sixes and sevens before Bush, with admirable tenacity, led the comeback by personal example. Three times he made breaks that opened up the defence only for the final pass or, ironically, bounce of the ball to go astray. The final moments were as memorable as anything that went before:

> '...There came in the final seconds a positively electrifying movement. The ball was heeled out beautifully to David, who passed to Bush – a grand pass splendidly taken – and the captain made a dodging run, passed to Gibbs, who threw to Nicholls, the transfers being given and taken brilliantly, and then Nicholls had a chance which he utilised magnificently. It was a great run of his, bang through the strongest point of the defence, and when he handed to [Ralph] Thomas the Penarth skipper had but to take the ball without losing his stride to score. The right wing took his pass grandly, and with a determined gallop, in which he swerved in the last step or two, he scored a try on the extreme verge of the goal-line.'

Winfield's attempted conversion kick that would have secured a worthy draw narrowly drifted wide of the upright and soon afterwards the final whistle went. Cardiff had lost by two points and the 40,000 crowd stayed in the ground for several minutes, hardly able to believe the evidence of their own eyes that the club had lost. The match post-mortems would inevitably focus on Bush's *faux pas*.

There was no shortage of encouragement from elsewhere in Wales as the letters poured in. A Mr WR Jones of Llanelli wrote advising that he should "Cheer up, old man ... the twentieth century will never see a perfect football player." From further west DG Lewis of Newcastle Emlyn wrote:

'Dear Mr Bush

I am very sorry to understand that you have allowed the slight error you committed on Tuesday [Boxing Day] to effect you to such an extent. Mistakes will happen. You played cleverly throughout and some of your runs were simply electrifying.

Yours faithfully

DG Lewis'

Much later, in his review of the season, Charley Arthur concluded:

'Of Percy Bush it is difficult to know how much to write; his play in some matches was positively brilliant, and he had extraordinary powers of dodging and feinting, and deceiving opponents as to his intentions, and has never had any superior in the art of dropping goals. He had unbounded confidence, and inspired his men with some of it, and this in a great measure carried them through the season with only one defeat.'

On balance, clearly, the pluses heavily outnumbered the minuses. Bush was indeed an inspiration and a season's record of played 32, won 29, drawn 2 and one solitary loss to the All Blacks speaks for itself. In the final week of the campaign the Barbarians were beaten by 38 points, Leicester by 13 and Llanelli by 40, all without the team conceding a point. This was a magnificent record and the ultimate confirmation of Bush's standing, if any was needed, was his re-election as club captain for two of the next three seasons. As we shall see, two more titanic struggles against 'Colonial' teams awaited in the immediate future – and with far more satisfying results that would establish Bush's reputation in the pantheon of Cardiff rugby.

Beyond that, there would be a wanderlust in Bush's personality that needed to be satisfied. He was, after all, from a family of achievers. When his rugby-playing brother Fred gave up the game to concentrate on his professional career, he moved north to become organising inspector of art for the West Riding of Yorkshire. Another art-loving brother, Reginald, became head of Bristol School of Art, and the oldest of the four brothers, Archie, travelled even further afield. He went to Mombasa to be chief engineer and designed the drainage system for the city of Nairobi. His job done, he went into the East African jungle to become a lion-hunter. There was also a sister, Ethel Maud, and her claim to fame was she was awarded the first Bachelor of Divinity at the University of Wales.

Percy's career path was equally impressive. Though he was to play four games for Cardiff at the start of the 1913-14 season, when he was 34 years of age, his blue and black days effectively ended after the game against Neath in February 1910. Restless for a new environment Bush moved to France, combining his work in the British Consulate in Nantes with, for a while at least, more rugby for the local club. In one game for Stade Nantais he famously scored 54 points against Le Havre. His flamboyance on the pitch was more than matched by his ambassadorial role off it. The coal port of Cardiff had close business contacts with its counterpart at Nantes and Bush was an invaluable coal agent because of his contacts in both centres. He was to stay in France for over 30 years, becoming Vice-Consul until 1937 before eventually returning to Cardiff. Thereafter he made a living as a part-time journalist and dabbled in public relations. He also held strong views on the post-war game in Wales and canvassed for the reinstatement of France into international rugby after its exclusion from 1931 to the outbreak of war in 1939. His contacts with the Cardiff club also remained close to his heart and at one stage he even became chairman of the supporters' club.

Further proof of the great ambassadorial role that Percy Bush had done on behalf of the Cardiff club in France comes from the honour bestowed on Bleddyn Williams and Dr Jack Matthews in later years. As a sign of the mutual respect and friendship between the two clubs, the two great post-war centres were made life members of Stade Nantais UC and they even played one game for the club against Wasps.

Percy had clearly left a lasting impression at Nantes as well. When Cardiff travelled there for a match in 1946, the messages of goodwill were conveyed back to Wales. The fixtures secretary Danny Davies wrote to him on 6 January 1946:

'... I must now personally convey to you from Nantes the best wishes of everybody, from the SNUC [Stade Nantais Université Club], Chamber of Commerce and the townsfolk, and particularly from Marcel Pedron and Henri Picherit [president and secretary]. The latter by the way told me you scored 54 points in one match – and even I marvelled.

However I can only tell you that your name not only lives on in France – it is very much alive and the best way I can put it perhaps is to say that it is synonymous with the Nantes UC. In a reply at the reception at the Town Hall I did appreciate that 'Cardiff gave you Percy Bush and Nantes gave us Marcel Pedron'.'

Percy Bush had long since been forgiven for his great slip-up of 1905 but memories of the All Blacks, and the one that got away, would live on until the elusive victory was finally delivered in 1953. Before then, though, New Zealand's rugby teams would again prove very difficult to beat.

2

Giving Second-Best

If the All Blacks tour of 1905 had proved one thing, it was that the great rugby countries of Wales and New Zealand were, along with South Africa, the pace setters in the world game. The only blot on the All Blacks' record on that trip was the defeat by Wales; but it was equally true that the other four fixtures in the Principality – against Glamorgan and particularly the club sides of Newport, Cardiff and Swansea – had all tested the visitors to the limit. Cardiff had come as close as any team to inflicting a second reverse on the All Blacks. Sadly the blue and black heroics were not repeated on the next two tours by full New Zealand sides in 1924-25 and 1935-36. It was more a case of the local fans, however reluctantly, having to sit back and admire the skills and winning ways of the tourists. That was particularly the case in 1924 when Cliff Porter's team of all the talents swept all before them in 32 matches to become 'The Invincibles'. No touring team before or since has matched their remarkable record.

The Cardiff team of the mid-1920s was ill-equipped to challenge such a side. The Golden Era had long since passed into the history books. In the first five seasons after the First World War the club had won only 124 of its 211 official fixtures, a record that was barely satisfactory after the vintage pre-war years. Yet there was no shortage of quality players and club men. Clem Lewis, Arthur Cornish and Idris Richards had led sides that included notable performers such as Wick Powell, Ossie Male, Charley Bryant and a young man destined for rugby league greatness, Jim Sullivan. The team in 1924 was no exception. The captain was Tom 'Codger' Johnson, a respected international approaching the twilight of his career. By trade a marine store dealer in Cardiff docks, Johnson had been one of the finest all-round backs of his generation. As well as 12 caps for Wales he played for the combined England & Wales team against Scotland & Ireland in the centenary match at Rugby School in 1923. He was considered to be the outstanding back on the field that day.

Five other members of the Cardiff team that would face the All Blacks were also internationals already. Arthur Cornish, a local teacher, was in the centre and was described in the international programmes of the period as 'a brainy attacker and clever exponent of the dummy ... [who] requires a fast colleague to anticipate his sensational bursts'. Unfortunately, Cornish had fallen out with the club committee in September 1924 and announced his retirement. He was only 27 years old and there was a degree of disbelief about this particular pair of boots being hung up. That was justified when Cornish re-surfaced 12 miles away at Rodney Parade and played half a dozen games for Newport. But as the All Blacks match drew ever nearer at the end of November the committee's team selection was very limited. Another of their centre stars, the richly talented 20-year-old Bernard Turnbull, was studying at Cambridge University and declared himself unavailable. So the rumours began that Cornish, who had turned out for Newport against Cardiff on 8 November, would be drafted back into blue and black colours. That was easier said than done given the inherent parochialism in the club game. One writer, 'Angel Entrance', a regular contributor to the club's programme, commented:

'There is a flutter in the dovecotes this week. Some people are asking questions as to why a Newport player is likely to be included in the Cardiff team. 'Haven't we enough men in the district?' and such like. For that matter, why should a Cardiff man be found in the Newport team? I wish we could all bear in mind that if a man wants a game, shows the form, and complies with the conditions laid down by the governing body, surely he can play for whatever team he chooses ... there are numerous rules and regulations that hamper amateur players in these days, but for goodness sake, give the amateur a little freedom at any rate.'

The writer accurately gauged the prevailing mood of the committee because when the team to play the All Blacks was announced, RA Cornish, having missed the club's last 10 games, was named at right centre. Alongside him in midfield was John Powell, a licensee who had won a solitary cap as a wing the previous year. At full back was the Irishman, Dr Tom Wallace, who had captained his country in 1920 against Wales at Cardiff Arms Park. In 1924 he was 32 years of age and very much approaching the veteran stage.

The personality of the Cardiff team was undoubtedly the pint-sized scrum-half, Bobby Delahay. Barely 5'4" in his stockinged feet, he was considered the supreme footballer of the decade and played for Wales in three different positions – both halves and in the centre.

Given the team's reputation for being forward orientated at the time, it is surprising that only one of the pack, the Glyncorrwg policeman W J Ould, had been capped before the All Blacks match. Subsequently, Idris Richards, Tom Lewis and Syd Hinam all received the national call. But this was not a Cardiff team to set the pulse racing. There was no great sense of anticipation in the weeks leading up to the game, rather as if the shadow of the heroics of 1905 hung over the team. Matters were not helped by three consecutive defeats by Blackheath, Aberavon and, horror of horrors, Newport in the month before the game. Spirits were lifted if only slightly by a 6-3 win over a modest United Services Portsmouth side at the Arms Park in the final warm-up. Yet the match programme that day contained the most sobering of previews of what lay ahead a week later:

'The question of how many points the All Blacks are going to trounce us by seems to be viewed from different angles. One week the prophets say 40 or more. A fortnight ago some Jonahs predicted a cricket score. We shall know all about it at about 4.30 pm on the afternoon of the 22nd inst., but if the players are in any way inspired by the best traditions of the club, there is every prospect of a thrilling and close game.'

On the day of the match itself, the prognosis was no more encouraging. Bemoaning the lack of players of the calibre of Nicholls and Bush, which seems more than a little harsh on men like Delahay, Cornish and Wallace, the programme editor concluded that 'We can hardly expect something so brilliant [as 1905] ... but a grim determination to follow as closely as possible in the footsteps of their illustrious predecessors.' There was also one whimsical piece of tactical advice to the team:

> 'Now, Cardiff, what about it? Remember, no taking the 'dummy'; no leaving a man unmarked in the line-out, and no collaring about the neck – fatal in each case.'

If the Cardiff team and officials were racked by uncertainty and self-doubt, the All Blacks, on the other hand, arrived in South Wales on the afternoon before the match having built up a full head of steam. They had already recorded 19 straight wins, including the first international of the tour against Ireland. Most recently they had swept aside Wavell Wakefield's much-fancied London Counties formation by 31-6 at Twickenham and 48 hours before the Cardiff match had again passed the 30-points mark against Oxford University. It is typical of the tour itineraries of the time that, having arrived in Cardiff at three o'clock on the Friday afternoon, their squad thought nothing of a spot of hand-shaking and what today would be called public relations. Following the precedent of Gallaher and Stead 19 years earlier, the 1924 All Black Read Masters wrote his own tour book and of his arrival in Cardiff he noted:

> 'Upon alighting from the train, [we] were given an enthusiastic reception by a large crowd that had gathered at the station. We then proceeded to the City Hall, where we were received by the Lord Mayor of Cardiff (Alderman WH Pethybridge), who accorded us a very hearty welcome, and reminded us that it was in his city that the 1889 and 1905 New Zealand teams were defeated. He hoped that the best side would win tomorrow's match, and that Cardiff Arms Park, in accordance with its traditions, would prove the field of Waterloo to us. Sir Thomas Hughes asked us to return to Cardiff to play a charity match on January 1st. This Mr Dean [the team manager] in his speech said we would be unable to do owing to our match with England being fixed for January 3rd. We then inspected the City Hall which is a magnificent building, and in the Council Chamber saw the flag which Captain Scott took with him on his last fateful expedition to the South Pole. We were also shown the jersey the late Bob Deans wore when he scored the famous try that was disallowed!'

Masters' jottings give us a valuable insight into how the culture, responsibilities and expectations of a rugby tour have changed. Imagine a modern day team being asked whether they could fit in an extra charity match in their schedule – and two days before they play England at Twickenham! Deans' jersey from the 1905 match against Wales, by the way, is today resplendent in the Cardiff club museum.

Whatever the downbeat mood ahead of the 1924 encounter, public interest was as great as ever. The All Blacks had already travelled into Wales for two games in the early part of the tour and had attracted record club crowds of 40,000 at Swansea and 28,000 at Newport. Now Cardiff was to follow suit with a 40,000-plus attendance of its own. The attraction was obvious. The All Blacks were more than simply a winning team; they were packed with personalities. First and foremost there was the remarkable full back, George Nepia. He was only 19 when the tour started with a preliminary visit to Australia on 5 July 1924. Between then and when the tour ended on 18 February 1925 in Victoria, Canada, he played in every one of the 38 matches. With his faultless tackling, kicking and catching of the ball he was considered to be the finest last line of defence seen in these islands. Almost equally eminent behind the scrum were players such as the five-eighth Mark Nicholls, who finished top scorer with 103 points, and the centre Bert Cooke, who scored 23 tries in 25 matches. The most celebrated names in the pack, apart from the captain Cliff Porter and the budding author Read Masters, were the Brownlie brothers, Cyril and Maurice. Great names in their own right, the sum of their parts was even greater.

So the big crowd, paying the princely sum of one shilling for the ground or two shillings for the enclosure, poured into the Arms Park on a dry but windy early winter's afternoon. The gates were locked half an hour before the scheduled kick-off at 2.45 pm but, reported the *South Wales Echo*, 'several hundreds occupied points of vantage on buildings overlooking Cardiff Arms Park'. The splendid 16-page match programme could not resist the temptation to reminisce yet again about the near miss of 1905:

'We wonder how many of the 1905 Cardiff team will see today's encounter. Percy Bush, of course, is in France, while Bert Winfield responded some time ago to the call of the Great

Scorer. The majority of the others are in the vicinity, although a few have taken seriously to golf and are only rarely attracted to witness the game to which they figured so conspicuously.'

It was also pointed out that Reggie Gibbs was now a club committeeman and Gwyn Nicholls had unofficially acted in a coaching capacity in the previous few weeks. What was not mentioned was that players such as Billy Neill and Dicky David had transferred to rugby league later in their playing days and, as such in the club's strict amateur constitution, had 'professionalised' themselves and were disqualified *sine die* from membership. Over half a century later this unforgiving attitude towards any association with rugby league was still written into the rules and bye-laws of Cardiff Athletic Club. Supporters applying for membership and a season ticket had to complete and sign an application form that included the clause, 'In applying for membership of the Football [Rugby] Section I declare I have not at any time been engaged in the Playing, Administration, Promotion or Fostering of Rugby League or other Professional Rugby Football'.

Whatever the changing fortunes of individuals from 1905, one facet of play was continued into the 1924 match. New Zealand's wing forward cum scrum-half role had passed from Dave Gallaher to Cliff Porter and the captain performed his duties to perfection. Universally regarded as a fine strategist, Porter was only 5'8" tall and weighed in at 12 and a half stone, but he and the official scrum-half, Jimmy Mill (all 5'7" of him), worked effectively together, especially around the fringes of the scrum. Cardiff's response was to keep Con O'Leary out of the pack to work alongside Delahay. This upset the All Blacks as Read Masters later wrote:

'We secured the ball in more scrums than our opponents, but owing to the obstructionist tactics of O'Leary – who, instead of playing in the pack, was invariably waiting off-side to pounce on our half-back – it was on many occasions inadvisable to let the ball out. Delahay, one of the opposing halves, was also waiting off-side on many occasions.'

Masters was obviously not prepared to admit that Delahay was apparently a kindred spirit. The opposing half-back, rover, wing forward – or whatever they wished to be called – certainly cancelled each other out in the early stages of the match as the game was little more than a dour forward struggle. The All Blacks had kicked-off with the wind at their backs but initially failed to gain any advantage. Cornish, Danny Davies and Delahay all contributed to a strong defence as two passing moves broke down and an attempted dummy by the elusive Cooke came to nothing. *The South Wales Echo's* reporter, though, sensed a turning of the tide after the opening exchanges:

> 'There were several occasions when the strain put upon the Cardiff defence looked like breaking it. It survived, mainly because of the good kicking of Delahay and Davies while Johnson and Cornish were also sound. Before Cardiff succeeded in driving their opponents back, Delahay incurred the displeasure of Captain Burge [the referee] by attempting to put the ball in a scrummage unfairly, and from the penalty given against him, straight in front of the posts, Nicholls placed a goal from 45 yards range.'

Having weathered the storm, the All Blacks used the wind to good advantage and expert kicking by Nepia kept them in Cardiff's half. Despite the temporary loss of one of their loose forwards, Andrew 'Son' White 'who was bowled over with such vigour that he was laid out' they were to establish a commanding lead by half-time. Fred Lucas scored the first try when he raced over unopposed after Jock Richardson had changed the direction of an attack and thrown him a long pass. Mark Nicholls narrowly failed to convert but he was to have more luck on the stroke of the interval when his side posted a second try. White had returned to the fray and he rolled over near the posts despite a last-ditch tackle by Tom Wallace. Nicholls' conversion had completed a satisfactory first 40 minutes for the tourists and they were well worth their comfortable 11-0 lead. The story of the half had been one of a gallant club side beaten for pace behind the scrum and weight within it up against a finely-tuned international team playing their twentieth match of a triumphant tour. It was to Cardiff's credit that they had to some extent upset their opponents' rhythm but there was still a sense of anticipation at the interval that the All Blacks might soon break loose and rattle up a high score.

That expectation gained further credibility in the opening minutes of the second period when a third try came from the captain Porter. He had changed positions at half time with Jim Parker and was now operating in the pack while the equally adept Parker took over as wing-forward. The score had been near enough to the posts for Nicholls' conversion to be a formality. Now Cardiff trailed by 16 points but the expected points avalanche never came. Instead it was the club side that finished the strongest. What Codger Johnson's team lacked in style they made up for in doggedness. Percy Rayer, Billy Ould and Fred Stephens took play into All Blacks' territory and a penalty was awarded which Wallace goaled from the touchline. This was the signal for several minutes of prolonged pressure from the pack but the try showed no signs of coming.

It was left to Delahay to break the cast-iron defence – the All Blacks were to end the tour with a clean sheet in no fewer than 12 matches – when he dummied and darted over for a fine individual try that was converted by Wallace. However, despite the vocal support of the home crowd there was no further scoring. The All Blacks shut up shop with long touch-finders and Cardiff threw away their best chances with speculative attempts at drop-goals in conditions where attacking with the ball in hand was the best option. The match ended with the visitors reportedly 'swept back helter-skelter to their own line' but again the defence held out.

After the match both teams were entertained at a formal dinner at the Grand Hotel in Westgate Street. Immediately after that Cliff Porter and six other members of the touring party went to the studios of the new Cardiff Broadcasting Station to speak to listeners in the locality and, incredibly, to perform the haka, the Maori war dance, on the radio. Read Masters assessed the audience to be one of four million people, which is hard to fathom unless there were listeners across the Severn in England and probably even further afield. George Nepia was also billed to sing two Maori songs but he failed to arrive in time. The All Blacks, however, rarely admit defeat and another Maori, a Major Dansey who was travelling with the team, stepped in and sang the songs having been introduced as Nepia. In the true tradition of the early tours the All Blacks did not dash off at the earliest opportunity. On the Sunday they visited Cardiff Castle before travelling to west Wales on the following day.

Meanwhile, Cardiff could take satisfaction from a brave second-half effort in the match itself. Codger Johnson and Bobby Delahay had done well enough to win selection for the Wales team that would play New Zealand seven days later in Swansea. The true worth of the club's performance was then seen in a better light as the national side was humbled by five tries and 19 points to nil. The All Blacks of 1924 were indeed the Invincibles.

Cardiff would have to wait another 11 years before their next attempt to make club history against the wearers of the silver fern – but the task would prove to be no easier than before. The respectable result in 1924 could not hide the fact that the club was still some way short of returning to the standards of the early years of the century. A disastrous experiment with the fielding of two parallel first teams, each fulfilling fixtures on the same day, for five seasons between 1926 and 1931 did nothing to enhance the overall standards or, in some respects, the standing of the club. Leicester and Northampton were prominent among the English opponents that complained that they were never quite sure whether they were playing the Cardiff 'first' or 'second' team. In September 1931 normality returned and, as we shall see, the visit of the Springboks that autumn concentrated blue and black minds wonderfully. Yet by the time the Third All Blacks arrived in 1935 there was no discernible improvement in Cardiff's playing fortunes. In the four seasons prior to the next encounter with the All Blacks the club had lost 72 matches and drawn 12 out of 193 they had played, a singularly unimpressive record.

As in the 1920s there had been a smattering of very good players but no great teams had emerged. Ronnie Boon, Harry Bowcott, Maurice and Bernard Turnbull, Tommy Stone, Bob Barrell and Archie Skym would rate as top performers in any generation but somehow the sides they played in flattered to deceive. The 1934-35 season had ended with only five wins in the final 13 fixtures and there was barely a marginal improvement as the new campaign opened. Once again there was an unsettled look to the teams selected from week to week, not least in the midfield backs where, a fortnight before the arrival of the All Blacks, there was still an uncertainty about the players available and which selections to opt for. The lynchpin of the operation was Harry Bowcott, a British Isles player in New Zealand in 1930, but one who had not been seen in Cardiff colours for two and a half years. He worked in London and had captained London Welsh but his expected return to the Arms Park was delayed until mid-October – the All Blacks loomed on the 26th of the month.

Fortunately, the senior Bowcott would have little trouble in finding his bearings as his partner at half-back was destined to be his dapper brother, Jackie. The scrum-half – 'Little Bowcott, himself scarcely larger than a football' was how *The New Statesman* described him – was like a breath of fresh air in an austere age. In 1933 he had partnered the gifted Cliff Jones at half-back for Cambridge University at Twickenham. Both had shone in a narrow defeat to Oxford but Jackie had been widely reported as man-of-the-match. After that he had gone on to play for Northampton, Wasps, Neath, with his brother for London Welsh, and had come close to an international cap after another impressive performance in the final Welsh Trial of 1934.

There were other formidable players that Cardiff could call on behind the scrum. The wings were the two Arthurs, Bassett and Jones. The former amassed 99 tries in 101 games for the club before eventually transferring to rugby league in 1939 and Jones had been a member of the first Wales team to win at Twickenham in 1933. The centres were even more interesting. For Arthur Cornish in 1924 read Ronnie Boon in 1935. Cornish had re-appeared at the Arms Park in time for the All Blacks after his brief sojourn at Newport. Boon's re-emergence was even more unusual. Undoubtedly a great player, like Arthur Jones he had made history at Twickenham in 1933, in his case dropping the goal and scoring the try that won the match. He had won his Cardiff club cap as a 19-year-old back in 1929 but had hardly been seen in Cardiff for the previous four years, playing only a handful of matches. This was not as unusual as it might seem because Boon was a high-flying educationalist who went on to become an inspector of schools. His vocational travels probably contributed to the number of clubs he played for, conservatively estimated at seven. Like Harry Bowcott he had particularly close ties with London Welsh but, at the eleventh hour in 1935, he answered Cardiff's call to face the All Blacks. It was to be both his first and last appearance for the club that season.

Alongside Boon in the centre was a young man by the name of Horace Edwards. Yet again there is an interesting tale to tell. In the autumn of 1935 he was barely 19 years of age, having captained the Llandovery College side the previous season. As Cardiff scratched around to find a pairing at centre worthy of the club's attacking reputation, they turned to the youngster only a fortnight before the All Blacks were due at the Arms Park. There was still no sign of Boon at that stage, of course, but the debutant acquitted himself well, albeit in a 0-3 home defeat to Gloucester. As Cardiff's two other games immediately prior to the touring team fixture, against Swansea and Newport, ended in scoreless draws, the side could hardly be accused of hitting a rich vein of form. Yet more could be said of young Edwards. He retained his place after the 'trial' against Gloucester, distinguished himself against the All Blacks, and went on to play in 29 games by the following April to comfortably qualify for his club cap. But the winning of the ultimate cap, an international one for Wales, was to prove tragically more elusive. His good form with the club continued into the next season, when he played another 33 times, and he inevitably attracted the attentions of the Welsh selectors. Having lost to England at Twickenham and Scotland in Swansea, six changes were made in the side to play Ireland in Belfast on 13 March 1937. When the former captain, Claude Davey, also withdrew injured the call went out to Horace Edwards for his first cap. At the same time, another established international, Vivian Jenkins, was unable to play at full-back and Edwards' club captain, Tommy Stone, was also sent for. Neither Edwards nor Stone ever took their places in a full international.

As the boat carrying the Welsh team steamed into Belfast Lough 48 hours before the game the area was hit by a blizzard. The international was called off and rearranged for three weeks later – by which time Davey was fit to resume his place in the team. Edwards lost out and so did Stone when the selectors had second (or was it third) thoughts about the full back position and gave it to Newport's Walter Legge. Stone, clearly disappointed, immediately signed professional forms for Barrow Rugby League club, abdicating his captaincy with two months of the season still to play. He had given the club fine service with 317 first team games over eight seasons to his name. Edwards, though, stayed in union and at least had the consolation of wartime international experience. In 1940, by which time he had joined Neath, he played twice for Wales against England in Red Cross representative games.

The hard luck stories in the Cardiff team didn't end there. One of the cornerstones of the pack was Eddie Watkins, a fine young former schoolboy international from Caerphilly. Now a police constable, he had made his senior debut for the club the previous season at the age of 18. The police force was a popular occupation in the hard years of the 1930s. Of the 56 players who made first team appearances during the 1935-36 season, no fewer than a dozen of them were uniformed constables. But even that regular employment was no cushion against the economic stringency of the age. When, in 1938, Eddie Watkins was selected for the British Isles tour to South Africa on merit, he was forced to withdraw because, quite simply, he couldn't afford to be away from his paid employment for six months. Less than a year later, with eight Welsh caps to his name, he finally succumbed to the call from the north and signed for Wigan Rugby League club. With him, on or about the same time, went four other first team players, including the dynamic flanker and eldest of the eight-man Williams brotherhood from Taff's Well, Gwyn.

Not all about the 1935 Cardiff team, however, was a case of doom and gloom. In the match itself the team would perform nobly. Other great characters in the pack included the Tongwynlais farmer, Ray Bale, and the vice-captain, Les Spence, who was another destined for long service with the club. Leslie Magnus Spence was once described as 'tall, craggy, endearingly clumsy and awkward', in other words suitably qualified to get under the skins of the All Blacks. In the following season he would become club captain and, after a war service that ended with him detained as a prisoner by the Japanese, he became successively chairman and president of the club. With a delicious sense of irony his term of office as president of the Welsh Rugby Union coincided with the national team's tour of Japan in 1975. He duly led the delegation and made many new friends. In 1935 he simply won admirers for his performances for Cardiff on the field of play.

The All Blacks had arrived in Cardiff on the Monday morning, six days before the game and spent an eventful first day in the city. A civic reception by the Lord Mayor, during which they also met the music hall star Sir Harry Lauder, was followed by an evening at the greyhound track and a quick visit to the theatre to see Lauder on stage. Then on the Tuesday they had travelled by train to Llanelli, arriving there at 1.30 pm – and 90 minutes later the team on duty was taking the field at Stradey Park to play the Scarlets. They won the match by 16 points to 8, attended a dinner at the Stepney Hotel where every one of the 120 guests were presented with 'sospans', caught the 9.00 pm train and were back in Cardiff in time for a good night's sleep. Such were the joys of rugby touring, 1935-style.

The three days leading up to the match at the Arms Park were as hectic as ever, with the touring team committing themselves to meeting the people and seeing new places with a relish that would be unrecognisable in the world of the modern professionals. On the Wednesday the team were taken to Bargoed Colliery where they went 650 feet underground and then walked for about half-an-hour to the coal face. This was followed on the Thursday afternoon with a guided tour of Cardiff Castle. Thankfully, there was some relaxation on the day before the match with time for a round of golf and a visit to the Park Hall cinema where a musical, 'Naughty Marietta', starring Jeanette Macdonald and Nelson Eddy was showing. The singing and dancing would continue for the All Blacks rather than the Blue and Blacks on the following day.

Match day dawned fine and breezy in the city with anticipation of a great occasion intensified after the touring team's four tries to one win over Llanelli. This had done much to restore their reputation after the defeat at Swansea in the early weeks of the tour, though the local correspondent in the *Llanelli Star* had his own explanation for this failure of his presumably beloved Scarlets to match the feat of the All Whites. 'Far be it for me to attempt to decry Swansea's meritorious achievement,' he wrote, 'but as comparisons, however odious, are being made it should be pointed out that the team which met Llanelli was more formidable than the fifteen which played at Swansea.' Some things in Welsh rugby never change.

The large crowd that gathered before kick-off were equally fervent (and probably one-eyed!) in their support of Cardiff. The new North Grandstand had been opened in January 1934 and over 5,000 of the estimated 35,000 in attendance had paid five shillings (25p) each for the privilege of the best view in any Welsh ground. Whether what they saw in the next 80 minutes or so was equally pleasing to the eye remains a matter of conjecture. The All Blacks lost the toss and played the first half against the stiff breeze, but within three minutes of the kick-off they took a lead they were never to lose. Tommy Stone had been hailed in the local press as 'the best uncapped full-back in the four home countries' but the New Zealanders were no respecters of reputations. Second five-eighth Pat Caughey launched a huge up-and-under towards the Cardiff posts and Stone was hustled off the ball for Caughey to regather and score. It was one of 18 tries he scored on tour, including a hat-trick against Scotland. The Cardiff team had barely caught their breath but were given some respite when full-back Mike Gilbert made a hash of the simple conversion. But four minutes later Caughey struck again, this time taking the running option to draw Stone and send right wing Neville Mitchell unopposed to the corner. Again the conversion was missed but after conceding two tries and six points in the first 10 minutes Cardiff's spirits were in urgent need of a lift.

There were some signs of life when Jackie Bowcott took full advantage of quick scrum ball to race half the length of the field before failing to chip over Gilbert's head – hardly surprising when a five-foot attacker sees a six-foot last line of defence in front of him. Bowcott's impossible task was replicated by his team in general. Unluckily for Cardiff a touring team that had struggled to click into top gear in several of its 12 matches so far, were now firing on all cylinders. More scores seemed imminent but Mitchell was denied a second try by a wonderful cover tackle from the far wing by Arthur Bassett and again Gilbert botched a straightforward penalty kick at goal. While the Cardiff forwards were sticking manfully to their task, the ball provided for their backs was wasted by sloppy passing and uncertain handling. It was this clumsy three-quarter play that contributed to the third try. A wild pass by Boon intended for Edwards was easily intercepted by Nelson Ball who sidestepped three would-be tacklers before sending Caughey on a race to the posts. Gilbert converted for an 11-0 lead and another home mistake widened the gap even further before half-time. This time the culprit was Harry Bowcott who failed to find touch and Gilbert, by now warming to his kicking duties, dropped a magnificent goal from 35 yards out and near the sideline. The four-point dropped goal had established an unassailable 15-points interval lead for the All Blacks.

The only question remained one of whether there was any spirit or skill left in the Cardiff team for the second period. Thankfully there was. Although the tourists almost scored again straight from the restart when scrum-half Joey Sadler was held up five yards short of the line, Cardiff then enjoyed their best 10-minute period of the match. Two of the All Blacks, Charlie Oliver and Eric Tindill, in their subsequent book *The Tour of the Third All Blacks*, noted:

'For the next ten minutes Cardiff gave us a wonderful exhibition, displaying football of the highest class. It was inspired, dazzling football, and it appeared as though they could pull the game round. Caughey dropped a pass as he was going through, and A Jones gathered the ball and punted ahead. McLean fell on the ball, but lack of support enabled the Cardiff forwards to carry on. Bowcott picked it up, cut through and handed on to Bassett, who raced down the centre of the field. When five yards from the line, and challenged by Mitchell, Bassett passed to Osmond, who although tackled by Gilbert, forced his way over for a fine try. Boon easily goaled.'

Unfortunately that was the end of Cardiff's purple patch. When they next attacked the ball was spilled and seized upon by Sadler who sent the 6'2" lock Tori Reid racing over for the try that settled the result conclusively. The club had finished strongly but the international tourists were worthy winners by 20 points to 5. In the great traditions of such tours a post-match reception and dinner was hosted in City Hall by the Lord Mayor, Alderman John Donovan and at which there were musical contributions by the Seion Glee Singers.

Curiously, there was some disagreement among the newspapermen present about the true quality of the All Black's victory. Clem Lewis, himself a former captain of Cardiff, reported in the *News Chronicle:*

'Here at Cardiff it was practically a case of master and pupil, and the spectators were left to decide as to how much the result was due to the brilliance of the New Zealanders or to the rank ineptitude of the Cardiff team. The losers had chances galore but alas! what a sad mess they made of all but one! The dropping of passes or knocking them on seemed like an insidious disease which permeated the whole Cardiff side. Such a fumbling exhibition as the Cardiff backs gave merely played into the hands of the New Zealand men and they extracted almost full toll.'

The ever-reliable views of 'Old Stager' in *The Football Echo* seemed more balanced as he rejoiced in the match he had seen:

'What does the mere winning or losing matter when we can have rugby of the type of that seen at Cardiff today? As a spectacle the game was well in advance of those in which the New Zealanders have so far participated in Wales. For that, too, the New Zealanders were not wholly responsible. Most of the gems of the game certainly came from them, but there was a glorious ten minutes early in the second half when the Cardiff backs toyed with the New Zealand defence in very much the same way as the New Zealanders had, earlier on, made Cardiff's defence look simple.'

Another observer at the game, E N Greatorex, was certainly of the same opinion as 'Old Stager', when he concluded:

'The man who was not satisfied with Saturday's exhibition of bright, open and almost reckless football should not go to rugby games. It was the sort of football that makes the result unimportant – rugby that sets the blood racing and brings the spectators to their feet. There was glamour and colour, because the players of both sides had the will to do and dare. The All Blacks alone did not make it so entertaining. That period in the second half when the Cardiff men, back and forward, sprang into action, and we saw those sudden and dramatic changes of fortune when defence was turned into attack in the twinkling of an eye, was the best of it all.'

On balance Cardiff, without ever threatening to win, had in most people's eyes come out of the game with some credit. The All Blacks, though, were still unbeaten against the club after three games of contrasting styles spread over 30 years. With a world war about to intervene, nearly two decades would pass before Cardiff and the All Blacks of New Zealand would meet each other again at Cardiff Arms Park. When they did it was in the match that would make reputations and establish legends that still stand over half-a-century later. The year of 1953 would indeed be the *annus mirabilis* in the long history of Cardiff Rugby Football Club – and for one man in particular it would be the year that sealed a remarkable playing career.

3

Bleddyn
The Man of Destiny

Bleddyn Williams has always said that he had no other ambition in rugby than to play for Cardiff. This will surprise no one. After all, he was a gifted schoolboy player himself and he had his eldest brother, Gwyn, to follow as a role model. As early as 1934 when he was barely 11 years old, he had gone to the Arms Park to watch Gwyn play for the blue and blacks. The following season, by then a regular spectator on the terraces, he had his first sighting of the All Blacks. He was immediately impressed by their play and their single-minded commitment to victory. What he could not have known in 1935 was that the New Zealanders' fortunes on the field of play would be inexorably interlinked with his own rugby exploits over the next twenty years. He would play against them in war-time services matches, put his growing reputation to the test against the post-war Kiwis in 1945 and then tour their country as a Lion five years later. But the ultimate examinations that would confirm the place of Bleddyn Williams, his club and his country in the history of the game would be set in the early winter of 1953. Somehow, it was a matter of destiny that he would take centre stage as great, never-to-be forgotten deeds unfolded.

Fourteen years earlier, Williams had first worn blue and black. He was still a schoolboy in the great North Wales sporting academy of Rydal School. Some might regard this as an unlikely Alma Mater for a boy born and bred in Taff's Well and one of eight brothers and four sisters. His first rugby ball, he admits, was an old shoe wrapped in paper but good enough to practise the passing skills for hours with Gwyn and his other elder brother, Brinley. His precocious footballing talent had attracted admirers from an early age, none more so than

Wilfred Wooller, arguably among the top two or three all-round sportsmen ever to come out of the Principality. Wooller had himself been transferred from the Llandudno County Grammar School to nearby Rydal at the age of 13 primarily because of his remarkable prowess in several sports; at the age of 20 he was playing for Wales at Twickenham, and sharing in the first-ever Welsh victory there for good measure. He had no hesitation in recommending the young Williams, then 14 years old, to be awarded a scholarship and to follow in his footsteps. The youngster had already played for Wales at under-14 level against England, albeit in the unfamiliar position of full-back, a selection that he still remembers wistfully: 'I had never played full-back before – and never did again,' he said. 'The strange thing was that in the final trial before they picked the team I was in the centre and the wings outside me scored a handful of tries. Still, we beat England 29-0 at Gloucester so it wasn't something I would want to miss out on even in an unfamiliar position!'

Bleddyn Williams may never have filled that last line of defence again, but the habit of providing try-scoring opportunities for those around him followed him throughout his career. Ironically, one of his first games for Cardiff was alongside Wooller against Chepstow. He was still barely sixteen but his famous partner was suitably impressed. Wooller, never one given to extravagant praise, later conceded that the youngster had shown 'all the power and strength of a future international but not yet the speed'. The pace would come later as Williams built up an impressive portfolio of representative experience. While still at Rydal he came back to Cardiff in April 1940 to captain an Anglo-Welsh Public Schools XV against the Secondary Schools of Wales at the Arms Park. Also on the pitch that day was another future Lion, the prop John Robins who was then a boarder at Wellington School in Somerset, while the opposition included one of Wales' and the British Isles' greatest ever wings, Ken Jones.

The schools match was to be the first of many high-profile opportunities during the war years. At the outbreak of hostilities, Williams was 16 and a half years old but by the time peace returned in 1945 he had served in the Royal Air Force and played for countless representative teams. At Cardiff Arms Park alone, as well as turning out for Cardiff in unofficial matches, he had appeared for various combinations, including East Wales, South Wales and, in a charity match for the Tenovus appeal, Sir Robert Webber's XV. These were no carefree exhibition events but serious competitive occasions where he rubbed shoulders with past and future internationals such as Eddie Watkins, Bill Tamplin, WEN Davis, Bunner Travers, Haydn Tanner and Arthur Rees. As the league/union divide could not be invoked for services matches, it also meant that some of the legends of the 13-a-side code, most notably Jim Sullivan, reappeared at Cardiff Arms Park.

Bleddyn Williams volunteered for the RAF as soon as he was old enough in 1942. By 1944 he had qualified as a pilot officer on single engine-powered planes near Phoenix in Arizona. Later that year as a direct result of the huge losses of Army glider pilots sustained at the Battle of Arnhem, Williams, along with a number of other graduates, was seconded to the newly formed RAF glider pilot regiment. They were trained specifically for what turned out to be 'Operation Varsity' on 24 March 1945. Further promotions made him a Flight Lieutenant in time for the crossing of the river Rhine that heralded the final push into Germany and the end of the war.

Throughout the war he was the most conscientious of airmen while always looking for the most unlikely openings to continue playing rugby. So, on top of his many representative games, he also turned out for clubs as far apart (in more ways than one) as Cilfynydd and Abercarn in the Welsh heartlands and Rosslyn Park in metropolitan London. By 1943 he had made sufficient an impression to be selected for Wales in the services internationals and, after that, the Barbarians. His debut for the famous club came on Boxing Day 1944 against JE Thorneloe's XV at Leicester. At that stage his preference was firmly for the fly-half position rather than in the centre and he partnered Tanner at half-back. The Baa-Baa's won the game 23-11 with both of them scoring tries. Three months later he returned to the Midlands in most unusual circumstances to play in another big game where he would come up against New Zealanders and their unique rugby skills for the first time.

The occasion was the grandly named Great Britain versus the Dominions match but Williams had to move heaven and earth to even get there. The war may have been in its closing months but the young Williams, by now a trained glider pilot, was firmly camped behind enemy lines along the river Rhine. Little more than twenty-four hours before the game he was still there, sleeping in a trench and waiting for further orders. Luckily, when they came they were from a fellow sports-loving officer:

'Though I had been invited to play in that game at Leicester and had accepted in principle my realistic assessment was that I would have to give it a miss. Fortunately for me, my commanding officer was Major Hugh Bartlett, a sports-mad county cricketer in his own right. To my amazement, on the Friday morning he told me to pack my bags and prepare to leave to play in the game that he had heard about. It was the start of an eventful day. By the end of it I had been driven across the Rhine and on into Holland and was flown from Eindhoven to the RAF base in Brize Norton, Oxfordshire. Suddenly the match was a reality but better still I was able to see my young wife, Violet, who had feared the worst as I had been reported missing in action. After that, it was pretty straightforward to travel cross-country to Leicester for the match the following day. We also won it by 30-odd points!'

The Dominions included five New Zealanders in their side, plus players from South Africa and Australia, so they were at least true to their title – but in reality they were not the strongest combination. Their best player was probably Williams' opposite number, Maurice Goddard, who turned out for England in the war-time matches and eventually played five tests for New Zealand. Before the end of 1945, however, Bleddyn Williams would encounter far sterner New Zealand opposition and with it would begin his admiration and respect for their rugby and its role in their everyday life.

Official international matches did not resume until the 1946-47 season but there was a hunger for organised sport by both players and spectators as soon as the war ended. Throughout South Wales crowds flocked to their local grounds to watch the games and nowhere was this more the case than at the Arms Park. The north stand had been badly damaged by a landmine in January 1941 and would not be fully repaired for several years but that did not prevent official club fixtures kicking-off promptly on 1 September 1945. Williams was seeing out his service days as a Flying Officer stationed at St Athan in the Vale of Glamorgan so he was available to immediately take his place in the Cardiff side. The club captain was his great soul mate, Dr Jack Matthews, and with another gifted player, Billy Cleaver, at fly-half they formed a devastating attacking midfield. They were well served by a formidable pack of forwards that included Maldwyn James, Cliff Davies, Bill Tamplin, Les Manfield and the vice-captain, Ray Bale. In no time at all the team hit top form and by Christmas had recorded 17 straight wins that included the taking of Coventry's 61-game unbeaten ground record that stretched back five years.

The constitution of the team was interesting because the young men came from all walks of life. Of the sixteen who made the most appearances during that first post-war season, two were doctors and another couple were medical students, there were three mining engineers and two more employed at the coal-face. Then there were two RAF officers, plus a policeman, an architect, a market gardener, a bank official and an industrial chemist. It was little wonder that they served up a brand of rugby to satisfy all tastes. They were undoubtedly marvellous ambassadors for the club with even their greatest opponents recognising the team's quality. The gates were locked an hour before kick-off at Rodney Parade on 10 November with the Newport committee noting that 'We are very mindful of the part [Cardiff] are playing in their successful endeavour to produce a standard of rugby so dear to the hearts of lovers of the game ... a team of unquestioned greatness, they have been delighting large crowds by their open, skilful and oftentimes brilliant displays'.

By the end of the season the team had scored 149 tries in 40 matches, 42 of them shared by Williams and Matthews and another 47 by the two regular wings, Glyn Jones and Graham Hale, outside them. As well as the domestic opposition there was the added ingredient of the large number of colonial rugby players still based in Europe who also welcomed the opportunity of competition before they were drafted home. Cardiff and the other Welsh clubs were happy to oblige. When they played the Royal Australian Air Force on 15 September, the match programme concluded:

'Sportsmen, like every other section of the community, will feel profoundly thankful at the cessation of hostilities and that we are permitted once more to enjoy an appreciable degree of

normality as far as civilian life goes. While we rejoice at this fact
and find it possible once more to resume our rugby activities,
our thoughts go out to those bereaved of their loved ones –
players and supporters alike – and we raise our hats in tribute
to those who made the supreme sacrifice.'

Cardiff won that game 25-11 and six weeks later added the New
Zealand Services to their unbeaten run but the plum fixture was to
occur on Boxing Day with the arrival of the Second New Zealand
Expeditionary Force team – the 'Kiwis'. It is doubtful whether any
such non-international side, except perhaps the Barbarians, have
captured the imagination as they did on their 33-match tour of
Europe. A similar touring team had been assembled immediately
after the Armistice of 1918 when the New Zealand Army team played
38 games, including a full-scale international match against Wales at
Swansea that they won 6-3. Now another squad was assembled, based
on an idea that had first been mooted as the Second World War
entered its final stages. It was an unusual endeavour in that it was the
brainchild of Lieutenant-General Sir BC Freyberg who approached
the New Zealand government in the summer of 1945 requesting
permission for the tour plus a guarantee of £7,000 to cover expenses.

Able-bodied young New Zealand sportsmen who had survived the
hostilities were dotted all around Europe and beyond awaiting their
recall home. But as news of a projected rugby tour spread, over 300
players based in Egypt alone applied for selection and as many again
in Italy. They were whittled down to around 120 who were put
through their paces in two trial matches in Austria and then reduced
to 85 who would attend a two-week training camp in Klagenfurt.
After that a favoured 61 were flown to England where they were
joined by three released prisoners of war for a final trial. It was a
remarkably well-structured process – the suggestion that it was
organised with 'military precision' is irresistible. Unlike their
predecessors in 1918-19 there were few All Blacks available so the
accent in the final party of 29 was very much on youth with a
smattering of pre-war provincial players. But the selectors chose well
because the Kiwis played an exciting brand of rugby that resulted in
only two defeats in their long tour.

Bleddyn Williams got to know them better than most. He played against them four times in the space of five weeks around the turn of the year – for the RAF at Leicester, the Combined Services at Gloucester, and Cardiff and Wales at the Arms Park:

'They were a very fine team and once news spread of their early victories at Swansea, Llanelli and Neath – all beaten by wide margins – there was a tremendous sense of anticipation from their future opponents as their respective fixtures drew closer. That was certainly the case at the Cardiff club, partly, of course, because we were playing such great rugby ourselves. Jack [Matthews] had instilled in us a marvellously positive approach. "Attack!" was his operative word – in fact it was the only instruction he gave the team week after week. Like him we all believed that you had to attack to win in rugby and we found every man in our team imbued with the attacking spirit.'

Victory over the Kiwis, however, was a tall order. Williams' first game against them for the RAF resulted in an 11-0 defeat despite the fact they had themselves fielded a strong side with several international-class players. He quickly appreciated the quality of his opponents. 'Charlie Saxton captained the side and he was a great half-back. In that game at Leicester I also came up against their fly-half Jim Kearney for the first time and Wally Argus and Jim Sherrett were on the wings. Add to that Johnny Smith in the centre and you can see that they had a fantastic back line – and Fred Allen didn't even play in that match!'

The Kiwis, for their part, were more than a little impressed with Bleddyn Williams. The commentator Winston McCarthy, who covered every match for the New Zealand Broadcasting Service, summed-up their feelings at the end of the tour when he wrote:

'We saw the celebrated Welsh centre, Bleddyn Williams ... we saw quite a lot of him in this [RAF] game, and a few games later. Bleddyn is a really grand footballer. He must rank as one of rugby's most accomplished centres: good hands, fine brain and a pair of feet out of this world – his side-stepping was a revelation.'

A fortnight after their first sight of each other Williams and the Kiwis locked horns again at Cardiff Arms Park. A capacity Boxing Day crowd of 30,000 turned up for what promised to be a classic encounter between two unbeaten sides. Four days earlier in Swansea eight of the Cardiff team, including no fewer than six of the backs, had played for Wales in the 8-0 win over France in the first of the 'Victory' internationals. Bleddyn Williams had scored one of the tries and created the other. Now for their club they found themselves playing at the same hectic pace. It had all the trappings of a fully-fledged international occasion with the Prime Minister of New Zealand, the Rt Hon Peter Fraser, in attendance and the singing of the national anthems before kick-off. McCarthy wrote:

'All my life I have been told of how the Welsh people sing before a match, and now I was privileged to actually hear it on the spot. Only one word can describe it – magnificent. Imagine both teams standing to attention in the middle of the ground while nearly 30,000 people, who sing because they love singing, stand and forget everything in their fervour to praise their native land! Be he as tough and as hard-bitten as he will, I contend that no man who has heard it can help but be really thrilled. As I sensed what was coming, I asked the BBC to record this unforgettable moment. The actual recording of the singing on this day is now in the possession of the New Zealand Broadcasting Service.'

The game itself lived up to expectations though to modern eyes the final score of 3 points to nil would not quicken the pulse rate. The solitary try came as early as the twelfth minute after a typical spell of continuous attacking by the Kiwis. Six players handled the ball before Argus, the smartest of wings, off-loaded in the tackle for Jim Kearney, in the move for the second time, to race the final 15 yards to the line for an unconverted try. Cardiff, as always, were threatening in the backs but there was also a heroic contribution from the pack, especially in the case of the back row where Les Manfield was outstanding. The game plan had been the one that had served the club well in its unbeaten run – to attack through midfield where Billy Cleaver, Matthews and Williams would orchestrate the moves but against a touring team with a well-drilled defence the strategy floundered. If anything, the three-quarters spent as much time in defence as attack. One of Williams' clearest recollections of the game is a tackle he made:

'It was on Wally Argus as the winger swept for our unguarded try-line like a vulture for its midday meal. I crunched him to the ground as he was going all out for the corner at the Westgate Street end and we both crashed into touch only a couple of yards from the line.'

Tragically, Cardiff could have saved the game in the dying moments when they were awarded a penalty in front of the posts and on the 25. The team's first choice kickers throughout the season were the forwards Maldwyn James and Bill Tamplin – neither Cleaver nor full back St John Rees were regular goalkickers. On this occasion it was the unfortunate James who took the kick and missed. There was still time for another, more difficult, penalty to be awarded and this time Tamplin was the kicker and again he missed. James, incidentally, finished the season as Cardiff's top points-scorer with 53 conversions and a mere 12 penalty goals in 37 games – a far cry from the penalty-ridden scoring patterns of more recent times.

Most observers accepted that the Kiwis were worthy winners but there was a consolation of sorts when Cardiff played them again in very different circumstances at the end of the season. Both teams were invited as guest sides to the Middlesex Sevens at Twickenham and they met in the semi-final. Bleddyn Williams, Jack Matthews and Billy Cleaver were expected to provide the running thrills but the unlikely hero was prop Cliff Davies who raced half the length of the field for the winning try. There was not a happy ending because in the final Cardiff lost to St Mary's Hospital, admittedly one of the top seven-a-side outfits of the time.

So when the Kiwis departed for home in the spring of 1946 Bleddyn Williams was left with a distinct feeling of business left unfinished. He had been in sight of victory for Cardiff, but less close to glory with Wales when the Kiwis won the unofficial international 11-3. He next came up against the pride of New Zealand rugby in 1950, when he saw everything they had to offer at close quarters as he undertook a 23-match tour as a British and Irish Lion. The four years leading up to the tour were ones when he firmly established his reputation as the best centre of his generation. Yet for a while he flirted with the idea of playing at fly-half where he had been a permanent selection at Rydal School. He had also played in the position for the Barbarians and he seriously considered the role at Cardiff. An agreement was reached at the start of the second post-war season that the midfield triangle would be switched so that Williams would be at fly-half (which in the 1940s meant he wore the number 6 jersey), and Cleaver would partner Matthews in the centre. For a while the new formation was a success – good enough, in fact, for the Welsh selectors to persevere with it in the international trial matches throughout the autumn. When the trio was then chosen en bloc for the first official international match for eight years – against England on 18 January 1947 – it signalled what appeared to be the confirmation of a successful experiment. It didn't quite work out that way. Wales, catastrophically, lost the game played at the Arms Park by six points to nine. Williams did not escape criticism. The leading correspondent, JBG Thomas of *The Western Mail*, while conceding that a slow scrum feed did not help Haydn Tanner's passing, continued:

'…Williams was marked down relentlessly by [Don] White, and the Welshman never appeared as his real self. Rarely did we see him flashing up-field with swerve and side-step, and far too often Williams passed before drawing his man.'

An added complication had been that the fly-half had pulled a thigh muscle in the opening minutes and, of course, this was long before the introduction of replacements during a match. An option to switch Cleaver back to fly-half had been declined and Williams played the rest of the game under a distinct handicap. The selectors, though, and for that matter a Welsh public that was shell-shocked to lose this first post-war international despite home advantage, had seen enough. For the next game at Murrayfield Williams went back to centre but Cleaver stayed there as well, with Matthews being sacrificed. The club selectors followed suit, though not of course in respect to Matthews, and for the rest of the campaign the status quo of the previous season was resumed.

What undoubtedly aided Bleddyn Williams in his rise to superstar status was the quality of the club team of which he was part. This was never better illustrated than in the 1947-48 season when the side won 39 of the 41 matches played – the two losses, rather bizarrely, were the away games at Pontypool in September and Penarth the following March. Among the scalps were the Barbarians, the touring Wallabies and Newport in all four matches. There had been nothing wrong with the team's backs in the two post-war seasons so far, but now was added another precious piece of the jigsaw. Haydn Tanner, a true legend of the game who had helped both Swansea and Wales to beat the All Blacks while still at school 12 years before, and was generally regarded as the finest player of his generation, had first appeared for Cardiff during the previous season. Now he was captain of the club as well as his country. Famously regarded as a master tactician – but one who some critics felt could be too loyal to a pre-determined game plan – the great scrum-half allowed his Cardiff team free expression as matches unfolded. The result was sensational and no one benefited more than Williams. By the time he played his 31st and final club game of the season he had scored 37 tries, three short of the record for a season set by Tommy Pearson in 1893. The opposition in the final game were Gloucester, formidable competitors who rarely conceded many tries. This, though, was Bleddyn's day as in front of an ecstatic crowd of 20,000 – and, helped, he still insists, by unnecessary passes from team-mates who could have scored themselves – he ran in four tries to establish a new record. He was at the height of his powers and was also an automatic choice for Wales.

If he had one regret during the late 1940s it was the lack of opportunities to play alongside Jack Matthews in international matches. This fact will surprise casual historians for 'Matthews and Williams' are generally regarded as the most successful and effective centre pairing of their era. Yet although they ruled the roost for their club and various invitation teams that they invariably supported with guest appearances, the national selectors quirkily found other combinations to their liking. True, they had been together for the Wales victory against Australia in 1947, with Cleaver at full back, but for the championship matches that followed Matthews had been shunted out to the left wing. That decision baffled Bleddyn who regarded his great friend as an out-and-out centre – 'Jack never let Wales down on the wing but he was not at ease in the position because his style was never suited to the flank'. And this, incredibly, was in the great Cardiff season of 1947-48 when the club back division based on Tanner and Cleaver at half-back and the Matthews-Williams duo at centre proved to be an ideal combination of complementary skills.

A degree of common sense returned to the national selectors, the infamous 'Big Five', for the championship campaign of the following season with the two of them paired against England who were beaten 9-3 at the Arms Park. They were also free to play in left and right formation. Despite their admiration for the Kiwis' second five-eighth and centre line-up neither of them held any truck then – and still do not when they watch modern-day rugby – with the inside and outside centre arrangement. 'I am left-footed' pointed out Williams, 'and it seemed obvious that if I was putting in chip or grubber kicks I would be more effective doing that on the left side. Equally Jack had deceptive pace and by playing as we did we kept our options open to test the tightest of defences.'

Unfortunately the 1949 internationals that had started so well faded away with narrow defeats up at Murrayfield and then in the home fixture against Ireland at St Helen's in Swansea. Tanner was still captain with Pontypridd's gifted practitioner, Glyn Davies, partnering him at half-back. Cleaver returned temporarily for the Irish match but the centre pairing was disrupted again for the fourth and final game in France when Williams was forced to withdraw in unusual circumstances. Never one to renege on a commitment, he kept a long-standing promise to appear in a charity match in Bristol six days before the international. The fates conspired against him: he strained a muscle in the closing stages and was ruled unfit for the big match in Paris. He was not to play for Wales again for two years – by which time he had fully reacquainted himself with the might of New Zealand rugby as a Lion.

The domestic season of 1949-50 had promised much for a centre who at the age of 26 was in his prime. Tanner had retired and his fellow players had no hesitation in nominating Williams for the club captaincy. The rugby committee happily concurred and he invited the full back, Frank Trott, to be his deputy. Little did either of them realise at the outset that the vice-captain would be left in charge for the best part of three months. The first half of the season had proceeded exactly as had been planned with the captain missing only two of the 24 matches played by Christmas – and those because of international trial matches. 'I felt that I was pencilled in to captain Wales against England in the New Year and was delighted to captain the Probables team in the first trial at Pontypool,' he said. 'But in the final trial I was tackled by Malcolm Thomas who fell across my knee as we went to ground. There was a sharp burst of pain and, although I didn't realise it at the time there was extensive ligament damage.'

The selectors went ahead with their original plan and named Williams as Tanner's successor as national captain but he was forced to withdraw injured. The captaincy was passed to the number 8, John Gwilliam, who was to stay in charge for 13 of the next 14 internationals. In the week between the Twickenham international and the next match with Scotland Williams turned out for Cardiff against Swansea in a vain attempt to prove his fitness. Unwittingly, he caused further damage to his knee and as a result his leg was cast in plaster from foot to knee. The remaining international matches would go ahead without him. The question now was whether the British selectors would consider him for the forthcoming tour to New Zealand and Australia. The answer was to be in the affirmative – but only if he proved his fitness by playing for his club.

The fateful day dawned on 25 March. Jack Matthews, Billy Cleaver, Rex Willis and Cliff Davies were playing at Cardiff Arms Park, helping Wales to beat France and complete a first international Grand Slam in 39 years. But Bleddyn Williams was turning out for Cardiff against Bath at the Recreation Ground. Inside him at fly-half was an 18-year-old newcomer, Cliff Morgan:

'Cliff was in his first season with the club and was already showing his extraordinary talent. Jack and I had given him a friendly piece of advice when he made his debut with us up at Cambridge University a few months before. Basically we reminded him that the occasional pass to his centres would be appreciated. So I don't suppose I batted an eyelid when he told me in the dressing room before we went out to play Bath that I would be alright, that he would give me a pass to score the winning try! Sure enough, that's exactly what happened in the closing stages and the week after it was confirmed that I would be going on the tour.'

There were more frustrations once the Lions reached New Zealand in early May after a month-long voyage via Panama. Williams had used the long sea journey to exercise and further strengthen his knee and he was buoyed by his nomination by the tour manager 'Ginger' Osborne to be the official vice-captain. Yet no sooner had he arrived in the South Island than he pulled a muscle in his other leg after stumbling in a pot-hole in training. Cursing his luck, he was forced to sit out the first three matches of the tour, and when he did play against Otago at Dunedin there was further disappointment. His injured leg continued to trouble him, forcing a half-time switching of positions with the left wing, Malcolm Thomas. However, Thomas was himself injured soon after the game resumed and Williams returned to midfield. Reduced to 14 men and with flanker Vic Roberts covering the wing vacancy the tourists slipped to their first defeat.

With the first test looming on the horizon, Williams knew he would have to bide his time to regain full fitness. He could only watch from the grandstand as the test was drawn 9-9 after the British Isles had held a comfortable six points lead with barely 20 minutes left to play. A week later he was ready for action against Canterbury in Christchurch. He was literally the centre of attention. Kiwi watchers wanted to see for themselves the man who had arrived in their country hailed as the best British back of his generation and this time they were not disappointed. The Lions won the match 16-5 and the local newspaper reported:

'It was a different Williams who took the field against Canterbury. His work this time was polished and it will be generally agreed that he was the best of the British backs. [He] is the ideal type of centre. Solidly built and weighing 13st 6lb he gathers speed very quickly and when in full stride has an elusive, weaving run that takes him through a line of backs. Williams had a hand in the three tries scored, for in the orthodox chain passing early in the game he missed his outside centre, Henderson, with a long pass to [Ken] Jones who outpaced the opposition for a fine try. In the next try he raced past Kyle to the blind side, took a pass from Rimmer and went over the line without a hand being laid on him. The third he was responsible for when he received the ball from Kyle to make an opening for Hayward to score. On this form it seems probable that Williams will be chosen to partner his old team-mate, J Matthews, in the second test.'

The performance could not have come at a better time, silencing as it did some ill-advised doubts about his future on the tour. The *Wellington Evening Post* conceded that:

'An impression was abroad that Williams' troubles had passed from the physical to the psychological. It was so long since he had been able to play his normal game that the possibility had to be faced of his confidence having been shaken permanently. [but] Williams did not take the brakes off on Saturday ... the taking and giving of passes with classic technique, some sure-fire tackles and several perfectly directed kicks to touch vindicated his reputation.'

Suddenly the rugby folk of New Zealand realised that the advance notices had not been an exaggeration. Rather, the false start against Otago had been an aberration influenced by injury and now the true class had been revealed. The reassuring thought for Bleddyn Williams, meanwhile, was that there were another 15 games in New Zealand plus another half-dozen in Australia, in which to really make his mark. And he seized his opportunity unhesitatingly, missing only two of the remaining fixtures before the Lions departed for Sydney. In the next game at Ashburton he scored a hat-trick of tries as the Lions won comfortably. His selection alongside Matthews for the second test in Christchurch four days later was then a formality. The *Wellington Evening Post* commented, 'BL Williams, the Welsh star, has come into the team like a Lion refreshed. If, as seems to be the case, his two outings in the past week have convinced him that his troubles are over, then he may be one of the stars of the match.'

Unfortunately, the expectations of the speedy British backs playing an influential part in the result of the test match didn't materialise. It was a dour game of 58 line-outs and 29 scrums, admittedly not unusual in the 1950s, and Williams, Matthews and Cleaver at the back spent most of their time tackling. Eye witness reports reveal that apart from one interception by Williams in the early stages the Lions never looked like scoring. They also played with 14 men for nearly an hour after the Irish flanker, Bill McKay, left the field suffering from a broken nose and concussion. Injuries were a feature of the tour – and that in an age when replacements were not sent for at the drop of a hat.

Several of the team had played only a handful of games, while the Scottish wing, Doug Smith, who was to be a notably successful manager of the 1971 Lions, arrived in New Zealand with a broken arm and did not appear until the eighteenth game. Billy Cleaver had impressed everyone with his all-round skills at full-back after the first choice, George Norton, had been injured in the fifth match and would not play again on the tour. By the time the tourists moved on to the North Island after the second test, it was realised that the onus on the fit backs like Cleaver, Matthews and Kyle who had barely missed a game in the first ten, was becoming too heavy. So history was made with the selectors sending an SOS for the precocious Llanelli full back, Lewis Jones. He would be the first Lion to fly to the southern hemisphere and the unfortunate Norton would stay with the team as an onlooker. The manager, Ginger Osborne, was effusive in his thanks. At the post-test dinner he said:

'It is my honour to acknowledge an action by the New Zealand Rugby Union which, I think, is unique, but is also an example of the most generous and splendid spirit of your football. I refer to the action of the New Zealand Union in agreeing to the replacement of our injured full back, George Norton, by bringing out another player from home, and to offer to retain him in New Zealand as your guest. Now the Australian Rugby Union has taken a similar course, and has asked George Norton to be Australia's guest. How much richer and more loveable is the spirit of our great game made by such actions.'

Whatever the prognosis of others to take some rest, what Bleddyn Williams needed more than anything was match practice so when the

Lions opened their North Island fixtures with the game against Wairarapa-Bush in Masterton he happily took over both the captaincy and the fly-half berth. He contributed what was reported to be 'a dashing display' as the Lions won 27-13 but reverted to centre for the 20-point defeat of Hawke's Bay later in the week. He scored tries in both games and then added two more in another important win over Wellington. He later admitted that the try he scored on the verge of half-time there ranked among the best team tries of his career with eight players handling in the build-up that Matthews had initiated. The *Evening Post* saluted Williams' all-round contribution as that of 'a great centre-three-quarter.' It continued, 'He played some of his most dazzling football, especially in the first spell, and his second try capped such a scintillating spasm by himself and his fellows that the crowd accorded it a special tribute'.

The scene was now set for the third test in Wellington and with the tour captain, Karl Mullen, unavailable through a leg injury, the captaincy passed automatically to Williams. Bearing in mind he had already led Wales in the unofficial international against the Kiwis in 1946, this was a notable double – but as in the earlier game at the Arms Park the New Zealanders' innate ability to snatch the unlikeliest victory was the crucial factor. The British Isles had taken an early lead through a penalty goal by the Welsh prop, John Robins, and were further boosted with their opponents reduced to 14 men from the fifteenth minute. The All Blacks had lost their prop, Simpson, to a leg injury. In a photograph that typifies the sportsmanship of the match, Williams and his opposing captain, Ron Elvidge, are shown assisting the limping prop from the field. On a heavy pitch, the visitors failed to take advantage of their numerical superiority – at one stage it was even a two-man advantage when Elvidge left the field temporarily. When he did return shortly after half time he was effectively a passenger with a badly injured right arm yet was in the right place to take a scoring pass for the equalising try. Fourteen minutes from the end Bob Scott kicked a straightforward penalty goal awarded for offside and the British challenge was finished. The All Blacks were two tests up in the series with only one test left to play. Another surprise to modern eyes was that there was then a gap of four weeks and half-a-dozen provincial fixtures before the final test in Auckland. During that time, more brilliant rugby was played with Williams sharing in handsome victories over Wanganui, Taranaki and Auckland. Mullen had returned to fitness only to be injured again in the preparation during the week of the match. The Welsh hooker, Dai Davies, therefore retained his place in the middle of the front row – and Bleddyn Williams was again the test captain at Eden Park.

There was to be no happy ending to the series. Though the British Isles played some stunning rugby, most notably in a famous length-of-the-field try by Ken Jones from a move started near his own line by his namesake, Lewis, New Zealand yet again had the knack of holding on to an early lead. The final 20 minutes was described by the correspondent of *The Weekly News* as 'the most exhilarating, exciting, brilliant rugby we could ever wish to see … the type of rugby we had always day-dreamed about but considered beyond the capability of mere humans.' But humans the tourists were, though their stand-in captain almost snatched the winning try in the dying moments only to be overhauled by the opposing wing, Peter Henderson, a speedster in his own right, with the line in sight. It was again a case of so near, yet so far against the New Zealanders. At the start of the tour, Bleddyn Williams had said that the prospect of playing the All Blacks in their own backyard was the biggest thrill of his football career. At the end, even in defeat, he was left with a feeling of excitement and, still, an appetite for perhaps one more attempt at defeating them. Over the next three years he would play against the Wallabies and the Springboks for club and international teams. He would be elevated to the captaincy of Wales at the beginning of 1953 for the championship matches against Scotland, Ireland and France, all of which were won. But at the back of his mind was the knowledge that in the closing months of that same year the All Blacks would be coming to Cardiff Arms Park again. And unlike the Kiwis of eight years before they would be fully representative of the best that their country's rugby talent could offer. This time, he would be in a position to ensure that Cardiff would be ready for them.

4

The Making of Heroes

'Dear Hubert

I just thought you would like to know that after seeing the All Blacks on Saturday I am putting my money on Cardiff. I believe they are going to be beaten more than once, but certainly by Cardiff, if only your boys play their normal game of throwing the ball about.

Kindest regards

Hywel'

The letter from Hywel Thomas, the fixture secretary of the famous London club, Harlequins, to Cardiff's chairman, Hubert Johnson, was written on 10 November 1953, eleven days before the Fourth All Blacks were due to step out onto the Arms Park to face Bleddyn Williams' team. Clearly, there was already a sense of history in the making. The Welsh-born Thomas had seen London Counties give the tourists a good game at Twickenham before losing 11-0 but he was already anticipating a red letter day for the blue and blacks – and obviously felt it was part of his Celtic duty to acquaint his old friend Johnson of the fact. Some clubs might regard this expectation as an unwanted pressure on them but that hardly applied to the Cardiff team of the time. Williams himself now admits that he had a 'gut feeling' that his team was about to deliver what he regarded as the ultimate victory. This is hardly surprising. Although the glittering post-war seasons had now passed into history, by the autumn of 1953 a new team was already taking shape.

The transition from the era of Tanner, Cleaver and Matthews in the late-1940s to the new generation had been relatively painless. The club unfailingly attracted aspiring young players and, indeed, more experienced campaigners as every new season dawned. For many years past the committee had sifted through the applicants in the most effective way imaginable – through a series of trial matches. These were remarkably well organised and invariably took place in the last week of August. In those civilised times no one even considered playing official rugby fixtures before September dawned. For that matter it would be heretical to contemplate the end of the same season extending beyond 30 April each year. And equally set in stone were the two and often three trial matches at Cardiff Rugby Club. The early ones would be staged at Sophia Gardens with the last, officially and impressively labelled the 'Final Trial', naturally played at Cardiff Arms Park. All of them received extensive coverage and detailed match reports in the local press. Thus a year earlier the *South Wales Echo* had reported that 'there was an obvious wealth of talent on show at this week's trial matches.' It continued, 'In fact, there was so many youngsters keen to wear the famous blue and black colours that Rex Willis, this year's skipper, vice-captain Sid Judd and the members of the selection committee were forced to stage an additional trial game and to postpone the final trial until this afternoon.'

That particular trial, watched, incidentally, by over 2,000 fans despite the counter attraction of Glamorgan playing Worcestershire in a county championship match on the adjoining cricket pitch, was to have a sad postscript. Willis, the 1950 Lion who had won the Triple Crown and Grand Slam with Wales earlier in 1952, tore a shoulder muscle after being heavily tackled. He would miss the first four months of the season and his club captaincy would be limited to a dozen games. The vice-captain, Sid Judd, took over at the helm. Both of them would be leading figures in the great events of 1953. So, too, would other newcomers who over the two-and-half seasons from the spring of 1951 to the arrival of the All Blacks came into the Cardiff set-up and duly won their club caps. In the backs they included the utility player, Alun Thomas, the gifted St Luke's College student, Gareth Griffiths, the goal-kicking wing, Gwyn Rowlands, and the solid last line of defence, John Llewellyn. The pack was also not without an influx of new blood. CD Williams, JD Evans and Eddie Thomas had all cemented their places in the first team at various stages but the question on everyone's lips as the 1953-54 season kicked-off was whether the emerging Cardiff side was strong enough in all departments to match the All Blacks.

Towards the end of the previous season, Reg Pelling, a respected journalist on the then authoritative rugby pages of the *News Chronicle*, wrote:

'The season's records show that once again Cardiff ranks as the best club side in Britain. Fixtures are eagerly sought by other clubs; and players from the Welsh valleys rush to offer their services. As with the Arsenal in soccer, few men leave the club having once made the grade. Cardiff serve as a model to rugby clubs everywhere.'

There was not, of course, an official league championship in the 1950s but the yardstick for success was *The Western Mail's* 'All Welsh Table'. This was a far from perfect device where positions were calculated on the basis of the percentage of matches won in fixtures against fellow Welsh clubs. There were 18 such clubs designated of first-class status, including London Welsh, but in 1952-53 Cardiff had official fixtures with only eight of them. That is interesting because it confirms that the majority of Cardiff's 49 matches during the season were against the top English clubs, together with two games in Ireland and home dates with Nantes & Cognac from France and Watsonians from north of the border. So in the final 'league' table Cardiff were top with a 72.2% return from winning 12 and drawing two of their 18 fixtures against Welsh opposition (bearing in mind that four of the matches were against Newport). Some clubs like Neath, Bridgend and Cross Keys had as many as 29 games each against other Welsh clubs and their final percentages were calculated on these great numbers. Yet no one could dispute Cardiff's pre-eminence because their overall fixture list had a depth of quality opposition from far and wide that the vast majority of other clubs in the Principality could only dream about at that time.

Not surprisingly, then, ambitious players flocked towards the Arms Park again in the summer of 1953. The *Football Echo* reported over

70 new applications for the trials and it even wondered whether, with the imminent arrival of the All Blacks, Dr Jack Matthews would be tempted out of retirement. By all accounts he was 'in strict training and looking fitter than ever.' In the end, the great centre resisted the urge to make a comeback. At 33 years of age he felt that his continuing services to the club would be best employed as a committee member. In fact he became its chairman 12 months later. Meanwhile, his great friend Bleddyn Williams had been appointed club captain for the second time and all the planning on and off the field for the first half of the season revolved around the challenge to the All Blacks. As if that was not enough to stir the heart beat for what was waiting around the corner, another visitor to Cardiff Arms Park caused further excitement.

Eamonn Andrews, the sports' broadcaster who was later to achieve fame as the presenter of *Sports Report* on the radio and *This Is Your Life* on television, spent a day at the club as the new season was about to get under way. He was researching material for his weekly radio programme aimed at a wider audience than merely sports-lovers. He interviewed several leading players and officials including the chairman, Hubert Johnson, the secretary, Brice Jenkins, and, of course, the captain and vice-captain, Bleddyn Williams and Sid Judd. Williams saw this as an omen:

'Eamonn Andrews was particularly interested in the history of the club and how we had already beaten the Springboks and Wallabies and, even though a non-rugby man, he immediately identified the significance of the approaching match with the All Blacks. I couldn't help but feel that everything was pointing towards us achieving what we wanted more than anything that season, victory over New Zealand.

When Eamonn asked me what pictures among the many on show on the walls of the club museum I would pick for myself, I remarked that the picture I wanted wasn't there. It was one of the 1953 Cardiff side which beat the All Blacks!'

So the captain and the club's ambition was public knowledge. The fixture was set for late November and meant that Cardiff would have nearly three months and 17 matches in which to fine-tune their preparations. For the All Blacks, it would be the seventh game of their 36-match tour. That could mean that they would still be settling in as a team and would be vulnerable against an experienced club combination. Equally, and particularly so in the case of any New Zealand side, they could already be in top gear and sweeping all before them. Time would only tell but Cardiff's priority throughout the month of September was to decide on their own best line-up.

Some selections were regarded as automatic. With Rex Willis back to full fitness no one questioned his partnership with Cliff Morgan at half-back. Further out in midfield matters were not so clear cut. Obviously the captain would be at left centre but who would partner him? There were several options. Gareth Griffiths had finished the previous season in the centre for the club and for the Barbarians but had won four international caps on the wing. Alun Thomas had played with Bleddyn Williams in the centre for the same Welsh team but was another with international wing experience. Then there were other promising youngsters like Howard Nicholls, Gordon Wells, Colin Bosley and Alan Barter. The fact that nearly all of these could also play on the wing only complicated matters because the strength in that position included Gwyn Rowlands, Haydn Morris and CL Davies. Morris had played for Wales in 1951 and would be a Lion in 1955 while Rowlands and Davies were future internationals in the making.

There seemed less conjecture at full back where John Llewellyn had played over 70 games in the previous two seasons and had also had international trials. Yet even here there were alternatives, particularly in the case of the 20-year-old Alun Priday who had already made a big impression in the Cardiff Athletic team. The inclination in the front row of the pack was to play John Phillips, who had considerable experience as a hooker, at tight-head prop alongside Geoff Beckingham and JD Evans. But the selectors knew that it would be hard to ignore one of the figureheads of the club, Stanley Bowes, who at the age of 36 had finished the previous season as first-choice prop. There were also various permutations to resolve in the back five positions of the scrum. The versatility of the three-quarters was replicated here with the likes of Eddie Thomas and Peter Goodfellow equally adept at lock or back row. The semi-retirement of the outstanding second-rower, Bill Tamplin, who had captained both club and country, was potentially a grievous blow but was offset by the continued development of the formidable Malcolm Collins. He was guaranteed one of the lock positions while the vice-captain, Sid Judd, and CD Williams would form two-thirds of the back row.

To their credit the selectors were not afraid to experiment in the early matches. The opening three fixtures against the District team, Cheltenham and Birkenhead Park were all at home on the Arms Park. Bleddyn Williams played in all of them, as he would throughout the autumn, putting him in the ideal position to weigh up the alternatives at first hand. Colin Bosley and Howard Nicholls were both given their opportunities with him in midfield and they were followed by Gareth Griffiths. At Leicester on the Midlands' tour at the end of September a late reshuffle due to injuries meant that Griffiths was moved out to the wing. The emergency centre drafted in was none other than Jack Matthews who had travelled with the team as a committee member. Cardiff won the game 12-3, including tries by Bleddyn Williams, Willis and Barter, their sixth straight win, but there were concerns about the quality of their performances. More sensibly, the *Football Echo* had already headlined a story, 'Don't write Cardiff off too soon as rugby's number one club'. It surmised:

'One of the penalties of possessing the reputation of being rugby's No. 1 club is that the slightest fall from grace in standards of play is seized on by certain critics as proof that Cardiff's post-war golden era is over. It is true that Cardiff looked anything but impressive in their two opening games against a District XV and Cheltenham and probably deserved the rude things said about them. But to write off the team completely on its showing in these early games is a trifle premature to say the least, particularly in view of the wealth of first-class talent available.'

The critics did concede that Phillips and Eddie Thomas had added mobility to the pack and they had been joined by an interesting newcomer at blind-side flanker, Des Walsh. He was another of the Rhondda recruits, offered real pace around the pitch and was outstanding in the win at Aberavon midway through the month. Likewise in the second row the early preference was for John

Maunder to pack down with Collins. He was a 24-year-old steelworker who had made his debut in the closing months of the 1952-53 campaign and had made a big impression as the new season gathered steam. Fate took a hand, unfortunately, and Maunder was sidelined by an industrial accident after only three games. Another exceptionally promising young lock, WR Evans, was fleetingly to play in a couple of matches before going off to pursue his legal studies at Cambridge University. Three years later Roddy Evans returned to the club and in 1959 toured Australia, New Zealand and Canada with the Lions as a fully-fledged test match lock. In 1953, however, the responsibility of line-out specialist in tandem with Malcolm Collins was eventually handed to Eddie Thomas.

Yet even as the season entered its second month, and with the All Blacks looming on the horizon, there remained a great deal of uncertainty about Cardiff's preferred line-up. The first match of four scheduled against Newport would normally be regarded as a key indicator of the selectors' intentions. But the team that took the field against the old enemy on 3 October bore no resemblance to the side that was eventually selected for the big match. This was partly due to injuries and eleventh hour changes that necessitated CL Davies replacing Haydn Morris on the wing – neither would play against the tourists – and the dependable Brian Mark playing instead of Rex Willis at the base of the scrum. In an unfamiliar pack formation, Judd was moved up to second row, the 24-year-old Glyn Morgan started at prop, and John Nelson, who had missed all but the opening match because of injury, switched from flanker to number eight.

In a dour encounter, Cardiff capitalised on Newport errors to score three converted tries and win by 15 points to 6. A crowd of 42,000 watched the game, the third highest attendance in the history of club rugby at the time. The blue and black fans among them would have been pleased with the final score if not the means of achieving it for still the team was not firing on all cylinders. Forty-eight hours later, in a re-arranged Monday evening fixture at Stradey Park, Cardiff lost their unbeaten record to Llanelli. The Scarlets deservedly won the match by 9 points to 3 – the attendance was this time a healthy 9,000 – with Dave Phillips in the *South Wales Echo* reporting that the home crowd was 'almost delirious with joy'. More encouragingly, he also noted that 'Cardiff looked more impressive in defeat than they have hitherto done in victory and their spirit was terrific throughout'. Several leading players, including Sid Judd, Geoff Beckingham, Rex Willis and Haydn Morris, had missed the game but the international centre Alun Thomas had made his season's debut.

The stuttering progress of the team continued throughout the next fortnight. A good win against Bristol at the Memorial Ground, with Bleddyn Williams scoring two fine tries, was followed by another defeat at Swansea. A 6-6 home draw with Neath, with the captain again rescuing his side with a brilliant late effort, suggested little cause for optimism as November dawned. More worryingly, there was still an unsettled look to the team. With Cliff Morgan injured, Alan Barter had played at pivot against Neath. With him in the backs were Alun Priday and Cowboy Davies and up front a young prop, John Dodds, with John Phillips hooking, and another new face, Bruce Thomas from Penarth, at number 8. Few if any of these young players would have been considered likely first-choicers at the start of the season. The uncertainty continued against Cambridge University at the end of the month with a narrow 14-9 home win.

By now the All Blacks had landed. On the day Cardiff were playing the University the tourists had opened their tour account with a 24-points without reply demolition of the Southern Counties at Hove. The home side had selected seven current or future internationals in their side, including CD Williams, but had been brushed aside. Four days later the All Blacks ran in six tries against a Cambridge University line-up that contained 14 of the players that had run Cardiff so close. Critics and fans were already attempting to establish worthwhile comparisons to forecast what might happen on 21 November. As if that was not enough to increase anticipation and concentrate minds ahead of the great day, tickets for the big match had also gone on sale. Grandstand seats were priced at five shillings, the enclosure at three shillings and the field – that is, behind the goalposts at either end – at two shillings. Season ticket holders were given first option to buy their tickets and reserve their normal seats before the remainder went on general sale on Monday 2 November. The rush that followed was phenomenal. Postal applications were not allowed so the personal callers to the Arms Park resulted in queues the length of Westgate Street. The original plan to allow payment for the enclosure and field tickets to be made on the gate on the day of the match remained in place though serious consideration was given to declaring the game 'all-ticket'. Still the demand continued with hundreds of fans destined to be disappointed.

'I never knew there were so many New Zealanders in South Wales,' said one club official in the *South Wales Echo*. Almost in a state of shock he pleaded, 'And please make it clear that we will not entertain applications for international match tickets until this business is over. We have enough on our hands now!'

Clearly a capacity crowd of 56,000 would pour into the Arms Park. Marshalling arrangements would be overseen by the Chief Constable of the city and special entrances would be provided for season ticket holders. The club's preparations were impressively thorough. The interior of the clubhouse was freshly painted and refurbished and extra New Zealand mementoes were brought out of the archives to be displayed in the club museum. A delegation of officials and players was chosen to meet the All Blacks on their arrival at Cardiff General Station at the start of the week. Blue and black touch judges' flags were embroidered, one of which would be presented to the touring team's management after the game. All that remained was for the team to be selected and prepared as thoroughly as possible.

The November fixtures had opened with a dispiriting loss at Northampton. The 9-22 score line marked Cardiff's heaviest defeat since 1936, hardly a good omen. Thankfully, there was an immediate improvement the following week at the Arms Park against Oxford University. The students were trounced by 30 points but even this failed to assuage the anxieties of the more pessimistic fans. The local press reported:

'Football crowds are strange assemblies and the 15,000 or so all-weather fans who braved the elements to watch Cardiff beat Oxford University 30-0 were no exception. Half of them left the Arms Park muttering gloomily that this was a one-sided, almost farcical massacre of the innocents – others were convinced that the Cardiff display in the awful conditions was a happy augury for the forthcoming New Zealand game!'

Some observers had obviously perceived a ray of light at the end of
the blue and black tunnel. The most significant fact that
understandably escaped them at the time was that the team that took
the field against Oxford would do duty again against the All Blacks a
fortnight later. One final club game remained away to Newport but
that coincided with the first Welsh international trial at Swansea. Six
of the club's backs were involved in that while two of the pack, Sid
Judd and JD Evans, were trial reserves and also unavailable at
Rodney Parade. Nevertheless, Cardiff won the match narrowly and
now there was just seven days left before the ultimate test.

Behind the scenes Bleddyn Williams and the committee had been
quietly resolving their selection headaches for several weeks. Typical
of their thoroughness was the choice of the best combination in the
front row of the scrum. No one was in any doubt that the hooker at
the heart of the operation would be Geoff Beckingham who was then
in his sixth season with the club and had played for Wales against
England and Scotland earlier in the year. Here was one of the great
characters in a team not short of characters. Like so many of his team
mates he had watched the Cardiff sides of the early post-war years
from the Arms Park terraces and formulated an ambition to one day
play in blue and black himself. He had particularly studied the play of
the leading hookers such as Newport's Bunner Travers, the England
international Bert Toft and Cardiff's own Maldwyn James. But
Beckingham had left Romilly Elementary School in Barry at the age
of 14 and eventually did his national service with the RAF. He stayed
in uniform for six years and was well past his twenty-second birthday
and back in Barry as a municipal gardener before he first tried his
luck at the Arms Park. A couple of games for the Athletic XV in 1946
and a first team debut the following year failed to satisfy his rugby-
playing appetite. Looking back, he said:

'My first senior rugby was with Barry and it was their club
secretary, Jim Hamber, who persuaded me to go to Cardiff for
the trials. When I did I was selected for the Rags and eventually
the first team. But I wasn't playing regularly because there were
five hookers, including the international Maldwyn James, and
only two teams. Even my mathematics told me that there was
little chance of a game every Saturday. So after two or three

games in the 1947-48 season I went back to Barry. Brice Jenkins [Cardiff's secretary] couldn't understand it and warned me that I was in danger of wasting my ability. I eventually went back to Cardiff in 1948, played over 20 games for the Rags to win a club cap and also had a dozen or so outings for the firsts. After that I never left until I hung up my boots ten years later.'

By 1953 Beckingham was one of the most respected front row practitioners in Welsh club rugby. As well as his international caps, he had played for Cardiff against the Springboks, and thought nothing of turning out for 40 club games a season. He also relished the challenge of facing the All Blacks. 'I couldn't wait to take them on,' he said. 'Whoever were the props – and I knew exactly who I wanted to go into battle alongside me – we would lack bulk as a unit but would have the scrummaging technique to come out on top. We would be shorter than them as well but we had short, hairy legs and they would have to come down to us because we would be packing low and hard!'

The Cardiff front row's scrummaging abilities were well-known to domestic opponents but would be a nasty surprise to the All Blacks. Beckingham tells a marvellous story about when the club played the Harlequins at Twickenham and his opposite number was the South African-born England international, Nick Labuschagne:

'He was another tall hooker, well over six feet, and ripe for the treatment. Again we scrummaged very low so he and his props were really struggling. Late in the game I even 'hooked' the ball back with my head. As it happened, Bleddyn Williams who was out in the centre spotted what I'd done. We won the game and as we were coming off the field he came over to give me a ticking off for illegal tactics. I protested, saying that I couldn't move my feet at that particular scrum. My props, 'JD' [Evans] and Stanley [Bowes] agreed. Bleddyn shook his head and said, 'That's the trouble with you flaming forwards, you always stick together – but don't ever do that again'. I muttered, 'not until the next time' … he wasn't amused'

Not surprisingly, then, Beckingham's preferred choice of props in 1953, on which he was duly consulted, were JD Evans and Stan

Bowes. 'Quite early on in the season when we were up in the Midlands playing Coventry and Leicester our vice-captain and pack leader, Sid Judd, had a quiet word with me and asked who should be the props against the All Blacks in November. I told him without a moment's hesitation that they had to be 'JD' and Stanley. We were not big but we were a unit with complete faith in each other. We were almost telepathic because when we were preparing to settle in a scrum I only had to move my finger a fraction as a signal and the two of them would come in around me. Someone once called us the three little pixies!'

There was nothing cherubic about John Evans, a hard-as-nails colliery welder from Mountain Ash. Beckingham regarded him as 'a thundering good scrummager' and, like himself, not afraid of hard work – in the previous season he had played in 40 of the team's 49 games and was still an automatic choice at loose-head prop. A knee injury picked up on the Midlands tour had caused him to miss seven games but he was up and running again by late October. What was more in doubt was the selection of the third member of the front row. Beckingham wanted Stan Bowes but whether or not he would get his way was at one time debatable. The former seaman from Llandaff was now in his 37th year and decidedly a veteran. He had made his club debut as long ago as 1937 and ever since September 1950 had been captain of the Rags. But as every year went by the selectors called him up from the Athletic XV to represent the first team. That had happened no fewer than 25 times in 1952-53 and, although re-elected Rags captain for a fourth season, it was still the case now. The truth was that normal rules didn't apply to ADS Bowes. A club wit of a later generation, Dai Hayward, called him Unsinkable Bowes, only partly because of his former career as a petty officer. Indeed the man himself was to have the most memorable of business cards in his eventual role as club chairman. It read:

STAN BOWES – A Legend in his own time
World Traveller   Bon Vivant   Soldier of Fortune   Oppressor of
Champions   International Lover   Casual Hero   All Round Good Guy
Philosopher   Wars Fought   Revolutions Started   Alligators Castrated
Governments Run   Uprisings Quelled   Tigers Tamed   Bars Emptied
Virgins Converted   Computers Verified   Orgies Organised.

Clearly with such a man in the team the All Blacks would be a pushover. So, after leading his Rags' side in nine games at the start of the season, Stan Bowes was once again promoted to the senior side a month before the All Blacks fixture. It was to prove an inspired choice. The courage of the front row trio was to prove crucial to the outcome of the match on 21 November.

Choosing a lock combination in the second row might at one time have been regarded as a difficult proposition for the selectors. The departure of Bill Tamplin and the unavailability of the promising youngster, John Maunder, had disrupted any early plans they might have had. Malcolm Collins, a fine forward in his fifth season at the club, would certainly be one of the locks. Though he lived in Newport Collins, like Bowes, devoted his rugby life to Cardiff. At over six feet tall he was the most reliable of lineout specialists and Beckingham describes him as 'sixteen and a half stone of solid muscle'. He added, 'Though Malcolm was a good jumper we did occasionally try a spot of lifting. He asked me to put my knee in his back when he went up and it worked a treat'. A brief spell out injured at the end of September proved temporary and he was firing on all cylinders again in the month leading up to the touring team game. At the same time Eddie Thomas had established himself as Collins' natural partner. The schoolmaster from the Rhondda had come to the Arms Park 12 months earlier after a distinguished career with Neath and he welcomed the opportunity to play against another major touring team.

'Basically, I was a back row forward,' he said, 'and had played at blind-side flanker for the combined Neath and Aberavon team against the Springboks in 1952. But at Cardiff the competition for places was stiff and I was prepared to play anywhere, especially against the All Blacks. As Tamplin had gone I filled the gap. Really I was a bit short for the position at only six feet tall and I was used mainly as a support player in the lineout. But I got around the field more than the usual locks and Malcolm and myself complemented each other pretty well.'

The back row selection was also fairly straightforward. With the vice-captain Sid Judd playing at number 8 the flankers would be CD Williams and John Nelson. CD, or Derek, Williams was a man of many talents on and off the field. Born and bred in Cardiff, he was educated at Canton High School and the local Technical College before further distinguishing himself in the academic world at Oxford University where he gained a First in Chemistry. Over the next forty years he was at various times a research scholar alongside a Nobel Prize winner, an industrial chemist, a fuel technologist for the National Coal Board, a marketing director for an international company, and a successful publican. He also brought a Corinthian spirit and considerable ability to his many sporting activities. These included athletics where he was a county half-mile champion and carried the Olympic torch near Wembley Stadium in 1948. That wasn't his only summer sport though, his cricket career included a double century for south Oxfordshire and numerous other big innings in club cricket, and added to that was a low handicap at golf that didn't prevent him still 'beating his age' when he was well past his seventieth birthday. At Oxford he won Blues at rugby in 1945 and at boxing three years later. In many ways he could have been one of the most vital contributors to Cardiff's pre-match planning for the match with the All Blacks because he had first-hand knowledge of their likely approach. Yet it didn't quite work out that way.

'I had played against them in their first match of the tour at Hove,' he recalled. 'At the time I was working for Huntley and Palmer's in Reading as an assistant chief chemist and played both cricket and rugby for Berkshire. That qualified me for the Southern Counties team against the All Blacks, a game I was really looking forward to as I had played for Oxford University against the Kiwis in 1945. As it happened the Counties' side was well beaten by the tourists but I left a little bit of a marker with them. My opposite number was their captain, Bob Stuart, and as we were packing down at the side of the first scrum I told him, 'Wait till you bastards get to Cardiff!' I came away from that game with one or two impressions. Firstly, I knew that their half-backs weren't quick enough and posed no real threat. That led to my second conclusion, which was that at Cardiff we could afford to employ a drift defence, shackling their backs across field. It was a strategy we had used very successfully in our matches with Newport – and they had an outstanding fly-half in Roy Burnett. So much for my master plan but Bleddyn didn't consult me anyway – but I was confident that we could win.'

Over-planning was not a feature of the age. A reliance on native wit and common-sense within a more general game plan was more the case. Players of CD Williams' sporting intelligence provided that and the captain obviously had faith in the ability of all the team to come up with answers on the field. Williams describes himself as the spoiler of the back row but other testimonies suggest there was far more to his play than that. His speed was undoubtedly an asset – in the summer of 1953 he had sprinted 100 yards in 10.5 seconds and covered a quarter-mile in 51 seconds on the running track. That made him a dangerous customer with the ball in hand or when he foraged among the opposition's backs. His team mate John Nelson preferred to describe him as blessed with 'an explosive burst that unfailingly disconcerted the fly-half he was marking'.

Nelson was the perfect foil to CD Williams and Judd. Though in the course of a 13-year career at the club he was to play in six different positions, he was essentially a blind-side flanker – and one out of the top drawer. Another product of the city's schools' rugby, in his case St Illtyd's College, he had also considerable experience of English club and county rugby. He had originally trained to be a teacher at St Mary's College in Strawberry Hill and played for London Welsh and Eastern Counties. In 1951 he had returned to Cardiff University to achieve further qualifications and enter the world of business.Establishing himself in the Cardiff side was a bonus but one that was thoroughly well deserved. Playing alongside Judd and Williams was something he particularly enjoyed. Though they were capped by Wales and he had to be satisfied with a final trial, a couple of selections as an international reserve and two games for the Barbarians Nelson was in 1999 one of the original inductees into the club's Hall of Fame. Speaking a few months before his untimely death in 2001, he recalled his memories of the All Blacks' match:

'As a back row, Sid, Derek and myself dovetailed perfectly. Derek always burst around the field to great effect while Sid was particularly dangerous when powering through the back of the line-out as a ball-carrier or disrupting the opposition's possession. We were also fortunate in that over the years none of us had suffered injuries that kept us out of the team for very long. It was a privilege to play with the other two because it was the best back row I was part of in my career. I was looking forward to the visit of the All Blacks tremendously and trained for 22 consecutive days, including weekends, in readiness for the match.'

Sid Judd completed the back row. In 1953 he was 25 years of age, a marvellous prospect who had already played for Wales. He had also taken over the club captaincy for a large chunk of the previous season when Rex Willis was injured. Tragically he was to die of leukaemia in 1959 but his contribution to the fate of the All Blacks against both Cardiff and Wales was considerable. His first caps for Wales had been at flanker but Cardiff preferred to use him in the middle of the back row. Geoff Beckingham remembers him with great affection:

'If that boy had lived he would have gone down in the history books as one of the all-time greats. He was incredibly skilful, especially at the back of the line-out, and with the ball in his hands he could be unstoppable. If he was running at the try line from 15 yards out then if Sid couldn't get there, nobody could.'

CD Williams agrees, describing Judd as 'both robust and intuitive'.

The All Blacks were to discover to their cost that Sid Judd was a prolific try scorer. The onus of the attacking, however, would surely come from the exceptional Cardiff backs. The chopping and changing had gone on throughout the autumn but the selectors had finally shown their hand on 7 November when Oxford University were trounced by 30 points to nil. The club's back division that day had John Llewellyn at full back, a three-quarter line of Gareth Griffiths, Alun Thomas, Bleddyn Williams and Gwyn Rowlands, and the international pairing of Cliff Morgan and Rex Willis at half-back. Between them they scored seven of the eight tries against the students, including a hat-trick for Rowlands and two from Morgan. The eighth was claimed by CD Williams who, it was reported in the *Football Echo*, 'followed up with a tremendous dash to score an unconverted try on the brink of half-time'. The prospects were good. With alternative selections such as Haydn Morris and CL Davies on the wing ruled out by illness and injuries, the selectors saw no reason to tinker further with the backs. Bleddyn Williams would want to run the ball at the tourists and there was no shortage of pace, skill or ambition in the players around him.

John Llewellyn's position as the last line of defence was unquestioned. Since the retirement of the international, Frank Trott, 18 months earlier, Llewellyn, a 26-year-old sales representative from Taff's Well, had taken his chance admirably, good enough in fact to be selected for an international trial by Wales. There was nothing flashy about his game but what he offered was the orthodox qualities of catching, kicking and tackling. A shoulder injury had forced him to miss several matches in October but he was now back to full fitness. The New Zealand match would mark his 90th first team match barely three years after his club debut.

The potential problem with the three-quarter line promised to be that of fitting five quality players into four places. That was avoided when the lightning fast left wing, Haydn Morris, who had been top try-scorer in 1952-53 with 26 in only 30 games, was given medical advice not to play for several months. A schoolteacher at Barry Grammar School, he declared himself unavailable for rugby and did not reappear until the turn of the year. With Bleddyn Williams at left centre and Gwyn Rowlands, a medical officer in the RAF, certain to fill one wing position, the question then was one of how to deploy Alun Thomas and Gareth Griffiths.. Both were internationals at centre and wing and equally adept in either position. In 1952 Thomas had played in four different positions, including fly-half, in consecutive matches but since his belated start to the season in early October he had concentrated on the centre position. There he offered a sound defence while Griffiths' greater pace, fine centre though he was, could be better exploited out on the wing in line with the team's expansive ambitions.

By November 1953 Morgan and Willis were as celebrated a pair of half-backs as any in European rugby. Cliff had made his blue and black debut at the age of 19 in 1949:

'My first game was at Cambridge University with Jack Matthews and Bleddyn Williams in the centre and although Dr Jack gave me a rollicking for delaying my passes I can safely say that I learnt more in one afternoon with them than I had in my entire career up to then'.

Cliff was a quick learner. Less than 18 months later he was selected for his first cap for Wales against Ireland at Swansea. His partner at scrum-half was Rex Willis and they were to go on to play together in a record-breaking 14 internationals. The fly-half was in particularly fine form that autumn, starting the club campaign with what was described as a brilliant try against Cheltenham, then one of the top English sides, at the Arms Park. The *Football Echo* reported:

'Cliff Morgan took a lone hand to score a brilliant solo try when Cheltenham's intensive network of defence seemed to have thrown up an impenetrable barrier. Morgan's twinkling feet carried him through where the defence seemed thickest and he scurried away in pursuit of his own kick ahead to score.'

Similar efforts followed against Gloucester and in the dress rehearsal for the big day against Oxford University but Morgan was a player for all conditions. When Cardiff won at Aberavon in dreadful weather, he it was who controlled a tight game with masterly tactical kicking. Throughout his career he was the first to give credit for his success to Willis, or 'Sexy Rexy' as he preferred to call him. Despite his glamorous persona as a multiple cinema owner and a free spirit off the field with an appetite for the good things in life, the 1950 Lions' scrum-half could be as self-deprecating as Morgan was flamboyant. He admitted that 'Playing for Cardiff was a privilege and there was always a few laughs – but if you woke up on a Saturday morning in mid-winter with snow on the ground and a match with Neath at the Gnoll looming later in the day you didn't exactly want to jump out of bed.'

The challenge of the All Blacks, though, was a different kettle of fish altogether. The experience gained by Willis on the tour to New Zealand with the Lions would prove invaluable. In a squad of three scrum-halves he had established himself as number one by the time of the final test in Auckland and had gone on to play in both internationals against Australia. In 1953, Rex Willis was still the top practitioner in his position in the British game, with his long pass, strong defence and protection of whoever was playing with him at half-back. Like his captain, Bleddyn Williams, he would want to finish off the job started with the Lions and beat the All Blacks. His injury-wrecked club captaincy season in 1952-53 made him all the more determined to achieve something memorable against them. And as Cliff Morgan still says of him:

'He was posh, drove fast cars, had long hair, and looked an unlikely scrum-half. But he also had big shoulders, a strong frame, and was prepared to defend you against all opposition. He was in every sense my better half. I first met him when invited to play for his team in a charity game against Porthcawl. I was only 19 and distinctly nervous but his almost laid back approach was infectious. He was a marvellous player and the ideal scrum-half to take on the All Blacks in 1953.'

So the Cardiff team was in place and ready for battle. Their opponents arrived at Cardiff General Station on the evening of Sunday 15 November en route to their South Wales headquarters at the Seabank Hotel in Porthcawl. Like their predecessors in 1935, they would play a midweek game against Llanelli before running out on to the Arms Park for the first time on the following Saturday afternoon. In time-honoured fashion several players and officials of the club met them at the station. Morgan and Willis were photographed sharing a joke with two of the tour party, the forwards, Bob O'Dea and Arthur Woods, while chairman Hubert Johnson warmly shook the hand of New Zealand's manager, Norman Millard. Behind the smiles and warmth, there was already an unwritten bank of knowledge about the perceived strengths and weaknesses of the illustrious visitors. For the past month, several blue and blacks and, of course, well wishers like the Harlequin Hywel Thomas, had been following their progress in their five matches in England. The club selectors had travelled across to Bristol to see them beat the Western Counties by 11 points to nil on the previous weekend. Bleddyn Williams, Rex Willis and Cliff Morgan would watch them again at Stradey Park.

What they had gleaned so far was that, as ever, the All Blacks were an efficient unit and one that seemed particularly strong in defence. They had won all five matches in England with something to spare, conceding only three tries. The three Counties sides put out in Hove, Twickenham and Bristol had failed to register any points at all against them. The strength was undeniably in their forwards and they were well led by the flanker, Bob Stuart, but there was a vein of inexperience running through the squad. Since their narrow victories over the British Isles in 1950, New Zealand had only played five international matches, all of them against Australia and only one of them had been lost. Stuart was a new captain and fifteen of the 30-strong party were new All Blacks. Kiwi supporters hoped they saw a blend of youth and experience in their composition. At the outset of the tour, the manager Norman Millard said, 'When we speak of the type of football we intend to play, we realise that if our opponents are too strong they will dictate the style of play in a game. No team can do well unless its forwards are strong, and we hope the forwards of this side will develop into a traditional New Zealand pack. If the forwards are strong we can concentrate on the typical style of New Zealand play. This is attack, not defence, and, after all, attack is the best defence.'

The early games in England had clearly gone according to plan for Millard. The performance of the pack, as expected, centred on the prolific line-out specialist, 'Tiny' White, and the marvellous scrummaging prop, Kevin Skinner. Others had come to the fore, including an exceptionally fast flanker, Bill Clark, a useful lock, George Dalzell, and in the front row another White, Hallard, who, for reasons even he couldn't explain, was known as 'Snow'. One of the more experienced back-rowers, Bill McCaw, had also shown up well against London Counties at Twickenham, where the home pack fielded five full international players.

Behind the scrum the focus of attention was the veteran full-back, Bob Scott. Arguably the most famous All Black of his generation, he was the only member of the team to have toured Europe with the Kiwis immediately after the war. Since then he had won the first of his dozen official international caps in 1946, had been a prolific points scorer on an otherwise unsuccessful tour of South Africa in 1949, and had been ever-present in the test series of the following year against the British Isles. But after that he had disappeared from the international stage, first through unavailability and then temporary retirement. Now he had been persuaded to make a high-profile comeback and he was regarded as the major attacking force in the team. Few full-backs attempted to come into the three-quarter line like Scott, though he had met his match in Lewis Jones in the final test of 1950. On tour he would again pose a threat but one that Bleddyn Williams quickly identified and countered. Cardiff's plan was simple, as he explained:

'We knew that Scott would come into the attack and try to run straight through the middle. We decided that the best course of action was to allow him to see the gap and go for it but then immediately be up on him and smother man and ball. I knew he would try to get past me at inside centre but I was confident that even if he slipped past me our back row would nail him.'

The other All Blacks known to Williams were the half-backs, Vince Bevan and Laurie Haig, and the centre, John Tanner, all of whom had played in the 1950 tests. Others, like the goal-kicking wing, Ron Jarden, another wing, Allan Elsom, the centre, John Fitzgerald, and the scrum-half, Keith Davis, had gained international experience since then in the matches against Australia. But none of them worried Cardiff unduly. Even after they had seen a sixth straight All Blacks' win over Llanelli, which the tourists regarded as a very good performance, and which led the Scarlets' skipper, Peter Evans, to conclude it was a sign that they would remain unbeaten on tour, the Cardiff leadership remained confident.

Bleddyn Williams now laid his final plan:

'I came away from Llanelli with a clear strategy in my mind. I knew that we had to score in the first 20 minutes. We needed to tear into them before they had settled down and before they had become inured to the nervous tension provoked by the atmosphere of the expected capacity crowd at the Arms Park. Against Llanelli we had closely studied their breakaway forward methods and noted how swiftly and efficiently they broke up their opponents' attacks. Then there was Bob Scott's habit of slipping in between his centres to make the extra man in attack. Our strategy was plotted and we had only one pre-match practice. Whenever it was Cardiff's throw-in at a line-out our wings would throw long to the tail. This would engage the attention of the All Blacks' fast wing-forwards who, hopefully, would be dragged in to the loose scrum or maul that followed. Then a quick feed to our backs would leave them man-on-man against their backs. If we got ourselves into that situation I was confident that we could score the tries to win the match.'

Eight years on from his tussles with the Kiwis, Bleddyn Williams and his team were ready for the ultimate challenge. All that remained was to put the master plan into action.

5

The Historic Day

'Between ourselves, we consider that our matches against Wales and England and the rest are secondary affairs. Our primary aim is to beat Cardiff.'

The speech by the All Blacks' captain, Bob Stuart, at a luncheon given by the Cardiff Rotary Club set the tone for the week of the big match. It was only Monday. The tourists still had to play Llanelli and Cardiff and still had to hold their final training session. But, if they hadn't appreciated the significance of the match beforehand, the listening audience was left in no doubt now. So too were the readers of the following morning's *Western Mail* as Stuart's comments were widely reported.

The build-up continued throughout the following days. The club secretary, Brice Jenkins, confirmed that ticket applications were still flooding in from places as far afield as Penzance and the north of Scotland. Newspaper supplements recounted the near miss and Percy Bush's gaff in 1905 and the history of the two games since then in 1924 and 1935 was graphically recounted, complete with archive photographs. The 1953 vintage of All Blacks were proving to be admirable ambassadors. There were several stories of fans visiting them at their Porthcawl headquarters with all manner of mementoes to sign. One enthusiast, Jim Carroll of the Llandaff North club, took with him a mounted photograph of a kiwi that had been presented to him by New Zealand soldiers while on active service in Korea. Every single member of the team was reported to have signed it for him. Later in the week the players were photographed performing the haka on a visit to Sully Hospital. The only potentially sour note was struck when Bob Stuart said he was concerned about the goal-posts on the Arms Park pitch that were made of tubular steel and not padded: 'Back home in New Zealand we pad our posts up to 5 feet 6 inches from the ground but these look dangerous.' Clearly match day couldn't dawn soon enough so that everyone could be put out of their anxieties.

With Cardiff's players completing their final preparations it only remained for the All Blacks to announce their team. This they did on the Wednesday evening and its most notable aspect was that no fewer than 12 of the team who had beaten Llanelli would play again against Cardiff just four days later. The three changes in personnel involved Doug Wilson replacing John Tanner at second five-eighth, and in the pack Snow White coming in for Ian Clarke at prop and Des Oliver for Bill McCaw in the back row. There was a deliberate attempt at continuity after what was considered one of the team's best performances so far at Stradey Park. They had finished that game strongly with the winger Allan Elsom claiming a hat-trick of tries in the closing stages. He would be in action again at Cardiff, as would his fellow wing, Ron Jarden, and, of course, Bob Scott at full back. The big guns of the pack – Kevin Skinner, Tiny White, George Dalzell, Bill Clark and Bob Stuart – all of whom were regarded as the nucleus of the team for the later international matches on the tour were all included. But one late change was to upset their preparation, New Zealanders would later claim to a decisive degree. Bob Stuart had received a nasty cut on his thigh in the game against Western Counties but had played again in Llanelli. But the wound had turned septic and he had reacted to a penicillin injection. Confined to his bed in Porthcawl he was reluctantly withdrawn from the starting line-up at the Arms Park and the vacancy handed to McCaw.

The only question raised by the team announced was what type of game were the tourists hoping to play. Would it be forward orientated, aimed at dominance up front and starving the club's dangerous backs of possession? Or would they attempt to surprise Cardiff by establishing an expansive approach of their own? The danger was that they might end up falling between two stools – and few people beforehand would accurately forecast the influence on the course of the match of eight unsung heroes in the blue and blacks' pack.

Saturday 21 November 1953 was a dry but dull day. The crowds began gathering outside Cardiff Arms Park at a very early hour. At ten o'clock, nearly five hours before kick-off, a group of 30 people formed the beginning of a queue outside the Gwyn Nicholls Memorial Gates in Westgate Street. By 11.30 am it had stretched almost the length of the street down towards the railway station. A quarter of an hour later the gates were opened and the fans began filtering into the stadium. Many of them were from New Zealand or were exiles domiciled in Britain. Local reporters' unearthed several interesting individuals among the early arrivals. Mr and Mrs Edwards, originally from Coity in Bridgend, had lived and worked for over two decades in Hawke's Bay and had returned home to shout for both Cardiff and Wales but their 22-year-old daughter was with them and said to be 'an out-and-out All Black fan'. The reporters also interviewed 77-year-old William Jones of Canton who proudly revealed that he had witnessed at first hand the great events of 1905. At 12.30 pm the standing room areas in the field and enclosure were filling up rapidly. By a quarter past two the ground was packed to capacity with 56,000 inside and it was decided to close all the entrance gates. Several thousand fans were left outside as the minutes ticked away to the 2.45 pm kick-off. Also in the crowd was a proud New Zealander, Sir Edmund Hillary, who had conquered Mount Everest earlier in the year, dignitaries such as Lord Moran and Sir Edward Williams and a legend from 1905, Rhys Gabe. Even the New Zealand ladies' hockey team had travelled from London as guests of the All Blacks.

Obviously the match had all the trappings of a full scale international match. The national anthem was sung and the haka was performed. John Nelson suddenly suffered a spasm of stomach cramp and was forced to kneel until it passed. Geoff Beckingham may have been a hardened international forward but he readily admits to having goose pimples as the home team lined up during the preliminaries. But he and his team-mates were totally focused on the 80 minutes that lay ahead:

> 'In the dressing room the three of us – Stanley, JD and myself – were sitting in our usual corner. Bleddyn had been going around giving his final few words to the rest of the team and then he came over to us. Standing over us, he said 'Now what do I say to you three?' Stanley turned to me and chipped in with 'He'll want us to give him 80 per cent of the ball instead of our

usual 75 per cent.' That was the signal for JD to comment that he thought we always did that. The final word went to Stanley who quickly calculated that if and when we'd given the backs enough ball to score the tries we could go home at half-time!'

The front row was to be at the heart of everything that was good about a classic team display. Like all the best props and hookers they were never slow in coming forward. No sooner had the acting captain, Laurie Haig, won the toss for the All Blacks and Cliff Morgan kicked off to the Westgate Street end than it was time for the first scrum. Beckingham was immediately up to his tricks:

'I quickly realised that the All Blacks front rowers were wearing leather shoulder pads that had been outlawed. We needed to know whether they were lace-ups or buckles and after the first couple of scrums JD was certain that they were lace- ups. I knew then we were in business because as they came down to pack against us at our very low angle the laces could be used to cut their throats very nicely! Not literally, of course, but in no time at all Snow White went to the touchline to take his pads off. When he returned Stanley was waiting for him with the priceless remark, 'Now let's find out how good you really are!"

Post-match reflections highlighted the contribution of all the lighter club pack. The goings-on in the scrums would have escaped their attention but there was also something of a comedy of errors in the line-outs. CD Williams at the tail of the line was well placed to recall the mayhem in that area and he still does so with a chuckle:

'The plan was for Rex Willis at scrum-half to call the line-out signals. If he shrugged his shoulders our wings, who were the throwers-in in those days, would throw long to Sid Judd or Malcolm Collins. The only problem was we had overlooked the fact that Rex had what might be called a natural shrug – so Sid in particular had a busy afternoon. Still, it worked in our favour because as Bleddyn had identified beforehand the opposition back row was tied in and there was space for our backs to move in.'

So much for the sub-plot. The dazzling back play was soon evident for all to see. After only six minutes Beckingham's razor-sharp heel at a defensive scrum on his own 25 allowed Willis to send Morgan racing out into open field. His kick ahead ricocheted back off a defender into his arms and on the little fly-half went. His link to Thomas and then Rowlands on his right was perfect. The winger, running out of space on the touchline had the sense to hoist another kick, this time a high one, towards the posts. As the posse of forwards from either side chased back it was the ace poacher Judd who got his hands on the ball first for a try within touching distance of the right goalpost. Rowlands' straightforward conversion gave Cardiff the early five points lead that they had wanted so much.

It was vital for the All Blacks that they struck back quickly and they did so through the boot of Ron Jarden. They had already squandered one penalty opportunity in the fourth minute when Scott teed the ball far too high from half way and the ball dropped well short. Now the goal kicking responsibility was handed to the winger and he responded handsomely from 45 yards and on the very edge of touch.

Cardiff continued to play at great pace. Morgan was in his element, darting around the field and forever probing for gaps. One reporter later likened his movements to pyrotechnics and it made for a thrilling spectacle. The visitors, wherever possible, attempted loose rushes from Cardiff mistakes but these were few and far between. It was already apparent that the home pack was rising to the occasion magnificently. If the scrums tended towards stalemate then the line-outs were a rich source of club dominance with Collins and Judd outplaying Tiny White, Dalzell and Oliver.

The vital second try came in the twentieth minute. Again it was a scrum in Cardiff's half and again a quick heel resulted in Morgan scuttling away to the right. This time he passed and Bleddyn Williams chip-kicked ahead. Thomas regathered and fed Rowlands who, with his head back and the ball tucked under his arm, raced 30 yards to the corner before the defenders could reach him. In the circumstances it was hardly surprising that he failed to convert but at 8 points to 3 Cardiff were not only ahead on the scoreboard; they had delivered a huge psychological blow. All the pre-match speculation about the deadly Cardiff backs had borne fruit. Yet there was still an hour's playing time left. There was a discernible change in tactics as the ball was released to the All Blacks' backs, only for their well-rehearsed move to be stifled by an interception from Alun Thomas. It was a pattern repeated throughout the game.

Gareth Griffiths had expected an afternoon of tackling but found himself under-employed: 'All the attacking action seemed to go to the right so my job on the left wing was to keep an eye on Bob Scott coming into the line and to stop their right wing, Allan Elsom. As he spent most of the afternoon swearing at me it was something I enjoyed doing!'

The young wing did have one opportunity to attack when Wilson was caught in possession by the flankers CD Williams and Nelson and Morgan worked it out to the left but Griffiths eventually ran out of room. Then it was the turn of Rowlands again on the right after another brilliant break by Morgan, only for him to be forced into touch by three defenders. The All Blacks were rattled and the club might have gone further ahead when a penalty was gained in the visitors' 25 but Rowlands' wide angled kick swerved outside the upright.

Though struggling in the line-out the indefatigable Tiny White led forward charges into home territory and the half-time whistle came after one last charge had been repelled by the combined efforts of Beckingham, Bowes and Evans. At that stage no one could have foreseen how heroic they would be again at the very end of the second period.

The belated All Black onslaught resumed after the restart. Now they were trying to bring their backs into play but Haig was pedestrian in comparison to his opposite number. Sooner or later moves invariably broke down because of kicking and it was the turn of John Llewellyn to make valuable contributions by his courageous catching and marking of high punts. When the All Blacks did cross the line it was almost inevitably by Tiny White, only for him to be recalled for an earlier infringement. The lock was again in action when McCaw and Clark had foraged well but he hesitated to pass with a two-man overlap outside him. Their frustrations were growing and now Scott was resorting to speculative drop goals. John Nelson recalled one incident where tempers were also becoming frayed:

'I was making a pretty good job of positioning myself among the All Blacks' back line and when Scott came racing through with the ball again he passed to me. Soon afterwards I nobbled Vince Bevan and that led to a bit of an altercation with McCaw.'

The minutes ticked by and the spontaneous choral singing from the terraces and stands were carrying the blue and blacks towards history. The defence held firm as Llewellyn stopped Tiny White in his tracks and Griffiths was equally safe as Elsom tried to run past him. One anxiety remained. The superior fitness of the touring team had overwhelmed Llanelli in the final twenty minutes. Would Cardiff suffer the same fate? They needed to play the game in the All Blacks' half but even when they did after a breakaway and kick ahead by Rowlands they were driven back on their heels. Fine inter-passing rocked them before Griffiths stepped in to clear. CD Williams was momentarily injured but played on after treatment and with little time left it was the extraordinary Bowes who led another foot rush. Llewellyn almost succeeded with an ambitious penalty attempt from half-way as the game entered its final five minutes.

The singing had now reached a crescendo and out on the pitch it was mayhem. Scott had abandoned all pretence of being a full-back, lining up and running with his three-quarters. A high kick by him to the posts could have led to a replay of Judd's early score but this time it was Morgan to the rescue, collecting the ball under the noses of the opposition pack and clearing to touch. A converted try would still secure the draw and rescue the tourists' unbeaten record and at the last breath they established two attacking scrums on the home line. At such moments are heroes made and games won or lost. It was a situation made for Geoff Beckingham and his pals.

'We knew that the All Blacks needed to score a try and convert it if they were going to pip us,' he said, 'and the word from one of the seagulls in the back row – that's what I called them – was that we should concede a penalty. But I was still thinking positively. Then John Nelson was whispering in my ear going on about how we needed this ball. I told him to get back to the back row where he belonged. Stanley, JD and myself knew what to do. The All Blacks had the crucial put-in but I had noticed during the game that their scrum-half, Vince Bevan, had a habit of spinning the ball in his hand then tapping the seam with his finger a moment before he fed it into the scrum. So the moment he did that I struck for the ball and won the ball on the tight-head. The heel shot back to Rex and then Cliff and he cleared to touch. The pixies had done their job again!'

Incredibly there was time for one more attacking scrum but this time the All Blacks were penalised. The ball was kicked dead for a final time and no-side was whistled to a stupendous roar from the crowd. The respected New Zealand writer, Terry McLean, noted, 'It was the match of a lifetime and no one could say it had not been a fair result.' Bleddyn Williams, the man of destiny, was chaired from the field on the shoulders of his victorious team.

The post-match reaction was almost unfailingly complimentary. In its leader column on the following Monday, *the South Wales Echo* concluded:

'Cardiff's victory against the All Blacks on Saturday was like a symphony on a football field, a masterpiece of design, an anthem of courage. These international matches are somehow above and beyond the game of rugby – they are the battles of the giants and Cardiff Arms Park is the Olympus. It is no exaggeration to say that it is the game of rugby more than anything else – including coal – which over the years has put Cardiff on the map of the English-speaking world.'

Rich words, indeed, and the rugby analysts were equally positive. In *The Western Mail* JBG Thomas's match report was headlined, 'Cardiff made history in triumph of traditional Welsh back play', but he did not overlook the contribution of the forwards. He wrote:

'Our fears were needless for the Cardiff forwards did not fail and gained in stature by their deeds. They were the heroes of the match. The backs, with brilliant running and anticipation, produced the tries, but it was the forwards who made victory possible. With the pack – and none played better than the veteran Bowes – doing so well the backs were given their opportunities to pierce the defence. Morgan touched the heights of greatness with running as swift and elusive as that of his great predecessor, Percy Bush ... For Bleddyn Williams it was a great personal triumph to lead a team to victory playing the traditional style of football.'

His colleague, Dave Phillips, in the *South Wales Echo* reached similar conclusions:

'For 80 minutes we saw the traditional skill and fire of what has rightly been termed the greatest rugby club in the world countered by the all-action enthusiasm of a determined All Blacks side who tried everything in their power to whittle down Cardiff's half-time lead of five points in a storming grandstand finish. Maligned and under-estimated before the game as a suspect pack, the Cardiff eight, well led by international Sid Judd, played the terriers against a larger and heavier eight and seemed to increase in spirit and fervour towards the end rather than wilt as had been freely forecast.'

The disappointed New Zealand journalists covering the tour might have been expected to be more temperate in their judgements but they found much to admire in the showing of the blue and blacks. Terry McLean was the official correspondent of the New Zealand Press Association and, in that role, travelled everywhere with the players and management. The first of the several reports he filed was to *The Wellington Evening Post* and he was generous in his praise. He wrote:

'One must pay proper and adequate tribute to the terrier-like qualities of the Cardiff forwards, who were only really contained in the last few minutes, and to the elegance and speed of the Cardiff backs. Rowlands, Morgan, Willis, Bowes, Beckingham, Evans and Judd were stars in what, to judge from the stupendous roar of the last whistle, will go down in history as one of the great achievements of Cardiff's long and illustrious rugby history.'

His subsequent reviews of the match that were published in the following Monday morning's editions back home followed a similar theme. In the *Christchurch Star* he pointed out features that confirmed Bleddyn Williams' pre-match analysis of the tourists and how to beat them:

'Cardiff used every opportunity to swing the play away from the All Black forwards, either by fast running or long kicking. This often resulted in breaks of up to seventy yards. The All Blacks pattern, on the other hand, was to keep the ball among or close to the forwards, and Bevan's many breaks from the scrum usually ended in turning the ball back towards the pack. This was punishing but not winning rugby.'

Working alongside McLean was the famous radio broadcaster, Winston McCarthy, otherwise known as the 'Screaming Skull' for the pitch and pace of his commentaries. His tour diary, 'Round the World with the All Blacks', recorded:

'They [Cardiff] were too good on the day. The Cardiff forwards hung on as a pack; the Cardiff backs were cleverer than their opposites both on attack and defence. The brilliance of Cliff Morgan early on seemed to panic the All Blacks, and he played merrily and mightily. Scott had a worrying day and he came out of it with credit, even though it was not his best match. He again had to leave his position many times to cover up inside. It was a bravely fought match, and as clean as a whistle. If only [Bob] Stuart had been there!'

McCarthy's last comment betrayed the one of only two or three 'excuses' put forward by the Kiwi camp for their defeat. Another was the possible effect of what they rather late in the day suspected was a debilitating air journey around the world. The Cardiff match was played nearly five weeks after they had first landed in London but back home in New Zealand the *Dunedin Evening Star* had its own interpretation:

'A factor which perhaps has not been sufficiently appreciated is that this team began its tour dangerously close to being jaded right at the start. The air trip so closely following a gruelling representative and trial match programme gave little opportunity for the freshening up that a sea trip would have allowed. For all that, New Zealanders will not be downcast because the Welshmen have once again risen to the big occasion. There was no disgrace in going down to the Cardiff stars, and there is the grit in our players to learn their lessons and regain their prestige.'

Elsewhere on the South Island *The Christchurch Press* was even more philosophical, seeing the benefits of defeat which, incidentally, was only the second to a club, combined or county side in 91 matches since the epic tour of 1905. It reasoned:

'The All Blacks' defeat at Cardiff on Saturday may be the very best thing that could have happened. Any good team will learn more from its defeats than its victories, of course, and it seems abundantly clear that the Welsh backs had much to teach the New Zealanders in the finer arts of attacking play. But the benefit may go much further than that. The ghost of the 1924-25 [Invincibles] record has been laid; and this team will no longer be haunted by it. The team will continue to try to win its matches; it will no longer be obsessed by the need to avoid defeat. The players themselves should enjoy their games more; and they may be encouraged to take the risks and to play the more open type of game which the spectators enjoy – and which wins converts to the game.'

So the Cardiff team had done the All Blacks a favour and they could now relax in their remaining 29 matches on the tour … somehow that sentiment doesn't ring true to the traditions of New Zealand rugby. What was more authentic was the reactions from the players and management. At the post-match dinner held in the Royal Hotel, Bob Stuart paid tribute to the quality of the club's performance when he said, 'We have no excuses to offer. We had our opportunities. We all admire the splendid spirit in which the game was played and both sides and the referee deserve credit for their efforts. Cardiff play the kind of football enthusiasts wish to see and it is hard to imagine a club side in New Zealand of such strength.'

In his response, Bleddyn Williams admitted, 'I am the proudest man in Cardiff tonight. The club has now beaten all three touring sides but I feel the greatest honour of all is to beat the All Blacks.'

Even as the immediate celebrations were reaching their conclusion in the long Cardiff night, congratulatory telegrams and letters were being prepared and despatched from all over the sporting world. The two Lions' props of 1950, Ireland's Tom Clifford in Limerick and Scotland's Grahame Budge from as far away as Vancouver, both had their telegrams read out in the Royal Hotel before 10 pm. They tell us much about the esteem in which the club was held. From within Wales itself dozens of letters eventually arrived from all the first-class and many of the second-class clubs. Pontypool's secretary, Clem Weeks, wrote:

'It is the unanimous wish of my committee that I write to you offering our heartiest congratulations and best wishes to the Cardiff club in view of the magnificent victory you so justly deserved on Saturday against the New Zealanders. Your victory is all the more pleasing to members of our club as the Cardiff team has always been held in great esteem in this area.

With kind regards and best wishes for your future success...'

Llanelli, Bridgend and Swansea all sent similar letters as did clubs from as far apart as Wrexham in the north, Chepstow in the east and Tenby United in the west. The greetings from the Monmouth club appreciated that the performance 'was a great contribution to rugby football in general and to the sport in Wales in particular ... it has done much to stimulate interest and enthusiasm in small clubs such as this one where enthusiasts work hard to keep the game alive ... may you go from strength to strength'.

From across the Severn, Adrian Stoop at the Harlequins and the leading officials of Bristol, Moseley, Lydney, Penzance and Newlyn, Totnes and Plymouth Albion were all sincere with their praise. Philip Woolf of Cheltenham sent a message to Brice Jenkins that was particularly poignant:

'My club were playing at Bath last Saturday and when the half-time score was announced on the public address equipment there, there was a cheer from the crowd and the players. The game was over and our chaps were dressing when the result was given to me in the dressing room and when I gave it out I wish you had heard the cheers which were given to your club on its performance.'

Significantly, the match attracted the attentions of organisations from outside the sport. Onto the desks of Brice Jenkins and Hubert Johnson arrived communications from not only the Cardiff Rotary Club but also the Rhondda Federated Chambers of Trade, the latter justifiably proud of the four players from those valleys that had been part of the Cardiff team. Others came from the BBC, from Kemsley Newspapers, the *South Wales Argus* in Newport and the *Evening Post* in Swansea, and scores of individuals who felt the need to record their thanks for the performance as much as the result.

Finally, there were the official letters from the Welsh Rugby Union and the Barbarians, whose venerable President, HA Haig Smith, applauded Cardiff as 'a wonderful side in the way they always seem able to rise on big occasions [and] it was especially a triumph for your forwards in the way they stuck at it to the bitter end'. Most important of all, the New Zealand team manager Norman Millard followed up a telegram from his home union in Wellington with the most sincere of letters to Hubert Johnson:

'I think you will know by now that although our boys were beaten, they thoroughly enjoyed the game, and greatly appreciated the manner in which the victory of the Cardiff side was gained. I am sure that we will not meet a side playing a better brand of rugby football during the whole tour, and certainly not a side with as great a team spirit … it is a pity that the All Blacks cannot leave a trophy such as the Springboks gave to you.'

There was indeed no trophy to put on display but Bleddyn Williams would soon have the photograph he had told Eamonn Andrews three months earlier he wanted to see more than any other hanging in the club museum. The Cardiff team of 1953 had indeed beaten the All Blacks.

One other tribute to the historic deed was established. It was decided to hold an annual reunion of the team for at least the foreseeable future. Arrangements were left in the capable hands of Stan Bowes – the match, after all, marked probably his greatest day and he soon imbued the occasion with a subtle mixture of style, formality, friendship and a sense of no one being allowed to take things too seriously. Thus the venues alternated between the Cardiff Athletic Club and the nearby County Club in Westgate Street or, especially on the occasion of subsequent All Blacks tours, the Banqueting Hall of Cardiff Castle. Sometimes there would be guest speakers as distinguished as the High Commissioner of New Zealand or Lord Brecon or the President of the Rugby Football Union; at other times merely a few recollections shared with the team members. Likewise those present might number several hundred or a much smaller gathering. Sometimes 'black tie' was *de rigueur* and at other times the blazer and tie – with the notable exception of Geoff Beckingham who has never worn a tie in his life. And the invitations might be on an impressively embossed card or in Bowes-inspired Kairdiff dialect – 'Tonite is the nite … Fryday 20th Oktowbur … U no ware … Kardiff Kasul'. What never varied would be that all the members of the 1953 team, together with the touch judge on duty, Billy Cleaver, and Dr Jack Matthews, would make it a priority to be present.

Sadly as the years have gone by it became more a case of the Survivors of 1953 meeting together. As the fiftieth anniversary approached in November 2003 seven of the history-makers were still alive – Gwyn Rowlands, Gareth Griffiths, Cliff Morgan, Geoff Beckingham, Eddie Thomas, Derek Williams and, of course, Bleddyn himself.

'We'll keep going probably until there's only a couple of us left and the last survivor will still have his unique memories,' he said. 'I wouldn't have believed back in 1953 that our win would have made such an impression and that we would still be celebrating it half a century later, but it's something to be proud of. Equally, I suppose, it's incredible that no Wales' international side has beaten New Zealand since then – and that is not such good news.'

6

The History Makers

The story of 1953 would not be complete without recording the careers and lives of the fifteen heroes.

Full back **John Edward Leighton Llewellyn** was 26 years old in 1953, 5 feet 11 inches tall and weighed 12 stones. His first experience of senior rugby had been with Penarth, playing for them against the Barbarians in 1949 and 1950. He then moved to the Arms Park and won his Cardiff Athletic cap in 1950-51 and his first team cap the following season. In November 1951 he was selected for the senior side, the Reds, against the Whites in the Welsh international trial match at Abertillery. After the All Blacks match he continued to play for the club until May 1957, by which time he had made 152 appearances for the first team. He then returned to his local club at Taff's Well and gave them great service. The annual match between the village and neighbouring Pentyrch is still played for the John Llewellyn Trophy. Originally a sales representative with the engineering merchants, GN Hunter & Co, he later worked with the international centre Harry Morgan as agent for the TW Lench company. He was a member of Whitchurch Golf Club but died tragically at the age of 42 while playing golf in the Midlands in May 1970.

Dr Gwyn Rowlands (24, 5'11", 12st 8lb) played on the right wing. He was born in Berkhamsted and thus was qualified to play for both England and Wales. While studying at and playing for London Hospitals in 1949 he was selected for two England trial matches. At the end of the same year he played for the Wales Possibles against the Probables in Maesteg. While on national service in the RAF he was stationed at St Athan, played in the inter-services matches at

Twickenham and joined Cardiff in 1951-52. An accumulator of points – he twice passed the century mark in a season and completed a career total of 66 tries in 99 matches for the club – his performance against the All Blacks won him international selection. Playing this time on the left he kicked a penalty goal and two conversions in Wales' 13-8 win over New Zealand and went on to win three more caps. Gwyn was vice-captain of Cardiff in 1955-56 before hanging up his boots a year later to concentrate on his medical career in Hertfordshire where he still lives.

Alun Gruffydd Thomas (27, 5'10", 11st 10lb) was selected at right centre. Originally from Cwmavon he joined Cardiff in December 1950. He had already played in international trials at fly-half and centre while a member of the Swansea club. It was as a Cardiff player that he won his first Welsh cap at Twickenham in 1952. After two games in blue and black in September 1954 he transferred to Llanelli and was selected for the British Isles tour of South Africa the following summer. He played in five games for the Lions, all at full-back, and finished his career with 13 caps for Wales and 82 games for Cardiff. A prominent contribution as an administrator followed, returning to South Africa as assistant manager of the Wales team in 1964 and manager of the unbeaten Lions ten years later. He was President of the Welsh Rugby Union in 1985-86. In his working career Alun began as a sales manager, became an oil company representative and then served as an appeals officer for the National Trust. He died in Swansea on 8 May 1991 at the age of 65.

Bleddyn Llewellyn Williams (30, 5'10", 13st 8lb) was the left centre, captain and guiding hand of the Cardiff team in 1953. Fifty years later he is still the *éminence grise* of the club, now the President of Cardiff Athletic Club. His achievements as a club man, Welsh international and British Isles test player are traced in detail elsewhere. He captained all these sides as well as the Barbarians but admits, unashamedly, that beating the All Blacks at Cardiff Arms Park ranks as his greatest day alongside the memories of his first Welsh cap in 1947 and his selection for the Lions three years later. The events of 21 November will forever be linked with his leadership and the dignity he showed in victory. Four weeks later he repeated the achievement at the same ground when he led Wales to another historic victory that has never been equalled. Bleddyn had a 100 per cent record of five wins as captain of Wales and scored seven tries in his 22 internationals. He played for the Barbarians against the Wallabies in 1948 and the Springboks in 1952. For the Lions he scored 13 tries in 20 games in New Zealand and Australia and his Cardiff career record of 185 tries in 283 games stood for 40 years. After retiring in 1955 he became a highly respected rugby correspondent for *The People,* a sought-after broadcaster and a successful Regional Marketing Manager for Wimpey Construction. In September 1999 he was one of the first fifteen inductees into the club's Hall of Fame.

Gareth Meredith Griffiths (21, 6'0", 12st 10lb), the left wing, was the youngest member of the side. Six days later he celebrated his twenty-second birthday and a few weeks after that another conquest of New Zealand for Wales, this time at centre alongside his club captain. Educated at Porth County School in the Rhondda and then St Luke's and Loughborough Colleges, the precociously talented youngster had made his Rags debut at the age of 18 in 1949. By 1952 he was a regular member of the first team, played in his first Welsh trial and represented the Barbarians. The first of his 12 Welsh caps came against England in January 1953 and he went on to score tries against both Ireland and France. He completed a hat-trick of appearances against the All Blacks by also playing for the Barbarians against them at the end of their tour. In 1955 Gareth was flown out as a replacement to South Africa and played three tests for the British Isles against South Africa. He also toured Canada with the Barbarians in 1957. His Cardiff career closed in 1960 with a total of 74 tries in 140 games. He was equally successful in his professional life, first as a teacher and then, after taking a Master's degree, in the business world with Amersham International. He was inducted into the Cardiff Hall of Fame in 2001. He now lives in Penarth.

Clifford Isaac Morgan (23, 5'7", 12st 0lb) was the fly-half and the inspiration for so much that happened at Cardiff Arms Park against the All Blacks. The game was a personal triumph after a difficult baptism against the Springboks in 1951. An icon of his generation, he captured the imagination of everyone who saw him play. In 1955 he took South Africa by storm as the British Isles tied the test series against the Springboks 2-2. He played 29 times for Wales and in 1956 he captained the national team in all four matches. He also completed a hat-trick of appearances for the Barbarians against the Springboks, All Blacks and Wallabies. His 16 games for the Barbarians also included overseas tours to Canada and South Africa. When his business interests took him to Ireland he played one season for Bective Rangers but returned to Cardiff for his final seasons. In all he played 202 games in eight seasons at the club and scored 38 tries. He retired from playing in 1958 at the age of 28 to begin a notably successful career in broadcasting. At first he was based with the BBC in Cardiff but eventually became Head of Outside Broadcasts. He was also a marvellous rugby commentator, most memorably on the 1973 Barbarians match with the All Blacks and the famous try in the opening moments by Gareth Edwards. Among his many awards Cliff has a CVO and an OBE and is a member of both the International and Cardiff club's Hall of Fame. He lives in London and is still in great demand as an after-dinner speaker and raconteur.

William Rex Willis (29, 5'9", 12st 7lb), the scrum half, was born in Ystrad and educated at the Cathedral School in Llandaff. He played for the Llandaff club before making his debut for the Rags in September 1947 and his first-class debut at the end of the same season. In 1950 he was selected for Wales at Twickenham without having played in a trial and before he qualified for his club cap. Later the same year he was a British Isles player in New Zealand and Australia, appearing in 13 matches, including three tests. He captained the club in 1952-53, Wales against France in 1954 and against Scotland the following year, and also captained the Barbarians against the All Blacks at the end of their tour. Rex retired from first-class rugby in 1956 but returned the following year to play for Cardiff against the Wallabies. He won 21 caps for Wales, played 208 games for Cardiff in 11 seasons, and later served on the committees of both Cardiff and the Barbarians. In 1999 he was inducted into the club's Hall of Fame. Rex described his life as 'a great adventure' and away from sport he was a successful entrepreneur and owned a chain of cinemas. He died on 19 January 2000 at the age of 75.

John Davies Evans (27, 5'11", 15st 2lb) played at loose-head prop. Another product of the neighbouring valleys, he was born and bred in Mountain Ash where he attended the local Pengeulan School. He captained Mountain Ash RFC for two seasons, playing mainly in the second row. After a failed attempt to gain a permit to play for Newbridge he eventually joined Cardiff in September 1951 and switched to the front row. He made an immediate impression, winning his first team cap at the end of his debut season. Originally a surface welder at Deep Duffryn Pit, John later became a sales manager for Scottish & Newcastle Breweries. He was a Welsh-speaker and described by his friend and fellow prop Colin Howe as a 'deep thinker and shrewd individual'. He played 338 games in 11 seasons for Cardiff and completed a touring team double when he helped the club beat the Wallabies in 1957-58. In the same season he played for the Barbarians against East Midlands and won two caps for Wales. In 1959-60 he was club vice-captain to Gordon Wells. John died at Velindre on 25 March 1989 at the age of 62.

Geoffrey Thomas Beckingham (29, 5'10", 13st 10lb) was the hooker and one of the great unsung heroes of the match. Held in great regard by all of his team-mates, Geoff provided the quick scrum heels that allowed the backs to create the two tries and remarkably stole the opposition put-ins at the unforgettable final set-pieces. All the match reports of the time also note the contribution made by the hooker and his two props in loose play throughout the game. He had won his first two international caps on merit earlier in 1953 but was not to win his third and final selection until the very end of his career in 1958 when he was an eleventh-hour replacement for Bryn Meredith against France. Wales' loss was Cardiff's gain as he played against all three touring teams from the Southern Hemisphere and a total of 331 games, joining his fellow front-rower J D Evans in the top ten of individual appearances in blue and black. After his playing days he coached both Barry College and Penarth with notable success. A proud son of Barry, he was a municipal gardener throughout his working life. He put his fitness down to the fact there was only one lawn mower for all the town's parks so he was pushing it for 15 hours a day in the height of summer. He still lives on Barry Island where he champions the cause of allotment owners against the curse of restrictive bureaucracy.

Arthur David Stanley Bowes (36, 5'10", 14st 7lb), the tight-head prop, told the player biography writers in 1953 that his age was irrelevant – 'a man is as old as he feels'. In fact he was born in 1917, made his Rags debut in the 1937-38 season and was still playing 24 years later. His final recorded appearance was for Cardiff Athletic at home to Glynneath on 9 December 1961. His profile however remained very visible for many years after that as committee member, touch judge and, in 1984, club chairman. At first a petty officer in the navy he later became an administrative worker at Whitchurch Hospital. As a club official he was a stickler for clubhouse etiquette where a gentleman should never wear a hat or swear in front of a lady. On the playing field his heart was huge. After forlornly chasing the legendary Irish wing, Tony O'Reilly, for 50 yards as he scored for the Barbarians, Stan was overheard telling the flame-haired wonder as he trotted back to half-way, 'I'd have caught you if your laces had snapped'. He kept running and scrummaging in 370 games for the club, including 179 in the first team and captained the Rags for four seasons between 1950 and 1954 and was vice-captain again in 1955-56. International honours narrowly eluded him though he played for Wales in two wartime Services Internationals against England in 1944 and 1945. A founder member of the club's Former Players' Association, he also was the chairman of Cardiff Youth. When Stan died in March 1988 his direct opponent in the All Blacks match, Snow White, journeyed from the North Island of New Zealand to be a pall bearer at his funeral.

Edwin Thomas (30, 6'0", 14st 1lb) who was known as Eddie, played at lock. He was born in Treorchy and returned to the Rhondda to teach at Pentre Grammar School where he became head of physics. His first senior rugby was for Neath and he played for the combined Neath and Aberavon side against the Springboks in November 1951. In the same season he was selected for a Welsh trial as a wing forward – his future team mate Malcolm Collins was on the opposing side. Eddie joined Cardiff at the start of the 1952-53 season and readily admits that he was prepared to play in any position to cement a place, although not over-enthusiastic about one suggestion that he should be tried out at prop. He acquired the nickname 'Toesy Thomas' because in the team photograph for the All Blacks match he can be clearly seen standing on his toes to make himself seem as tall as Malcolm Collins! After the heroics of that game he eventually returned to the back row and was at number 8 in November 1957 when he captained the club to a 14-11 victory over the Wallabies. He was considered to be a very good club captain because he knew the game inside out and led from the front. He retired with 217 games for Cardiff to his name and for a while served on the committee. Eddie still lives in Treorchy.

Malcolm Collins (25, 6'2", 16st 7lb) partnered Eddie Thomas at lock and was the chief middle of the line-out jumper in the team. Originally from Monmouthshire, he made his club debut for the Rags in September 1949, played eight games for them and was immediately promoted to the first team. He then played in 30 of the remaining 34 matches that season to qualify for his club cap. The following season he played in all three international trials and two more in 1952 but Wales never picked him. He played for the Barbarians against the East Midlands in 1954 but first and foremost he was a blue and black. He became club captain in 1955-56 and played in an almost unimaginable 50 of the 52 first team fixtures. The two games he missed were against Watsonians at Christmas, when there were five matches in eight days, and St Ives on the Cornish tour, when again the team had eight fixtures in a fortnight. His durability, understandably, was legendary and he finished his career with 306 appearances for the club. He also played for a while for Ebbw Vale but soon returned to Cardiff and became a highly respected committeeman. He was club chairman in 1977-78. Originally a ganger platelayer on the Great Western Railway he later became a manager at the rail depot in Canton. Malcolm died suddenly in December 1985.

John Daniel Nelson (28, 6'1", 13st 7lb) played at blind-side wing forward. A native of the city, he was educated at St Illtyd's College and Cardiff University as well as completing his teaching qualifications in London. He played for London Welsh and Eastern Counties and after leaving the Royal Navy he applied for the Cardiff trials. He made his first team debut in September 1948 against Bristol and went on to play 291 times before his retirement in 1959. His Irish ancestry attracted the attention of the Ireland selectors after John had starred for Cardiff in matches against Bective Rangers and Old Belvedere but an opportunity to stake a claim with Wales came first. In 1955 he played in the final international trial, was chosen as a reserve against England and Ireland and only missed a cap against France when he didn't have his passport readily available after Clem Thomas had dropped out injured. John was a gentleman of the game and an obvious selection for the Barbarians, for whom he played twice on their Easter tour in 1958. After his playing days John became synonymous with the club as a committee member and its secretary and unashamedly declared it was a responsibility 'to maintain the heritage of the club and the game'. As well as his work for a building society John was recruited by the BBC's Saturday evening 'Sports Medley' programme. In September 1999 John was inducted into the club's Hall of Fame. He died on 10 January 2000 at the age of 74.

Charles Derek Williams (28, 5'11", 13st 0lb), the open-side wing forward, was the perfect foil for John Nelson. Another son of Cardiff, he had attended Lansdowne Junior School and Canton High School before furthering his distinguished academic career at the Technical College and Oxford University. His game for the University against the Kiwis had given him an appetite for playing touring teams. He was playing for London Welsh in 1947 and missed the chance to take on the Wallabies but was back in Cardiff for the arrival of the Springboks in 1951. 'CD' had first worn blue and black in an unofficial wartime fixture against Cardiff Medicals in 1942. His official debut was against Swansea in the first post-war season but because of his travels he didn't gain his club cap until 1951.By then he had already played in international trials – though his Wales appearances were to be limited to two games against France in 1955 and 1956. The latter is remembered for his infamous 'try in the Taff' when he chased a cross-kick to claim the converted try in injury time that won the match 5-3 for Wales. The touchdown may or may not have been before the ball crossed the dead-ball line at the river end of the Arms Park.

There was nothing uncertain about CD's contribution to rugby at Cardiff, despite a year's sabbatical in 1955 when he went to Neath.

He made a pact with Rex Willis to come out of retirement and play against the Wallabies in 1957 and stayed on to become club captain at the age of 34 in 1958-59. When he finally retired he became a committee member, was chairman when the club first won the Welsh Cup in 1981 and is still a respected trustee of Cardiff Athletic Club. His varied career in industry culminated in stints as landlord of three public houses, the last at the Butcher's Arms in Llandaff from where he retired in 1989.

Sidney Judd (25, 6'2", 14st 12lb) was the number 8 forward and vice-captain of the team. Everyone who saw Sid play testifies that if he had not been struck down by a cruel illness he would have gone on to become of one of the all-time greats of Cardiff and Welsh rugby. All the evidence suggests that this is no idle assessment. Sid attended Cardiff High School and he was still a student teacher at Trinity College, Carmarthen, when he played in his first international trial match, as a lock, in 1949. He was never far from the national selectors' minds, featuring in half-a-dozen more trials before playing for Wales against England in January 1953. He missed only one of the next 11 internationals before his deteriorating health became a factor. Sid had made his club debut for the Rags in September 1946, a fortnight after his eighteenth birthday, and his first-team baptism followed on Boxing Day against Wasps. While away studying he played as a guest for Carmarthen Athletic but returned to the Arms Park to win his club cap in 1950. In the following year he played against the Springboks and the Lions, the 75th anniversary game in which he scored one of the club's four tries. His crucial try for Cardiff against the All Blacks was followed by another, almost a carbon copy example of his opportunism, when Wales beat New Zealand the following month.

After two seasons as vice-captain, he became club captain in 1954-55 but having played in 24 games he missed the last three months of the season. His last international match was at Murrayfield on 5 February and up to that point he was a strong candidate for that summer's British Isles tour to South Africa. A year later he appealed to the club to play on the end-of-season tour to the West Country. His last game was against Newton Abbott on 11 April 1956. It was his 184th game for the first team; he had also won 10 international caps

112

and appeared four times for the Barbarians, including their match with the All Blacks. Sid Judd died of leukaemia on 24 February 1959 at the age of 30. At the end of the season a Past v Present match was staged at Cardiff Arms Park in his memory. A galaxy of stars came out of retirement to play, including Dr Jack Matthews, Billy Cleaver, Cliff Davies and the Irish international, Des O'Brien. In an appreciation in the souvenir programme, JBG Thomas wrote:

'Sid Judd was a great footballer and a brave man...He had all the qualities and physical attributes which go to make an outstanding back row forward. His knowledge of the game was considerable and his love of good rugby immeasurable ... he will be missed by rugby men everywhere but never forgotten.'

7

All Black Aftermath

As the dust settled on the great deeds of 1953, everyone involved in the Cardiff club looked forward to the next time the All Blacks would play on the Arms Park. That would be some considerable time in the future, of course, because in the days of long tours the international teams from the Southern Hemisphere only came to the British Isles every ten years or so. No one really minded that because it served to enhance the mystique of the All Blacks, Springboks and Wallabies. When they did arrive it would be a special event in the rugby calendar, seeing them play something to cherish, and to occasionally beat them an achievement to proudly celebrate.

Undeniably the Cardiff team of 1953 had set a standard that subsequent blue and blacks would seek to emulate. Modern professional sportsmen might be irritated at the inevitable comparisons between their performances and the teams of the past. But for forty years after the heroics of Bleddyn Williams' team, subsequent generations of Cardiff players saw it differently: they were happy to try and follow in their footsteps. It was a marker to be proud of. As one later player admitted, 'I wish we had a reason to hold a reunion in memory of beating the All Blacks.'

The next opportunity for the club came exactly ten years later on 23 November 1963. Again the Cardiff side was reasonably well equipped to consider a victory as a real possibility. A good mix of youth and experience in any sporting team may be dismissed as a cliché but there was every reason to apply the description to the 1963 vintage. There was a battle hardened seam of experience in abundance. The captain was Dai Hayward, a buccaneering flanker who had terrorised opposing fly-halves at the Arms Park and grounds all over England and Wales for the best part of a decade. He brought the same spirit and *joie de vivre* to the club that was typical of Stan

Bowes and his contemporaries in the previous decade. Dai's playing career, in fact, had overlapped those of Cliff Morgan, Willis, Beckingham, JD Evans and CD Williams from the late-50s. Having already played for the club against the Wallabies and Springboks, he dearly wanted the scalp of the All Blacks, if only to add another glorious chapter to the club's history.

Since joining the club in 1957 after national service with the RAF and college rugby at Loughborough, Hayward had bought into the Cardiff identity in a big way. As he says, 'Even in the 1950s the club was professional in the sense that every one of its players as well as officials were charged with a responsibility to respect its traditions, to foster its image, and to never forget that to represent Cardiff on and off the field is as good as it gets.' Defeating the All Blacks would fit in very nicely to Dai Hayward's scheme of things.

He had an able lieutenant in the future Lions prop forward, Howard Norris, and eight other internationals in the side. None of them were survivors from 1953, though two of Bleddyn Williams' younger brothers were in the team – Lloyd at scrum-half and Elwyn at blind-side wing forward. Lloyd Williams, who had succeeded Rex Willis as Cliff Morgan's partner and had himself captained the club for two seasons, played 13 times for Wales. Elwyn Williams might have also won international honours but for a serious leg injury after an outstanding final trial – the more ironic because this fine clubman played 339 first team games over a period of 15 seasons almost without interruption.

The experienced players formed the spine of the team and were typified by Alun Priday at full back. Here was another local boy steeped in the history of the club. He was smitten by its glamour and style from the moment his father had taken him to the Arms Park as a 12-year-old in 1945 and almost the first action he saw was a spectacular try by the winger, Dr Glyn Jones. 'I knew from that moment on that I wanted to play for Cardiff Rugby Football Club,' he admits, 'and my ambition could only be strengthened after being privileged to see at first hand the great rugby of Haydn Tanner's team in 1947-48.' By the spring of 1953 Priday had achieved his ambition and might have played against the earlier All Blacks as well but for the reliable presence of John Llewellyn. But in the ten years since then he had become a fixture in the team and had won two international caps. Like Hayward he had enjoyed beating the Wallabies in 1957 but had emerged battered and bruised from a torrid game with the Springboks three years after that. Now with these latest All Blacks he, too, sensed a chance of glory.

'Matches with the major touring teams simply have to be the highlight of any club player's career. The buzz of anticipation is almost indescribable. I had sensed it when we played the Wallabies and the Springboks and here it was again. We weren't a great side but we were a club side – and that meant our team work and spirit, that all-for-one, one-for-all approach, must give us a chance and I was looking forward tremendously to playing them for the first time.' Unfortunately, fate was to deal Alun Priday a cruel hand that afternoon.

Meirion Roberts in the centre was another international, Cliff Ashton was alongside Lloyd Williams at half-back, the Monmouthshire toolmaker Billy Thomas was at hooker, and two British Isles test players from 1962, Kingsley Jones at prop and Keith Rowlands in the second row. The pack was completed by the lock, Graham Davies, a schools international who had taken his chance when the senior player, John Price, was sidelined by injury, and at number 8 the reliable Cliff Howe. The two wings, Steve Hughes and Richie Wills, were real opportunists. All these players had many miles on the clock after several seasons of club rugby in Wales and would not panic in a high profile match. Youth was represented by one player, but no ordinary one, in Maurice Richards. In 1963 the Rhondda-born flyer was still only 18 and in his first full season at the club. But he had already given notice of a rare talent. The previous spring he had been part of a Welsh Secondary Schools back division, including Gerald Davies, which ripped their English counterparts to pieces. The Cardiff selectors wasted no time giving him a senior run-out before the end of that season and now he was establishing himself at centre. Incredibly, and despite playing in nearly every international trial in the meantime, Richards would have to wait five years before winning his first Welsh cap but within another three months he was touring South Africa with the Lions. A year after that he scored four tries in one match against England and made a huge impression on New Zealander critics with his displays in an otherwise struggling Welsh touring team.

The presence of Richards and the pacey Wills in the three-quarters gave hope for an attacking approach by Cardiff. The team had made a disappointing start to their domestic season, losing consecutive games to Ebbw Vale, Bridgend and London Welsh, and suffered further defeats against Coventry, Bristol and Oxford University but there had been some improvement prior to the arrival of the All Blacks. The tourists, on the other hand, had arrived during yet another golden period in their history. New Zealand were unbeaten in 10 international matches spread over three seasons and had a nucleus of several great players. They were led by the highly respected prop, Wilson Whineray, as they had been since 1958. With him he brought the cream of Kiwi forwards – Colin Meads, Ken Gray, Denis Young, Kel Tremain and the newest star, the flanker Waka Nathan. Predictably, they ran up big scores in England and Scotland, most especially when thrashing a star-studded London Counties side 33-0 at Twickenham. But they had lost by three points at Rodney Parade, so to some extent Newport had stolen Cardiff's thunder. Yet Hayward and his men felt that the All Blacks were vulnerable – and the first hour of the game bore out that belief.

After a sombre preamble in which the 50,000-strong crowd stood in silence as a mark of respect for the American President John F Kennedy who had been assassinated 24 hours earlier, the game took an unusual pattern. Against expectations, the club decided to play the game tight, taking on Meads and company up front, and the half-backs kicking the ball to touch or putting it in front for the pack to chase – bear in mind that in 1963 direct kicking to touch from any part of the field was still allowed. They had an early setback when Clarke kicked a towering penalty goal from 50 yards but still Hayward stuck to the pre-match plan. It almost worked. When back row pressure forced fly-half Mac Herewini into a fumble, Cliff Howe pounced on the ball for a try, converted by Priday. But the full-back, a fine servant of the club as player and later administrator, was to play an unwanted part in the eventual outcome. Crucial to the success of the team strategy was that the All Blacks would concede penalties and that goals would be kicked. There was no shortage of penalties but the second part of the equation collapsed around one man's boot. Alun Priday, the neatest and most dependable of full backs, was playing as well as ever as the last line of defence. A marvellous catcher of the ball and the possessor of a trademark screw kick to touch, one aspect of his play was not going at all well.

'To explain why I missed four penalty kicks at goal in the first half is almost impossible,' he explained. 'Some days the ball goes between the posts every time, on others they just don't strike home. All I can say is that week in, week out, for season after season, I – like all goal-kickers – followed exactly the same routine but for some unfathomable reason there are occasions when the timing isn't right. Goal kicking is an almost frightening responsibility – but one I was happy to accept wherever I played. I realised that if only one of those kicks had gone over we would have been eight points to three up and in those days of the three-points try the All Blacks would have been hard pushed to overhaul us. I have to admit that I was never so upset as I was after that game.'

Priday is being unduly hard on himself. He might point out that his opposite number, Don Clarke, who had kicked six penalty goals in an infamous 18-17 victory for New Zealand over the British Isles in 1959, also failed with three of his four goal kicks in the tricky wind of the Arms Park. More importantly, the tactics employed were arguably flawed. Taking on the All Blacks' pack was courageous but it was also foolhardy. Well as Dai Hayward's men played it was never likely that they could sustain a forward dominance for the full 80 minutes. To their credit all the pieces fell into place in the first half. The giant Keith Rowlands had the upper hand on Meads in the line-out; the scrum was impressively comfortable; and the back row chased any loose ball like dervishes. One lovely box kick by Lloyd Williams almost led to a try by Wills in the corner but the flag went up for touch in goal. The well-deserved half-time lead held for another 15 minutes of the second period. And then the pack blew up. Suddenly Meads and Stewart were dominating the line-out; then the Cardiff scrum was going backwards; but still the tackling was rock solid. Yet even as they achieved territorial dominance there were no frills from Whineray's men. Herewini ignored a triple overlap to drop a scruffy goal and gain a one-point lead. That was the end of the scoring. The tourists' one intention was to put the record straight after 1953. They achieved their aim but the general reaction was that a draw would have been a fairer result.

'We were desperately disappointed,' said Dai Hayward, 'because we all knew it was a game we should have won. The rub of the green went against us and perhaps we wasted a couple of chances. But I was proud of the boys because every one of them had played their heart out. We weren't up there with the 1953 team in the folklore of the club but we had let no one down and had maintained the reputation of Cardiff in the wider rugby world – and we had scored the only try of the match!'

What no one could have foreseen in 1963 was that the great tradition of Cardiff against the All Blacks in front of 50,000 crowds was almost over. The games of later years never seemed to have the indefinable magic touch of what had gone before. The players involved and the club's most intense fans would disagree but for the general rugby public there was rather less sense of anticipation outside the Arms Park fraternity and the matches themselves were certainly less memorable. Between 1972 and 1980 Cardiff played the All Blacks three times. True, in 1972 an impressive crowd of 45,000 turned up at what was by then the National Stadium at Cardiff Arms Park to see whether the blue and blacks could repeat the medicine dished out by Llanelli in beating the tourists earlier in the week. What they saw was an ugly match totally out of tune with the prevailing optimism of Welsh rugby in the sparkling 1970s. Punches were thrown, bodies were trampled on and both teams were culpable. The match was a betrayal of the great traditions of the past. The All Blacks won the game 20-4, Gareth Edwards claiming the club's points with a try when the side was already 20 points behind. As he scored the great scrum-half was apparently rabbit-punched. Somehow it seemed to sum up the whole day.

The teams met again in 1978 and 1980. Over-familiarity was becoming a problem, though there were some nice touches. In the first, Cardiff officials realised that the world-class wing, Bryan Williams, was about to make his one-hundredth appearance in an All Black jersey. An inscribed commemorative silver salver was ordered and presented to him by club chairman, John Davies, immediately before the kick-off. A grateful Williams returned the compliment by leading the haka and brilliantly creating the last of his side's three tries in a comfortable 17-7 victory.

Two years later the All Blacks were back to celebrate the centenary of the Welsh Rugby Union. Matches were scheduled against the established clubs of Cardiff, Llanelli, Swansea and Newport and an international against Wales. Cardiff had the honour of staging the opening fixture and in a salute to the great events of 1953 invited the veteran radio commentator, GV Wynne-Jones, who had captained the Rags in the 1930s, to come out of retirement and describe the opening exchanges. The distinctive voice was as resonant as ever but the match itself less memorable. As in 1978 the All Blacks were led by Graham Mourie, Cardiff for their part by the charismatic John Scott. But neither could inspire a great match on this occasion. Scott's side was in the early stages of developing into a team that would dominate Welsh domestic rugby in the next half-dozen years; the All Blacks were not yet in the form that would overwhelm Wales by a then-record 23-3 margin a month later. Cardiff failed to register a try for the first time in eight matches against the All Blacks and lost 16-9.

One last match remained. By 1989 the long tours of the past were shrinking but Cardiff was still the venue for the first fixture of a 13-match trip. Again the club performed respectably, losing only 25-15, but the goal-kicking gremlins that struck Alun Priday a quarter of a century earlier now visited Mike Rayer. Two vital chances were missed and an interval lead, thoroughly merited in the circumstances, was overhauled by three second-half tries by the tourists. The final whistle on 14 October 1989 signalled not only the end of a match but the end of an era. Cardiff had played the cream of New Zealand rugby for the ninth and last time. Every one of the individuals who had worn blue and black in those games would have memories of their own. But the fifteen players of 1953 remained the special breed.

PART TWO

SOUTH AFRICA

8

The Greatest Victory?

Cardiff's victory over the All Blacks in 1953 completed a full hand of victories over the major touring teams from the southern hemisphere. The accepted wisdom among the club's followers of the last half-century is that it was its greatest victory. But was it? It certainly has a special place in the hearts and minds of a now older generation of fans who were lucky enough to be at Cardiff Arms Park that November day. Add to them those of us not there but who have heard the tales of great deeds re-told by those who were and those who played in it. As the years go by, however, and the eye-witnesses dwindle in number, a more detached review may throw up other candidates for the title of 'Greatest Victory'. As we shall see, six wins in six matches against the Wallabies is a remarkable record and contains within it some outstanding matches in their own right. But there is an even more eye-catching score line from the early years of the twentieth century: on 1 January 1907 Cardiff Rugby Football Club beat the Springboks of South Africa by 17 points to nil.

The Cardiff team of 1907 was of the same vintage that had so narrowly failed against Dave Gallaher's All Blacks the previous season and the parallels between the two matches were almost uncanny. Once again Cardiff was playing host to a formidable international team from the other side of the world; the club's own Golden Era was still in full bloom; there was even the same match referee. With only a 53-week gap since the frustrations of the All Blacks' defeat, 12 of the Cardiff team would be playing again, including the legendary names of Gwyn Nicholls, Rhys Gabe, Johnnie Williams and Billy Neill. Percy Bush was still captain and had done a fine job in the intervening 12 months. Since the departure of the All Blacks the club had played 35 matches and lost only three, all of them away fixtures. At the Arms Park they had won 23 consecutive games, the most recent on Boxing Day 1906 when they had swept away the Barbarians by scoring 35 points without reply.

Not everything had been sweetness and light, however, in the early months of the season. Nicholls, having again gone into what turned out to be temporary retirement, missed the first nine games and the defeats at Swansea and Devonport Albion. He had also declined an early invitation from the national selectors to lead Glamorgan against the Springboks at the Arms Park at the end of October. But he had given the first signs of a change of plan by returning to the Cardiff side against Penygraig on 24 November. A week later he was once again captaining Wales but South Africa had proved too strong for the conquerors of New Zealand, winning by 11 points to nil. Bush had also made sporadic appearances for the club, in fact only seven in the first 20 fixtures. The back division had struggled in the absence of his guiding hand, with even the prolific try-scorer, Williams, finding it difficult to be regularly on the score sheet. But his reputation, like those of Nicholls, Bush and Gabe, was good enough to retain his place in the national team. South Africa's comprehensive victory in the international match was enough to send shock waves around the club which, allied to its own mixed bag of results, created an unusually pessimistic feeling about prospects for the big game.

Charley Arthur, still recording the annual fortunes of the team, noted:

'During the first half of the season, the games in which we were successful were not won by that clean and scientific football associated with our club, and little portended the triumph we obtained over the South Africans on New Year's Day. The South Africans had, as everybody knows, beaten every club, county and country except Scotland, and had caused consternation by defeating Wales. Cardiff was their best fixture, and to Cardiff everybody looked to beat them, so that one Welsh team should stay their triumphant career.'

The turning point in the club's preparations came over the Christmas holiday. First London Welsh came to the Arms Park and went down to defeat by 9 points to 5. Then the performance against the Barbarians made people believe that success against the Springboks was a real possibility. Although Bush and Gabe were again absent, the team had ran in nine tries, including a hat-trick by Johnnie Williams, against an experienced team captained by the club's former international, Boxer Harding. The three newcomers to the team from the previous season were also making a considerable impact. The change behind the scrum had been occasioned by the return of the wing, Ralph Thomas, to the Penarth club. His place had been reclaimed by Cecil Biggs, one of the six brothers to play for the club, who had been ruled out of the All Blacks' match by injury. Biggs was generally considered unlucky not to have played for Wales, but had been a first teamer since 1899 and had been club captain in 1904-05. Like Johnnie Williams he was a serial try scorer, eventually finishing his club career with 111 in 173 games.

The two projected additions to the pack were even more interesting. Ernie Rumbelow and Llew George had been replaced by Alf Brice and Joe Pugsley who represented the opposite ends of the age spectrum. Brice, known as Bobby for no better reason than he was a policeman, was 35 years old but had only been with Cardiff for three seasons. He had won the first 15 of his 18 caps while with Aberavon but had been suspended from all rugby for eight months after swearing at the referee when playing against Ireland in 1904. Now he was available again and an extremely useful performer. Pugsley, on the other hand, was still only 21 years old as the Springboks match approached. But he was a labourer in Cardiff docks and already a strong scrummager. In due course he would play seven times for Wales in 1910 and 1911 before turning professional with Salford and winning further international honours. Unfortunately, after playing throughout the season, Pugsley was injured in the Boxing Day fixture with the Barbarians and his place went to Jim Casey, who had made a big impression since joining the club from Pill Harriers.

The one tactical decision to be made was also a repeat of the All Blacks' match the year before. Once again Cardiff elected to play seven forwards and eight backs. Charley Arthur records that this was because 'we had eight backs and did not know which one to leave out [so] it was decided to play all of them'. Another story going around at the time was that it was because Gwyn Nicholls would only play if none of the regular seven backs were left out. The Springboks, however, had another theory. Their vice-captain and chronicler, Paddy Carolin, claimed that 'they [Cardiff] decided that the only way to beat us was to play eight backs'. To which one might add, ergo, Cardiff had only seven forwards against the Springboks' eight. Whatever the reason, the decision was a good one. Though Arthur states that Reggie Gibbs would again be the 'rover', in the event Bush often assumed the duty once the game was under way and did so with telling effect.

The Springboks were still the pre-match favourites and deservedly so. The Cardiff game was the final match of their tour of the British Isles, though the following week they would go to Paris and hammer a French XV by 55 points to 6 in an unofficial international. They had, admittedly, lost to Scotland and only drawn with England, but both matches were blighted by atrocious weather that literally caught the South Africans cold. Twenty-five other matches on the tour had been won, several of them by big scores – 44 points against Northumberland, 37 against East Midlands, and 34 against Yorkshire, all without reply. In Wales they had beaten Newport, Glamorgan, Monmouthshire, Llanelli and, of course, the national team and they had conceded only two tries. By the time they came to play Cardiff their reputation was based on a powerful pack, spearheaded by their captain, Paul Roos, and an adventurous ball-handling back division inspired by gifted half-backs such as Fred Dobbin, Dirk Jackson and Paddy Carolin. In the five days before the Arms Park showdown they had comprehensively beaten Monmouthshire at Newport and Llanelli at Stradey Park. But the bad weather that had followed the touring team around the four countries, most particularly at Crystal Palace in London and Hampden Park in Glasgow for the two internationals where victory eluded them, struck again on New Year's Day 1907.

In Ivor Difford's impressive *History of South African Rugby Football*, Paddy Carolin had his own vivid description of the state of the Arms Park that day:

'Owing to a hard frost the ground was covered with straw, and this was not removed when the thaw came. It looked as though a river had overflowed the ground which was literally a sea of mud at least a foot deep. A strong wind blew from end to end, and to add to our misery we lost the toss and had to face it.'

These appalling conditions would no more suit the Cardiff backs than it did the visitors – but what could not have been anticipated was the marvellous exhibition of running rugby that was to be put on by Percy Bush and his team. From the first whistle the club's tactics were to mix forward rushes with swift ball to the backs. Though the Springboks had kicked off they were soon back on their heels as the kicking of Nicholls and Gibbs put the ball deep in their territory. Biggs was forced to leave the field limping after a collision with the flank forward Bill Millar but still Bush insisted on running with the ball. Johnnie Williams, Biggs in the lead-up to his injury, and Rhys Gabe had all threatened the line before the breakthrough came. A scrum was forced in the visitors' half and a long pass out to midfield was gratefully accepted by Gwyn Nicholls who spotted half an opening and swerved through and around the cover defence for a classic centre three-quarter's try. Bert Winfield, still smarting after being dropped by Wales for the international match, kicked an excellent conversion from wide out on the left.

A feature of the game was how Winfield's opposite number, the highly regarded Arthur Marsberg, was struggling to come to terms with the conditions and the pressure put on him by Cardiff. He was at fault when his side conceded a second try, a direct result of another breakaway from a line-out, with the ball being taken on by Reggie Gibbs. The rover lived up to his appointed role by dribbling the ball past Marsberg and the winger, Anton Stegmann, to dive on the ball for a spectacular touchdown. Though Winfield narrowly failed to convert, the eight-point lead was a significant one in the conditions – and the first half scoring was not yet over. Biggs was back on the field but a virtual passenger with torn knee ligaments and Fred Smith was also in the wars after being knocked out in a heavy tackle. Marsberg continued to make unforced errors and the Springboks were literally bogged down in their own 25. On the stroke of half-time, the half-back, Dirk Jackson, played the ball almost in desperation in an offside position. Again Winfield defied the tricky wind and heavy ball to kick a fine penalty goal from a wide angle.

The 11 points lead at the interval was a good one but the

Springboks would have the wind at their backs in the second half and they were famed as strong finishers. As the Cardiff players trooped to the dressing rooms at half-time to seek dry jerseys they could have expected nothing less than a green-and-gold onslaught in the second 40 minutes. What they could not have realised was that their opponents had already almost thrown in the proverbial towel. Paddy Carolin later wrote:

> 'Owing to the wind it was next to impossible to clear our lines and gain relief by kicking [in the first half] and at half-time, when Cardiff led by 11 points to nil, we had all had more than enough … Under the conditions we could never have beaten any side, let alone such a magnificent fifteen as Cardiff fielded'.

This uncharacteristic defeatism by a South African side was dealing Cardiff a significant psychological advantage and one that, unaware of it though they probably were, they exploited to the full. Cecil Biggs had insisted on returning to the field for a second time, his knee heavily strapped and little more than a passenger, but somehow representative of the spirit and determination of the entire team. Equally, the sodden crowd of 30,000 had sung Welsh hymns throughout the interval as the visitors attempted to dry themselves with towels in the centre of the pitch and an impromptu rendering of the national anthem as the Cardiff team re-entered the arena. Amidst scenes like this on dark winter afternoons is sporting history often made. So it was as the second half unfolded.

The vice-captain, George Northmore, restarted the game for Cardiff but the Springboks were soon camped in the club's half. Scrum followed scrum near the home line until a break-out was led by Bush and Gibbs only for Marsberg to use the wind expertly to pin back the blue and blacks again in their own 25. To the visitors' consternation, however, Winfield, Nicholls and Bush were proving perfectly capable of finding touch with their own kicks into the wind and as every minute went by the situation became more desperate – not helped by two missed penalty goal chances by Dougie Morkel.

Midway through the half there was a noticeable change of tactics by both sides. The Springboks resorted to handling in the icy conditions with the inevitable result of a succession of mistakes. The wily Percy Bush, in contrast, realised the importance of tactical control and his field kicking was of the highest order. And his side still had two more tries up their sleeves that would finally break the Springboks' hearts. First Bush and Gabe worked their magic in midfield and released Johnnie Williams with the line in sight. In *The Western Mail*, the match report of 'Forward' memorably described what happened next: 'JL Williams diddled Marsberg very cleverly with a pretty run and scored wide out'. The report continued: 'There was no longer any doubt as to the result, Cardiff being infinitely the superior team and outplaying their opponents at all points with only 14 men.'

At the very end the Cardiff pack made one final surge into the Springboks' 25. Marsberg was again found wanting, failing to collect the loose ball and allowing Gabe to dribble past him, re-gather off his toes, and dive over for a magnificent score. Winfield's attempted conversion, blown away in the wind, hardly mattered as the game was well and truly decided in Cardiff's favour. It was, indeed, a famous victory.

Charley Arthur's conclusions were clear cut:

'No Cardiff team ever played better, or achieved so great renown, and the best man on the field, as he had been so often before, was Gwyn Nicholls. He never played a better game in his life, and never scored a better try than the one he opened Cardiff's score with. The South Africans took their defeat in a most sportsmanlike manner, and confirmed the opinion that had been formed that they were a great team of gentlemen and athletes.'

Paddy Carolin was making no excuses afterwards admitting that his side was thoroughly and absolutely outplayed or, as he put it, 'whacked to the wide' and 'utterly routed and smitten hip and thigh.' Roughly translated, we can assume that he realised the better side had won. The adverse conditions continued to be a discussion point among his team mates but there were no excuses. With the benefit of a period of quiet reflection, he wrote:

'Nothing but the very best we were capable of would have been good enough to stave off defeat if we are to judge from what the

The Pioneers

Percy Bush with his team for Cardiff's first fixture against an international touring team, the All Blacks of 1905. Some of the greatest players of the era are in the line-up.
(Back row, left to right): Johnnie Williams, Jack Brown, Ernie Rumbelow, Billy Neill, Llew George and Fred Smith (Middle): E Gwyn Nicholls, George Northmore (vice-captain), Percy Bush (captain), Rhys Gabe and Reggie Gibbs
(Front): Ralph Thomas, Bert Winfield, Dickie David and Jack Powell
The two officials are interesting. On the back right is Gil Evans, of Birmingham, who was to referee all three of the club's first matches against the All Blacks, Springboks and Wallabies. On the left of the back row is one of the two umpires, Mr W Phillips. Umpires were the forerunners of the more familiar touch-judges.

The Cardiff team has hardly changed from a year and a week before, but now the opponents are the 1907 Springboks. The blue and blacks go one step further and triumph by 17 points to nil. Percy Bush is still the captain and this time the committee obviously want to be in the picture. The three new players are Jim Casey (second player on the left of the back row), Alf Brice (back right) and Cecil Biggs (second from the left in the middle).

A Warm Welcome for the Wallabies

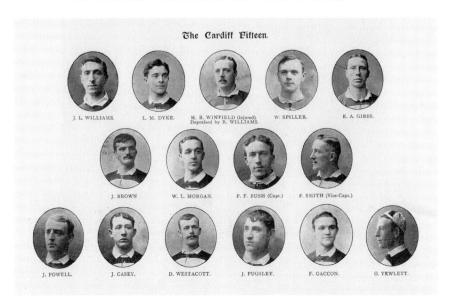

The Cardiff Fifteen.

J. L. WILLIAMS.   L. M. DYKE.   H. B. WINFIELD (injured). Deputised by R. WILLIAMS.   W. SPILLER.   R. A. GIBBS.

J. BROWN   W. L. MORGAN.   P. F. BUSH (Capt.)   F. SMITH (Vice-Capt.)

J. POWELL.   J. CASEY.   D. WESTACOTT.   J. PUGSLEY.   F. GACCON.   G. YEWLETT.

The match programme for the 1908 game against the Wallabies shows the triumphant Cardiff team in close-up. Bush's new half-back partner is Willie Morgan. Six of the forwards are along the front row and the other two, Brown and Smith, flank the half-backs in the gallery. The unfortunate Bert Winfield was replaced by Bobby Williams at full-back.

A more informal team line-up for the opposition. No one warned the Wallabies about the weather but at least it was a white Christmas. Later in the day the temperature rose as Cardiff opened the Australian chapter of their touring team book with a comprehensive 24-8 victory.

The Second All Blacks

The closest that Cardiff got to the Invincibles of 1924 was the joint team photograph before the match. The All Blacks won by 16 points to eight. The Cardiff players in the line-up are: (Back row) William Ireson, Frank Stephens, Sid Hinam and Idris Richards; (middle row) Tom Wallace, Bobby Delahay, Arthur Cornish, Tom Lewis and Percy Rayer; (front row) Con O'Leary, WJ Ould, Tom 'Codger' Johnson (captain), Jim Brown and Jack Powell; while Danny Davies sits on the ground at the front.

The All Blacks' outstanding vice-captain, Jock Richardson, heads for the line in the move leading up to his side's first try. There are several recognisable buildings outside the ground in Westgate Street.

A Golden Era

The Cardiff team that developed after World War Two was the greatest since 1905-08. By the time they played the Wallabies in 1947, they were a match for any team in the land. Eleven of them played for Wales during the season.

(Back row) Billy Jones, Gwyn Evans, Les Manfield, Bill Tamplin, Roy Roberts, Elvet Jones, Cliff Davies; (Middle row) Stanley Bowes, Doug Jones, Jack Matthews, Haydn Tanner (captain), Bleddyn Williams, Billy Cleaver, Frank Trott; (Front row) Maldwyn James and Les Williams.

The committeeman at the back right is Duncan Brown while between Tanner and Bleddyn Williams sits the 1924 fly-half, Danny Davies, who was now the club chairman.

The captain, Haydn Tanner, fires out a typical dive pass before the Wallabies defence can get near to Cardiff's backs. Tanner was a golden star in a golden era. As a schoolboy in West Wales he had helped both Swansea and Wales to defeat the 1935 All Blacks. In 1938 he toured South Africa with the Lions. Six years of war, when he was a lieutenant in the Army, had not blunted his skills. In the background can be seen the packed south stand and enclosure of Cardiff Arms Park.

Billy Cleaver was Tanner's partner at half-back and a great player in his own right. Misleadingly nicknamed 'Billy the Kick', he was no slouch as a runner and was in his element against the Wallabies. In the course of three months he helped Cardiff (as a fly-half), Wales (at full back) and the Barbarians (in the centre) beat the tourists at Cardiff Arms Park.

They tamed the tourists in Cardiff but were also famous tourists themselves. In 1950, five Cardiff club players were selected for the British Isles touring team that went to New Zealand, Australia and Ceylon. From left to right they are Rex Willis, Jack Matthews, Bleddyn Williams, Billy Cleaver and Cliff Davies. All five of them won test match places during the tour.

The One That Got Away

So near yet so far in 1951 as the Springboks escaped with an 11-9 victory against Jack Matthews' team. But things were looking good when Bleddyn Williams careered over the line for a text-book try after a brilliant combination with Cliff Morgan, Alun Thomas and Matthews.

And then the victory was snatched away in the dying moments. Full back Frank Trott can't get close to flying Springbok wing, Chum Ochse, as he crosses for his second try of the game.

The History Makers

Half a century after they defeated the All Blacks by eight points to three, the names of the fifteen players that wore blue and black on 21 November 1953 are still among the most revered in the club's history.
(Back row) Gareth Griffiths, John Llewellyn, Eddie Thomas, Malcolm Collins, John Nelson, J D Evans; (Front row) C D Williams, Stanley Bowes, Rex Willis, Sid Judd (vice-captain), Bleddyn Williams (captain), Cliff Morgan, Alun Thomas, Gwyn Rowlands, Geoff Beckingham

For Haydn Tanner in 1947 read Rex Willis in 1953. Another quick heel enables the scrum-half to send out a pass to Cliff Morgan as the team continues its marvellous attacking game plan during the opening 20 minutes.

Sid Judd's great moment. They have attacked and attacked and finally the defence is breached. Cardiff's vice-captain has pounced on the bouncing ball near the All Blacks' line and he has scored the opening try. The club is on the way to a famous victory. Four weeks later Judd repeated the medicine for Wales against New Zealand with a similar result.

When you beat the All Blacks, you celebrate. Captain and hero Bleddyn Williams is chaired off Cardiff Arms Park shoulder high.

As the years go by, the celebrations continue – and everyone joins in. Cliff Morgan tinkles the ivories to the delight of an impromptu choir. Eddie Thomas, Gareth Griffiths, John Nelson, J D Evans, Stanley Bowes, Bleddyn Williams and Rex Willis are in this reunion of 1970. With them, standing between Bleddyn and Rex, are the match referee, Viv Llewellyn from Llansamlet, and the club chairman, Hubert Johnson.

From Cavaliers to Roundheads

The 1960 Springboks won few friends with their relentless approach. A rare sight against Cardiff is that of scrum-half, Dick Lockyear, passing the ball to his fly-half. Racing around the blind-side of the scrum is Cardiff's skipper, Lloyd Williams, and the scrum-capped Howard Norris looks on. Further out are fly-half Tommy McCarthy and wing forward Dai Hayward.

Anything the Springboks could do....the 1972 All Blacks were cast in the same mould as the earlier Springboks. Win at all costs was their motto and the result was an ugly match with the blue and blacks. Roger Lane guards the blind-side and Carl Smith is on stand-by duty as Gareth Edwards tries to gain territorial advantage with a tactical punt.

Not So Memorable

Dai Hayward's Cardiff team of 1963 came as close as any side to repeating the heroics of 1953 against the All Blacks but suffered for their own reluctance to spin the ball wide.
(Back row) Haydn Wilkins (touch judge), Maurice Richards, Elwyn Williams, Graham Davies, Keith Rowlands, Cliff Howe, Richie Wills, Billy Thomas, Tom Holley (physiotherapist), Denzil Hughes (referee)
(Middle row) Lloyd Williams, Meirion Roberts, Howard Norris, Dai Hayward (captain), A T Thomas (chairman), Alun Priday, Kingsley Jones (Front row) Cliff Ashton, Steve Hughes

At the end of the decade the game against Dawie de Villiers' beleaguered 1969 Springboks was quickly forgotten. Starved of possession, the order of the day for Cardiff was one of tackle, tackle and tackle again. Never far from the call of duty were skipper Mervyn John and fellow flanker, John Hickey, as Lyn Baxter (number 4) arrives to provide back-up.

And Again…..!!

The 1966 Wallabies went the same way as their predecessors, going down 14-8. This time it was scrum-half Billy Hullin's big day. The ever reliable John Hickey and Lyn Baxter look on as he conjures up another piece of magic.
© *Western Mail & Echo*

Joining in the fun is Tony Pender, a number 8 who could also play at prop. His chip ahead wins the approval of the supporting John O'Shea.

Wallaby woe continued in 1975 and this time another blue and black starlet burst onto the scene. Gareth Davies was to play four times and score a record 30 points against the major touring teams. Here he marks his debut with a second-half try as Cardiff headed for a 14-9 victory.
© *Western Mail & Echo*

Not even the Grand slam Wallabies of 1984 were safe against Cardiff. Adrian Hadley collects Alun Donovan's pass and heads for the corner and the try that settles the 16-12 result – and six wins in six matches against the pride of Australia.
© *Huw Evans Picture Agency*

The Last Tries For and Against

Another close call against the 1989 All Blacks, with number 8 Mark Edwards powering over for the try that gave the club a 9-3 interval lead. Enjoying the moment are Mike Rayer, Andrew Booth, Howard Stone, Mark Ring and, on the ground, Richie Collins. It was Cardiff's last try against a touring team.

As Steve Ford watches and Emyr Lewis attempts a cover tackle, the final touchdown of all is claimed by the 1994 Springbok scrum-half, Joost van der Westhuizen. Fittingly it was a brilliant individual effort by a world-class performer – and the end of the touring team era at Cardiff Arms Park.

Cardiff backs did under the most adverse conditions. Better handling and combination we had rarely, if ever, seen on a dry day. E Gwyn Nicholls himself had been disappointing in the previous games in which we had seen him, and, though it was at our expense, we were all highly delighted at seeing him at his very best. A prince of players and the best of good sportsmen, no world side could be complete without him.'

In victory the Cardiff club and its supporters did not forget that the Springboks had themselves reached the end of a long tour and would be leaving for France within 24 hours. In his post-match interview, Bush congratulated them on the overall results of the tour, adding, 'We realise that the South Africans have taken their defeat like true sportsmen and have nothing but admiration for the spirit they have shown'. An official dinner for the touring team was hosted by the club at the Queen's Hotel in St Mary Street and no expense was spared in the lavish eight-course menu. But while these formalities were being concluded a large crowd had gathered to give the Springboks a spontaneous send-off. *Reuter's News Agency* reported that 'A crowd numbering 9,000 assembled outside the hotel at which the Springboks were staying and escorted them to the [railway] station amid tumultuous cheers. Marsberg was the most popular member of the team with the crowd. He was carried shoulder high to the station.' Shortly after seven o'clock that evening Paul Roos' Springboks departed South Wales for the last time. Their tour had been an undoubted success but they left behind a Cardiff team that could justifiably claim to have delivered to their club one if its greatest victories.

Nicholls had grabbed the headlines, and deservedly so, but the real triumph was for the entire team, not least the captain Percy Bush as he swept away the shadow of his unforced error that had cost his side the earlier match against the All Blacks. Now they could bask in the glory of a truly great win and the prospect of yet another match with an international side when the Australian Wallabies arrived in Britain in 1908. For later historians the challenge of accurately assessing the true worth of the 1907 victory alongside that of Bleddyn Williams' side in 1953 is an almost impossible one. Were, for instance, the Springboks of the early years of the century a stronger side than the All Blacks who came in a totally different rugby age? Were they, indeed, unhinged by the atrocious playing conditions – or should great teams be winning teams in all situations? Were the Springboks simply exhausted at the end of a long tour? On the other hand, with the focus more on the 1953 All Blacks, were they of the best vintage from a great rugby country? The New Zealand critic, Terry McLean, christened them 'The Incomprehensibles', presumably because no-one in his own country could decide how good, or bad, they were. By the end of their tour they had lost four and drawn two of their 36 matches, an unacceptable debit column by their countrymen's exacting standards.

All these points are academic. Better, perhaps, to evaluate from the Cardiff club's point of view. Undoubtedly the teams of 1907 and 1953 were both great ones in their different ways. Percy Bush captained the first for four of the five seasons from September 1905 to April 1909 and the teams of those years were remarkably consistent, well meriting the accolade of a 'Golden Era'. The defeat of the Springboks in the middle of that era was the jewel in the crown. All contemporary accounts acknowledge the remarkable skills and ambition shown in the climatic circumstances of the match. The overall team performances were rather different in 1953. Bleddyn Williams, like Bush before him, had been part of another halcyon chapter in the club's history. There are still many people alive who testify that the style of rugby served up by the men in blue and black in the late 1940s was as good as anything from the later television age of the 1970s when the Welsh national side was on a pedestal. By 1953, no one was pretending that there was a week-in, week-out consistency of performance from the Cardiff team. But what Bleddyn's team did on 21 November 1953 was raise their game on a particular day against specific opponents and achieve a victory that they wanted more than any other – and, like their predecessors in 1907, did so in a style that won admirers from near and far. The truth of the matter is that both teams enhanced the standing of the Cardiff club throughout the rugby world. In the first decade of the twentieth century, Percy Bush may well have captained the greatest ever Cardiff team. In 1953 Bleddyn Williams oversaw the club's greatest victory.

9

Dr Jack and the Springbok Head

In the Cardiff Rugby Football Club's museum, officially known as the Hubert Johnson Room, there are many splendid club and international caps, jerseys, boots, photographs and mementoes recalling the history of the club and its players right back to its foundation in 1876. The most imposing single trophy by far is a Springbok head. Rugby followers everywhere will know exactly what it symbolises: victory over a South African touring team. The obvious conclusion is that this particular head dates back to the marvellous triumph by Percy Bush's team in 1907. Yet, oddly, it doesn't. As it happens the tradition of awarding the trophy, a stuffed and mounted head of a real springbok, did not commence until the second touring team from South Africa to come to Britain, Billy Millar's side of 1912. Cardiff's proud trophy dates from more recent times when it was presented at the end of the 1951-52 tour. Yet in that season Cardiff lost to the Springboks – but such was the quality of their play once again that the South African management presented the head to the club. The circumstances of the match are themselves fascinating.

As with the All Blacks two years later the Cardiff team of 1951 focused on a famous victory over a top-class touring team. The Springboks of that year were definitely that, arguably the very best ever to undergo a full 30-match tour of the British Isles. Better even than the 1905 All Blacks and their three Springbok predecessors. That in itself was a considerable compliment. The 1907 team had lost only twice. The two tours since then had been equally impressive: 24 wins in 27 matches in 1912-13 and only one loss in 26 outings in 1931-32. More importantly, over the span of the two tours they had won nine consecutive international matches. Not even New Zealand could match that. Cardiff at least had the consolation of putting up creditable performances against them on both tours.

In 1912 the club, captained by Billy Spiller, held them to one point. This was no mean feat because these particular Springboks were the first touring team to win all their international matches against the four home countries and France and conceded only one try along the way. They were famed for a monster pack though their backs did not have the brilliance of their predecessors of five years before. There was also a lack of strength in depth and their three losses were all outside the test matches – against Newport, Swansea and London. In the circumstances the Cardiff team would have been disappointed not to inflict another defeat on them but there had been many changes in personnel since the heady days of the 1900s. Not one member of Percy Bush's teams of 1905 and 1907 was around in 1912. The captain, Spiller, was a good player in his own right, a policeman from St Fagans who won four caps as a centre for Wales. He had four other internationals in the team with him – the 5 ft 5 in full back Bobby Williams, whose diminutive size belied a deadly tackling ability, Clem Lewis at fly-half, and in the pack Jim Birch and Billy Jenkins.

This was not a Cardiff side to set the pulse racing – it was to be beaten 24 times over the next two seasons – but to its credit it reserved one of its best displays for the showpiece match against the Springboks. It was played in perfect conditions and Spiller's team could easily have snatched victory. It was the captain himself who scored the only try of the game, a brilliant effort early in the second half that put his side 6-4 ahead. Unfortunately, a later penalty goal, awarded for obstruction, won the game for the touring team by a single point. The Springboks had achieved their stated aim of avenging the defeat of five years before.

There was a long gap of nearly 20 years before the next Springbok tour in 1931-32 and it again coincided with a somewhat mediocre period in Cardiff's history. The controversial policy of fielding two first teams between 1926 and 1931 had won the club few friends and done little for individual player development. At least in 1931 the principle had been abandoned but the results were only slowly improving. The team had already lost half-a-dozen matches before the Springboks arrived in late November and would lose 20 in all during the season. The tourists' match, not unexpectedly, was one of them but at least it was again a case of defeat with honour against a top international side. That is hardly surprising because, however unsatisfactory the progress of the team in terms of results, there were several individuals within it who were quality players. Five internationals behind the scrum – the entire three-quarter line of Ronnie Boon, Graham Jones, Bernard Turnbull and John Roberts and fly-half Harry Bowcott – were complemented by the talented Maurice Turnbull, brother of Bernard, at scrum-half, and Tommy Stone at full back. Bowcott had taken over the captaincy from the injured Howard Poole, a scrum-half who had been good enough to tour New Zealand with the Lions in 1930 without ever winning a cap for Wales. The vacancy left at half-back went to the younger Turnbull who was ranked among the finest all-round sportsmen produced by Wales. A county and test cricketer, an international hockey and squash player, he eventually won his international rugby cap at exactly the right time – as part of the first Wales team to win at Twickenham in 1933. Sadly he was killed in action in Normandy in August 1944.

The club pack was also well blessed with several internationals – Tom Lewis, Archie Skym and Bob Barrell were already capped and Iorrie Isaacs and Don Tarr would follow them later. But the Springboks of 1931, led by Benny Osler, were a dour team. They had come to win everything and they almost succeeded, again winning all their internationals and losing only to East Midlands. Their heavyweight pack and two capable scrum-half options, Pierre de Villiers and Danie Craven, provided the perfect platform for Osler to kick the leather off the ball. He did so with a vengeance. It was not pretty to watch but stunningly effective. Cardiff at least had the satisfaction of contributing to one of the more entertaining matches of the tour. One of the highlights was the match within a match between the opposing wings, Ronnie Boon and Maurice Zimmerman, two young men with a hunger for try-scoring. Boon had won the first of his 12 international caps as a 20-year-old the previous year and the Springbok was himself only 20. He struck first with a typical piece of opportunism, seizing on a bouncing ball to race away for a converted try. Not to be outdone, within five minutes Boon wriggled out of the tightest of corners near halfway and showed Zimmerman and three other Springboks a clean pair of heels for a breathtaking try in the corner that Stone converted from the edge of touch.

Cardiff were deservedly on level terms at the interval but squandered a couple of further try-scoring opportunities. The tourists punished them as all good teams do, with two late tries completing a 13-5 victory. The Springboks were now ahead in the three-match series with the club but when they next met in 1951 the drama would equal anything served up in the epic games with the All Blacks in 1905 and subsequently in 1953 and the defining blue and black triumph over the Springboks in 1907.

In 1951-52 Cardiff Rugby Football Club was celebrating its 75th anniversary season. The fourth visit of the Springboks would be the centrepiece of the jubilee but there were other unique events arranged as well, including a match against the British Isles touring team of 1950 that would be specially reconvened for the occasion. Only the Cardiff club would even contemplate the arranging of such an ambitious fixture. The games with the Lions and the Springboks were barely a month apart and so, once again, the club would be in the eyes and ears of the entire rugby world. They could have had no better figurehead than their captain, Dr Jack Matthews. His two seasons at the helm immediately after the war were among the greatest in the club's history, both in terms of results and the sheer enjoyment and style of the play. Now he would lead the club in its celebration season and there were many great days.

Forever bracketed with Bleddyn Williams as a great centre partnership, Jack Matthews was a great player and leader in his own right. He was nearly three years older than Williams and was originally from Bridgend. There he attended the Oldcastle Primary School and later the County School for Boys. His dynamic speed off the mark soon marked him out as a rugby player of considerable potential as well as a good track athlete. His first appearance at Cardiff Arms Park was as a 14-year-old in 1934 when he helped the Bridgend Schools district side beat Newport to claim the prestigious Dewar Shield. He was still in the sixth form when senior clubs came knocking on his door and matches for Bridgend, Neath and Aberavon soon followed. Already his devastating running allied to trademark tackling was attracting an even wider audience and he was selected to play in a senior international trial while still at school. His meteoric rise showed every sign of matching that of the multi-talented Wilfred

Wooller until the outbreak of war in September 1939 intervened. He still hadn't played for Cardiff in an official match but his appetite for top-class rugby was further whetted in April 1940 when he was selected to play for Wales against England in a Red Cross international match at Gloucester. His captain and centre partner was Wooller.

'That was a great experience,' said Matthews. 'Wooller was a very commanding figure and a powerful runner. He had incredibly long strides and a phenomenal kick ahead and my job was to chase them. Unfortunately the war meant that he had to go off to the Far East and after being a prisoner of war under the Japanese he never played first class rugby again. As for myself, my medical studies meant that I was sent back from my RAF camp to the Welsh School of Medicine to complete my training. That was frustrating but the consolation was I could carry on playing rugby. I captained Cardiff Medicals and we had, among other matches, wartime fixtures with Cardiff at the Arms Park.'

As the war years continued, various invitation teams were put together for matches in South Wales and it was in one of these that Matthews and Williams combined for an East Wales XV against the British Army at the Arms Park in January 1943. He knew by then that if and when normality returned he would set his sights on playing for Cardiff. When it did in the autumn of 1945 Matthews was not only playing for the blue and blacks but was chosen by the Emergency Committee of the club to be its first post-war captain:

'I considered it to be the greatest of honours and, despite all the other teams I played for and captained, I still do. The way the team responded to my overtures to play attacking rugby in those early post-war seasons was marvellous. Leading Cardiff out onto the Arms Park against the likes of the Kiwis, the other representative sides and the Barbarians made me very proud.'

It is hard to appreciate looking back that, because of six years of war and another season when official internationals were not staged, players like Jack Matthews had to wait so long before they had the opportunity to play for their country. There had, of course, been Services Internationals during the war and a season of Victory

Internationals after that but, competitive as they were, they weren't quite the real thing. As it happened, Matthews had captained Wales in the first of the Victory matches, against France, in December 1945. But it wasn't until January 1947, in the first official international since March 1939, that he won his first full cap. The schoolboy wonder was already fast approaching his 27th birthday. Yet he still had several seasons of top class rugby ahead of him. The national selectors, unfortunately, found it hard to plump for the obvious and pick Matthews and Williams as a pair so there were matches when Bleddyn would play at fly-half and Jack on the wing. In 1949, fortunately, they played as a partnership against England, Scotland and Ireland before an injury sidelined Williams for the French match. The British selectors, however, had seen enough – allied, of course, to their perennially brilliant club pairing – and they both went on the great tour to the Antipodes a year later.

In the opening month in New Zealand, Matthews made a big impression on the watching critics. His partner was injured but he played in the first four games and, even when the team lost, his personal qualities were recognised. The 23-9 defeat against Otago was the first setback of the trip but Matthews was commended for 'his dash and vigour' and was pinpointed as the outstanding back on the field. When the Lions returned to Dunedin to play the first test, the special correspondent for the local paper, profiled him in glowing terms:

'Iron Man they are calling him now – the one and only Jack Matthews of Cardiff. New Zealanders love to bestow nicknames upon their favourites. Nearly every rugby team to visit this country, for instance, has had its Iron Man … But the record of the sturdy Welsh doctor looks like surpassing those of all the earlier ones. He celebrated his 30th birthday during this tour and by his magnificent all-round displays he has given the lie to any suggestion that he is past his best … As far as I can recollect, he has missed only the game against Southland, which possibly would have gone the other way if he had been present to stiffen a defence which on that particular day was lacking in the centre position.'

The mistake often made when assessing Jack Matthews' qualities as a player is to highlight his deadly tackling. To some extent that is quite understandable because on the field he took no prisoners. He recalled how when Cardiff kicked off against the Wallabies in 1947 he chased the ball so hard that he collided with his scrum-capped opposite number, Trevor Allan. No one realised at the time that he was concussed.

> 'Almost immediately I started asking Bleddyn what the score was and he couldn't work out why I kept repeating the question throughout the game. Then during the early hours of the Sunday morning I jumped out of bed to get dressed, telling my wife that I had to hurry because I was due to play against Australia in a few hours!'

His indestructible reputation was further enhanced by an illustrious amateur boxing career that included climbing into the same ring as the heavyweight legend, Rocky Marciano, at RAF St Athan. But there was also a telling attacking side to his game. Geoff Beckingham recalls a chance meeting with the champion sprinter, E MacDonald Bailey:

> 'MacDonald Bailey was doing some running along the touchline at the Arms Park and Jack joined in. To my amazement he was more than holding his own over at least 50 yards. Bailey couldn't understand why Jack didn't take athletics seriously. He told him, 'If I had your start I'd be world champion', but Jack wasn't interested. He replied, 'It's easier playing rugby, all I have to do is sprint 40 yards then pass the ball for someone else to score'. The look on Bailey's face was a picture.'

And Bleddyn Williams is the first to admit that his great friend was the perfect partner in midfield:

> 'Sometimes my sidesteps could surprise even myself and I wasn't sure where I was going – but every time I ran out of options or space Jack was invariably at my elbow ready for the pass.'

The Lions' tour was certainly a triumph for Matthews. He played in all six tests against New Zealand and Australia and 14 provincial matches, captaining the side three times. He returned home hungry for yet more international rugby. His four games in the 1951 championship culminated in the captaincy against France but that turned out to be his swansong. He might have played again at Twickenham the following year but his rejection of a last-minute summons to go there as a replacement says much about the integrity he brought to all his sport:

'I was not selected in the original team to play England – Bleddyn and Newport's Malcolm Thomas were in the centre – and I was due to captain Cardiff at Bath the same afternoon. But Bleddyn dropped out injured and I received an SOS from the WRU via our chairman, Hubert Johnson, to catch the early train to London on the Saturday morning. Not sure what the situation was I reached the team hotel and travelled up the road with them to Twickenham. I changed ready to play but 10 minutes before the kick-off the selectors, who had been huddled in a meeting with the captain, John Gwilliam, told me that the travelling reserve, Alun Thomas, would play instead. I had no problem in principle with Alun playing, especially as it was his first cap, but something had to be said. So I gave them the benefit of a piece of my mind and told them never to pick me again. They never did.'

That was half way through the club's jubilee season and Dr Jack had plenty to keep him occupied. As he says, 'The special matches with the Lions and the Springboks were fantastic occasions and we also had our eyes on four wins over Newport. We had lost a few senior players since my previous captaincy four years before – especially Haydn Tanner and Billy Cleaver in the backs and Maldwyn James, Les Manfield and Gwyn Evans from the pack – but we were still strong. As well as Rex Willis and Cliff Morgan taking the places of Billy and Haydn, we had three outstanding replacements up front in Geoff Beckingham, CD Williams and the Irish international number 8, Des O'Brien.'

The acquisition of O'Brien was typical of the way the fame of the

Cardiff club attracted even the biggest names long before the modern day cheque books were waved around to entice the unlikeliest players to the Arms Park. O'Brien was a player of stature in the game who had first played international rugby in 1948, sharing in Ireland's Grand Slam triumph and, the following year, a Triple Crown. While with Cardiff he would also captain his country five times.

'Joining Cardiff at that stage of my career hadn't been planned,' said O'Brien. 'I was already way past my thirtieth birthday and was thinking of retiring. I had been very disappointed when I wasn't selected to tour with the Lions in 1950. But I was employed by Guinness and was moved to South Wales to work as an inspector. Vivian Jenkins, the great Welsh full-back who I had played with at Wasps during the war, took me in hand and said, 'If you are selling Guinness in Wales then you have to play for Cardiff!' So I did and didn't regret it for one minute. I have to admit though that their fixture list frightened me to death. When I played for London Irish we had about 26 games a season. Cardiff's was more like 56 so I didn't start until the end of September. Going to the Arms Park was a perfect pick-me-up and I have some wonderful memories of my time there and the friends I made.'

O'Brien's debut for the club came in unusual surroundings – for the Rags away to Blaenau-Gwent and he says he made sure he played well enough so that he wouldn't be needed for such tough opposition again. He needn't have worried as he soon made his mark and Matthews impressed him as a captain and player:

'Jack was a quiet captain with a tremendous presence. It was obvious when he took over in the 1951-52 season that he already had everyone's respect on the basis of what he had done before. His tackling, of course, was incredible. I remember playing at Rodney Parade and he flattened his opposite number who was one of Newport's up-and-coming stars. The tackle was only a fraction late, if you follow me. Any way the home crowd was baying for his blood. At the final whistle the rest of the team surrounded him for his own safety. We thought we were in the clear once we were changed and socialising afterwards. But Jack was carrying a full tray of drinks across the bar – he was always generous – when a young lady stepped forward and tripped him up calling him a blue and black so-and-so!'

Des O'Brien finally retired in the summer of 1952, declining an invitation to take the club captaincy. But he stayed in South Wales for another seven years. He had bought a six-acre farm in the Gower but eventually moved to Oxford and is now living in Midlothian. In 1966 he was manager of the British Isles team on their tour of Australia, New Zealand and Canada.

In 1952 no one was in any doubt that the match with the Springboks at the beginning of October would mark the serious business of the season, but equally the date with the Lions was sure to be an historic occasion unique to the Cardiff club. The date was set for Saturday 22 September 1951, exactly 75 years to the day since the Cardiff Football Club, as it was originally called, was formed out of an amalgamation of the Cardiff Wanderers and the Glamorgan Football Club. It was a marvellous sense of timing on behalf of the organising committee, chaired by Hubert Johnson. The very fact that the four Home Unions agreed to the fixture in the first place was partly due to the overtures made by Bleddyn Williams and Jack Matthews – and, of course, the three other Cardiff Lions of 1950, Billy Cleaver, Rex Willis and Cliff Davies. A proud Matthews recalls the background to the match well:

'We approached the Lions' manager, Surgeon-Captain Ginger Osborne, with the idea of the match and he had no hesitation in recommending to the four Home Unions that for the first time ever the Lions should play a match on home soil. Unfortunately Ginger couldn't be with us in person because he was back on active military service in Korea but 20 of our fellow Lions from 1950 were there at the Arms Park.'

Too often when such celebration matches are staged there is a host of late withdrawals from the published team, but that was never the case with the Lions in Cardiff's jubilee season. To look at the Lions' line-up now is, to say the least, impressive. The touring team's skipper, Karl Mullen, led a pack that had John Robins of Wales and Tom Clifford of Ireland propping either side of him; two more Welshmen,

Roy John and Don Hayward were at lock, and in the back row there were Ireland's Jim McCarthy and Jim Nelson alongside Vic Roberts of England. The Lions were equally powerful in the backs with a three-quarter line comprising two Irishmen, Martin Lane and Noel Henderson, plus Malcolm Thomas and the Scot, Ranald Macdonald. In a team of stars the real attractions were Lewis Jones at full-back and arguably the player of the tour, Jack Kyle, at fly-half. With Rex Willis playing in the Cardiff team the Lions had Billy Cleaver at scrum-half. All the visitors were *bona fide* Lions, with not a 'guest player' in sight.

Not surprisingly the match captured the public's imagination. From late summer ticket applications flooded in from all over the British Isles and there was every prospect of a huge crowd. The previous February a record attendance, variously estimated between 48,500 and 50,000, had turned out for a Cardiff v Newport fixture and no one even blinked when there were several 30,000-plus crowds for other club matches. To their credit the club committee declared that season tickets were valid for the visit of the Lions; match tickets on general sale were priced at the normal admission rates of one to three shillings. The actual attendance on the day was in excess of 45,000 and, in perfect conditions, they were treated to 80 minutes of top quality rugby. Beforehand, both teams were introduced on the field to the Lord Mayor of Cardiff and the ceremonial kick-off was performed by Sir Wavell Wakefield. The fact that the Lions were wearing the same numbered jerseys from the Antipodean tour – for instance, Kyle was number 11 and Vic Roberts number 25 – added to the special atmosphere.

Cardiff soon established an early lead through two tries by the right wing Derek Murphy. Both were near the corner flag and Bill Tamplin narrowly failed with the attempted conversions. Before half-time the Lions hit back with three tries of their own, all by forwards. Roy John, Clifford and McCarthy went over in quick succession. Lewis Jones converted the second beautifully from the edge of touch and also stroked a penalty goal over from long range. His kicking was to prove the vital difference in the final result. For Cardiff the Matthews-Williams duo was at its exuberant best and their inter-passing at speed set up a try for Bleddyn. Then he jinked through again to give Sid Judd the scoring pass for a try under the posts. To everyone's amazement Malcolm Collins missed the point-blank conversion and the Lions won the game 14-12.

The scoreboard didn't matter on this occasion. The Springboks' match a month later would be something different altogether. First, though, there were the jubilee celebrations undertaken in style with the post-match banquet for 400 guests, including 124 former players, held at City Hall. Proposing the toast, Sir Wavell Wakefield said, 'Cardiff stands for all that is best in rugby football. No club in the world could quite stage such an occasion as this.' To set the seal on a perfect weekend, the *Football Echo* paid its own tribute:

'In these days of frustration and lacklustre living, the virile chapter of sporting achievement written by the Cardiff club must encourage and revive the confidence of many who may have doubted the trend of modern British sport in general and of the rugby game in particular. Here is a club that has fashioned for itself a great reputation by clean and clever play alone, inheriting a glorious tradition which must spur them on to even greater efforts in emulation of the almost legendary figures of the past.'

On the Monday after the jubilee weekend, preparations for the arrival of the Fourth Springboks began. The day of the match, Saturday 20 October, was by any standards set to be a massive one for the city. As well as Cardiff playing the Springboks at the Arms Park, less than a mile away at Ninian Park Wales would be locking horns with England in a British Championship soccer international. Once again one can only salute the authorities of half a century ago. In 2003 the staging of a Cardiff club match at the Arms Park, with a likely 6,000 attendance, and Cardiff City playing a second division game in front of 12-13,000 fans, sent all sorts of safety officers, traffic police officials and even local media into a mini-panic about possible congestion. One can only refer them to the events of that October afternoon in 1951. The organisation undertaken by both the soccer and rugby clubs was exemplary. Tickets for the soccer international went on sale on Saturday 6 October and rugby tickets two days later. They were equally popular – queues stretched towards Leckwith from Ninian Park and the length of Westgate Street outside the Arms Park. There were the usual human interest stories in abundance. In the *South Wales Echo* it was reported that one lady, who had queued for rugby tickets for her husband and son from before dawn, reached the front of the queue by 11.00 am only to discover that she needn't have bothered because they were season ticket holders anyway! *The Western Mail* praised all concerned:

'Cardiff is preparing for the invasion of approximately 120,000 people on Saturday [and] Cardiff City police are planning to ensure that traffic on the big day is kept on the move and certain streets will be subject to special provisions. There is little doubt that both Ninian Park and Cardiff Arms Park will be filled to capacity for the matches ... In an outstanding day in the history of Welsh sport Cardiff will do its best to cope with the immense influx of visitors.'

Meanwhile the Cardiff team had to make its own preparations for the biggest game of the season. The Lions extravaganza was followed by four consecutive wins, including an 11-3 home victory over Newport in front of another big Arms Park crowd of 43,000. The only setbacks were a succession of injuries, most notably to Bleddyn Williams when he fractured a cheekbone at Aberavon. Preliminary reports suggested that he would not have recovered in time to play the Springboks. Further complications arose when on the Saturday before the big day an almost full strength blue and black team lost unexpectedly at Wasps. Two absentees were Williams and Matthews. Behind the scenes on the following Monday an even bigger drama was secretly unfolding. The club selectors were giving serious consideration to doing the unthinkable: they might not select the captain to play against the touring team. Matthews had been carrying a niggling injury but was fit again and available for the match but word leaked out that the four-man committee were about to make an amazing decision. Dr Jack, for once, was almost speechless though he ruefully admits now that he might never have played for the club again. Thankfully, sanity prevailed – with a little help from an impressive player delegation of Bleddyn Williams, Cliff Morgan and Rex Willis. 'The thought of Jack not leading the team out against the Springboks was ridiculous,' added Williams.

So Matthews and Williams took their rightful places. The rest of the team had a settled look. Willis and Morgan were at half-back, another international, Frank Trott, at full back, and the wingers, Alun Thomas and Haydn Morris, completed a near all-international back division. Thomas, of course, would play for Wales three months later at Twickenham. Cliff Davies, another 1950 Lion, would anchor the scrum alongside Geoff Beckingham and Arthur Hull. Bill Tamplin and Malcolm Collins formed an impressive second row with another illustrious back row formation made up of Sid Judd, Des O'Brien and CD Williams. On paper it looked a particularly strong club side but Cardiff would need to be at their very best.

The Springboks of 1951-52 were themselves a great touring side. 'I still consider them the best-ever', said Bleddyn Williams. 'They were strong in every department, from Jackie Buchler at full back right through to Hennie Muller at number 8. He was their captain after Basil Kenyon was injured and an incredible forward, so mobile with great skills. They also had Stephen Fry and Cliff Morgan's great adversary, Basie van Wyk, in the back row. The admirable thing about them was they were positive and sought to play 15-man rugby. Jack and myself particularly enjoyed playing against their centre pairing of Tjol Lategan and Ryk van Schoor, partly because they were being compared to ourselves. Lategan was the dazzling runner and van Schoor the crash tackler – but as I keep saying, both Jack and myself had all round games rather than one of us being an attacker and the other the defender.'

The Springboks soon came to see the wisdom of this claim for themselves. From the outset the Cardiff backs ran at every opportunity and Morris, Williams and Matthews all came close to claiming an opening try. Finally, Tamplin put the club ahead with a pinpoint penalty goal after 12 minutes. A particular feature was the duel between the two fly-halves, Morgan and Hannes Brewis, both of them only 21 years old and both instinctive attackers. It was the Springbok who drew first blood in the 20th minute when he darted around the blind side of a scrum to put the left wing, Chum Ochse, over in the corner. Buchler's superb conversion was to prove crucial in the final reckoning. As in the very different circumstances of the Lions' match, Cardiff's goal kicking was proving unreliable. By half time, Tamplin had failed with three penalty attempts, one, admittedly from long range and another hitting an upright. But their attacking instincts had not deserted them. Matthews and Williams were in prime form, making the predilections of the selectors earlier in the week all the more unfathomable. The captain did suffer one major disappointment however:

'I charged down a clearance kick by Brewis, picked the ball up and crossed the line for the try. There was nothing wrong with it – even the Springboks lined up behind the posts for the conversion. But to my amazement the referee, Cyril Joynson from Caerleon, ruled the charge-down a knock-on and disallowed the score. At half time I reminded him that the law about charge-downs had changed and that what I had done did not constitute a knock-on. What was doubly infuriating was that in the second half exactly the same thing happened in reverse when their scrum-half charged down a kick by Cliff [Morgan] and the try was awarded.'

By half-time, however, the two centres had worked their magic to the satisfaction of the referee. A lightning fast scrum heel by Beckingham allowed Alun Thomas to take the ball on the burst from Willis and Morgan and Matthews were in the move before Bleddyn Williams dived over for a classic try. With the conversion again drifting wide of the mark the club had to be satisfied with the 6-5 interval lead. The gods, unfortunately, were against the blue and blacks in the second period. With the prop Arthur Hull little more than a passenger, Malcolm Collins was forced to pack down in the front row, leaving Hull to do little more than hobble around the field as a token back-rower. Yet in the opening minutes of the half Tamplin at last succeeded with a penalty goal, a fine one from 45 yards into the wind. Now, surely, victory was in sight. To the chagrin of the 53,000 crowd it was snatched away, first by Oelofse's charged-down try and then another touchdown five minutes from the end.

Brewis was increasingly using tactical kicking to establish territorial advantage and Cardiff had fallen into the trap of too much kicking themselves. The Springbok fly-half was a master of the art and his diagonal kick to the open-side left corner cruelly exposed Cardiff's lack of pace out wide on the right. As the ball bounced away from

Frank Trott, Chum Ochse flew along the touchline to reach the ball a fraction before it reached touch in goal. It was a great opportunist try but a dagger in the heart of the blue and blacks. At 9-11 down there was time for one last attack but Matthews was thwarted as he was stopped by four Springbok tacklers. His was a captain's effort but the Springboks had won.

The touring team were the first to admit that they were lucky winners but they also realised the importance of victory. Their touch judge on duty at the Arms Park was the utility back, Basie Viviers, and he told their assistant manager, Danie Craven, of the depth of his feelings:

> 'Something happened to me today over which I had no control. When Chum [Ochse] scored that try and the referee gave it I started crying loudly. When I got to the goal-posts for the conversion kick I had to turn my back on Cardiff's touch-judge for fear that he should see what was happening to me. I never saw what happened to the kick.'

Craven recalls the episode in his book, *Springbok Story, 1949-1953*, and he endorses the feelings of Viviers and the team, when he concludes that, 'Our elated feelings were mixed, for we realised only too well that the fates had been kind to us that day.' Cardiff and Jack Matthews, on the other hand, could only rue the wasting of a golden opportunity to again tame a touring team – but there was one more twist in the tale. Frank Mellish, the South African manager, had brought with him two Springbok heads as trophies for any team that beat the Springboks. Most observers, particularly at home in Cape Town and Johannesburg, might have decried him for his gloomy pessimism. They would have been half right because in the event only one of the 31 matches was lost – unexpectedly to London Counties at Twickenham. All five internationals had again been won, as on the tours of 1912-13 and 1931-32, with Scotland well and truly annihilated by 44 points to 0. Wales lost narrowly 6-3 with Bleddyn Williams again scoring a brilliant try, and when the Springboks returned to the Arms Park for the third and final time they won again, this time against the Barbarians. Enter the strange story of the Springbok head.

Twenty four hours before the Barbarians' match the Springboks had already decided that, win or lose the following day, their second trophy would be presented to Cardiff Rugby Football Club. The ceremony was arranged for the Saturday evening and the accompanying letter from Frank Mellish to Hubert Johnson was self-explanatory. It read as follows:

'Dear Mr Johnson

On the eve of our departure for home we should like to take this opportunity of thanking you, Dr Matthews and the members of the Cardiff Rugby Club for their great kindness to us during our various visits to Wales. I can assure you that we will take back with us the happiest of memories, not only of the games we have had in your country but all the pleasant and happy times with you off the field.

We felt extremely fortunate that our game with Cardiff resulted in a narrow win for us, and we all realise that it was just that little bit of good fortune which permitted us to be the victors.

As a memento of our visit and the very happy time we spent with you, we would ask you to accept a Springbok head which we would like to present to the Cardiff Rugby Club, and may it be a lasting reminder of the excellent game and the even better spirit that has grown up between us.

May you go from strength to strength and may you continue to play the excellent hard, clean rugby that you are playing today.

Yours very sincerely

Frank Mellish
Hon Manager.'

The very special trophy was received on behalf of the club by Hubert Johnson and Jack Matthews. A month later the *South Wales Echo* reported that the South African Board had invited the Cardiff team to conclude their 75th anniversary season with a short tour to the union. Sadly, time was against the proposed visit. Fifteen years later a Cardiff team did go to South Africa and brought more glory to the club with their sparkling back play.

At the end of the 1951-52 season, Dr Jack Matthews decided to give up playing to concentrate on his medical career. His own links with South Africa and the friends he had made from there would continue without interruption. The centres who were said to be the mirror image of Bleddyn Williams and himself, Tjol Lategan and Ryk van Schoor, still play host to him on his regular visits. He has also been the official guest of the South African authorities – and in 1980 he returned to South Africa as a Lion. This time he was the doctor travelling with the British Isles Rugby Union Touring Team. Blessed with a global perspective of the sport, rather than the narrow parochialism that handicaps so many of his and later generations, Dr Jack remains a fine ambassador for the Cardiff club. By the time he officially retired, he had played 180 games for the first team and scored 54 tries. Two years later in 1954 he became club chairman and still turned out occasionally for both the first team and the Athletic XV. He even played for the Barbarians against the club in the prestigious Easter Saturday fixture. Now he is a respected trustee of Cardiff Athletic Club and president of the Former Players' Association. Ask him about how much he enjoyed the match against the Springboks in 1951 and his answer is succinct: 'We should have won.'

10

Springbok Sadness

The matches in the first half of the twentieth century between Cardiff and the All Blacks and Springboks – and, indeed, as we shall see, the Wallabies – had a romance and a vibrancy peculiar to themselves. The matches since then have rarely recaptured these almost intangible qualities. The game's historians remain fascinated by the context and the ebb and flow of the great tussles of 1905 and 1907, and they accept that the matches of the inter-war years were less exciting but remain a credit to the endeavours of the club's players against superior opponents. After the Second World War, the fans, many of who are still alive today, must have felt that they were watching a re-run of the early years of the century: for Gwyn Nicholls and Rhys Gabe there were now Bleddyn Williams and Jack Matthews; for Percy Bush read Billy Cleaver or Cliff Morgan; for Billy Neill perhaps Stan Bowes or JD Evans. Here again was rugby with flair, with a smile on its face, and epic victories mixed with glorious defeats. After 1953, the matches were never quite so glamorous. To be frank, the teams of Haydn Tanner, Matthews and Williams between 1945 and 1953 were a hard act to follow – but, being Cardiff, the wave of expectation every time the major touring teams appeared on the horizon would continue for many years yet. The reality of the matches themselves, unfortunately, was often less palatable. Never was that more the case than in 1960 when the Fifth Springboks and Cardiff literally went into battle.

Yet the game played on 29 October 1960 could have been so different. For the first time since the match with the All Blacks in 1905 Cardiff approached a touring team game with a season's unbeaten record. Only Northampton on their own ground had held them to a draw in their thirteen fixtures. The side was well led by Lloyd Williams, one of Bleddyn's younger brothers. That was regarded as a good omen because the tall scrum-half was another respecter of the club's traditions and of the need to perform well in the full glare of a touring team match. He had succeeded Rex Willis in both the club and national side but he had waited a long time for his first game of this nature. He had been incredibly patient:

> 'I had made my debut for the first team eight years before but then I went away on national service and when I returned there were two other top-class scrum-halves at the club. As well as Rex there was Brian Mark so my opportunities at first were limited. In fact for a while I played at fly-half – at six feet I was one of the tallest around – and playing in the position gave me a better understanding of the need for good passing from the base of the scrum and line-out.'

Lloyd Williams was certainly a good passer of the ball, like Willis particularly adept with the dive pass, and he was also a considerable physical presence. He would need it against the Springboks. Unusually, after winning his first two caps for Wales alongside Cliff Morgan in the spring of 1957, he failed to win a place in the Cardiff team that beat Australia the following December. Willis came out of retirement during that autumn and got the nod from the club selectors for the match with the Wallabies. A week later Williams was back in the team and eventually played all four international championship games for Wales that season. He still maintains a diplomatic silence about being dropped for the club's big game.

By 1960 there was no question of him missing out again. He was a fine captain and a good tactician with the ability to read a game. After a couple of seasons in the doldrums the back division was beginning to click again. The fly-half, Tommy McCarthy, was no more than a good club player but he was an effective one. Ray Glastonbury on the right wing was a try-scoring opportunist while on the left was Gordon Wells. Like Gareth Griffiths before him he was equally effective in midfield or out on the flank but in 1960 there was little doubt that he should be on the wing. The club had found their best centre pairing since the days of Williams and Matthews, though no one was talking about the new combination in the same breath yet. Meirion Roberts and Cyril Davies were as different as chalk and cheese. Roberts, a product of Cardiff High School, was a ruthless tackler who went in low on his opponent but also an effective attacker with a good pass. Davies was at five feet seven inches the archetypal pint-sized sidestepper and all-out attacker from West Wales who had already won international caps before joining the club. Their partnership in the early part of the season had been one of the features of the team. Completing a useful back division at full-back was the ever-reliable Alun Priday but everyone accepted that the old cliché about games being won or lost up front applied more than ever against these particular Springboks. Lloyd Williams remembers them well:

'When we look back at their pack of forwards I can almost still feel the pain. Their captain, Avril Malan, was at lock with Johann Claassen, who had been playing for South Africa for several years. Behind them in the back row were two physical wing forwards in Martin Pelser, who only had one eye, and Hugo van Zyl, both of them well over 15 stones, and the outstanding Doug Hopwood at number 8. But the real crunch was in the front row where the hooker, Abe Malan, was propped by Piet du Toit and Fanie Kuhn. Ask Colin Howe about Mr du Toit!'

Colin Howe was one of the life and souls of the Cardiff team in the second half of the 1950s but he wasn't chuckling on the day he played the Springboks. He thought he had seen it all in the half-dozen years he had been packing down in the Cardiff front row but this was a new experience altogether. He said unashamedly:

'Piet du Toit was by a long way the hardest prop I ever scrummaged against. Not dirty but just plain hard. He was incredibly strong as you'd expect from an Afrikaans farmer but he also had a great technique. I had switched from tight-head prop to the loose-head side at the start of the season so it was just my bad luck. But life was not exactly a bed of roses on the other side either. There they had Kuhn who was another stone heavier. He was up against Kingsley Jones, who was to play against them again with the Lions a couple of years later. It was without doubt the hardest game of rugby I was ever involved in.'

On paper the Cardiff pack appeared capable of competing with the Springboks. The front row was completed by the hooker, Billy Thomas, who had succeeded Geoff Beckingham and was no shrinking violet himself. The Welsh international Danny Harris was in the second row with Graham Davies and in a good back row Elwyn Williams and Dai Hayward were on the flanks and Howard Norris at number 8. They would bear the brunt of the furious Springbok onslaught:

> 'With the back division we had I felt that we needed to win regular possession and we were in with a chance of beating the Springboks,' said Lloyd Williams. 'What I didn't bargain for was the absolute hammering we were about to receive from their pack of forwards. It was an incredibly physical match and I was flattened time after time. But others fared even worse.'

The debate still lingers as to who started the mayhem. The most obvious sign of trouble occurred after about 12 minutes when Priday fielded and cleared the ball to touch on the north stand side of the ground. As always, it was one of his inch-perfect screw kicks but little did he realise that he was about to be hit by a human torpedo. As he half-turned to take up his position at full-back he was hit by a very late and shoulder-high tackle by the wing Francois Roux, the 21-year-old jack-in-the-box of the touring team. It was a flying tackle in every sense and one that laid Priday out a few yards in from the touchline. He obviously needed considerable treatment that only served to the increase the crowd's anger as they shouted for Roux to be sent off. The tone was set for an ugly hour ahead that bore little relation to the glorious deeds of the past.

The Springbok version of events starts at the very first line-out where they claimed that one of the Cardiff back row men punched Hopwood. Also, they said, du Toit had a finger bitten at a scrum and Claassen an eye scratched. Cardiff's counter-claim to that was that someone in the Springbok front row was consistently putting a finger in Billy Thomas' eye. Whatever was going on out of the sight of the 50,000 crowd it was not a good advertisement for the sport, for the tour, and, unfortunately and however indirectly, the reputation of the club. By half-time McCarthy had left the field with a serious elbow injury; he also had a black eye and a cut nose. Cyril Davies was moved to fly-half, Wells came in to the centre and Elwyn Williams was permanently withdrawn to play out on the wing. Hayward was trampled on and played the second half with one arm hanging limp. Six-and-a-half club forwards against the Springboks' juggernaut pack should have been no contest but, against all odds, they held out for most of the game.

The only score of the first half was a turnover try when the centre Ian Kirkpatrick pounced on a loose pass and linked with Hopwood, Roux and fellow centre John Gainsford for Pelser to score a try converted by scrum-half Dick Lockyear. In the second period Lloyd Williams was harshly penalised for offside at a scrum and Lockyear kicked the goal. He then converted a penalty try awarded when Roux was impeded chasing a kick ahead over the Cardiff goal line. The booing and unpleasant atmosphere continued right up to the final whistle with the Springboks winners by 13 points without reply. The media reaction to the match was equally unforgiving. In the *News Chronicle* Reg Pelling took no prisoners:

'Brutal. Unsporting. Stampeding elephants. All-in wrestlers. Anything but good rugby types. Those are some of the more printable terms being used in Wales to describe the Fifth Springboks. The complaint is not that they beat Cardiff, but that they should use such borderline, strong-arm, and ruthlessly negative means to accomplish it … This match was nothing better than a slogging brawl punctuated by late tackles, obstructions, line-out barging and heedless, needless trampling upon men.'

In *The Western Mail* JBG Thomas was more measured but also highly-critical. He wrote:

'The course of the play was a tragedy for South African rugby and could have a vital effect upon what promised to be the happiest of tours. Cardiff were battered into submission … the tourists were never in danger of defeat but they did not win any friends by their display. I cannot fully express my disappointment at the course of the game.'

South African correspondents were more concerned with the failure of the Springboks to fully exploit their one-man advantage in the last hour of the game and were baffled by the inflexible adherence to 10-man rugby. There was also a conclusion that it had been unwise for the Cardiff pack, as they saw it, to try to dust-up their bigger opponents. In his tour book, *Springboks in the Lions Den,* Maxwell Price of the *Cape Times* wrote that 'It is a fact that when lighter men try out bigger, stronger opponents and move them to vigour it is always the lighter men who will come off second best'.

By all accounts the scene in the Cardiff dressing room after the match bore testimony to that law of the jungle. Reg Pelling wrote, 'I saw the red-rimmed gouges made by football studs when [Dai Hayward] was helped out of his jersey afterwards ... and Alun Priday came out of the bath to tell me that every tooth in his head was loose and he didn't know which leg to walk on.' In the *Daily Mail* Wilfred Wooller revealed that 'the Cardiff dressing room after the contest looked like a battle clearance station.'

In these circumstances the post-match ceremonies were, to say the least, muted. As Lloyd Williams said, 'The Springboks were not by nature great socialisers and the events of the afternoon had left everyone feeling very subdued'. It was no consolation for the club that the rest of the Springboks' long tour followed a similar pattern, remaining unbeaten until the final match when the Barbarians lowered their colours. Appropriately that match was played at Cardiff Arms Park.

There was definitely a sense that fences had to be mended after the dark days of 1960-61. Luckily, the wounds didn't last long. Personal friendships still flourished. Alun Priday, for one, has kept in close contact with John Gainsford. The centre from Cape Town had only just turned 22 in 1960 and was on his first overseas tour. He went on to become one of the great Springboks and today is a notable wine merchant. Tommy McCarthy went to live in South Africa and still has his home in Johannesburg. Even Dai Hayward has family connections in South Africa. Most important of all, an invitation for the club to tour there, originally mooted in 1952, was received again and this time a tour materialised. And there could have been no better way for the club to re-establish any lost reputation than by the performance of the young team that went there in 1967.

Overseas travel was no stranger to the club but before 1967 it had been almost exclusively to France – a team went to Paris in 1906 and Bordeaux three years later – with one adventure to Bucharest in 1957. The latter merits a footnote in the club's annals because the first of the two matches in Romania was watched, in the closing stages at least, by a crowd of 80,000 – it was staged as a curtain-raiser to the Romania v USSR soccer international. The trip to South Africa, where the club would play five matches, was an exciting development. It was the first time that the South African Rugby Board had officially invited a club side to visit the republic and in his official message of welcome the Board's president, Danie Craven, hailed 'the most famous rugby club in the world'. Happily for the club the visit coincided with a mini-revival in its back play.

Looking now at the back division, in particular, it is hard to imagine a more exciting set of players playing together at the same time. The first-choice three-quarter line read: Keri Jones, Gerald Davies, Ken Jones, Maurice Richards. All four were at some stage in their career British Lions and, more than that, they were all dazzling runners and game-breakers. At fly-half there was a choice between the St Luke's College student, Phil Morgan, and another of the Williams dynasty, Tony. Both were fine linkmen for the try-hungry stars outside them. The scrum-half and captain was Billy Hullin who had won a cap for Wales earlier in the year, and the full-back, Ray Cheney, was a sensational goal kicker. There was another name to consider when choosing the best line-up behind the scrum. Gareth Edwards was only 19 years old and still studying at Cardiff College of Education but he had already played for his country. With the captain playing at scrum-half where could the exceptional Edwards be fitted in? In 1905 Gwyn Nicholls or Percy Bush would have had the perfect answer: play eight backs with one of them employed as a 'rover'. That was not an option in the more structured (or stereotyped) modern game. On a short tour Hullin could understandably expect to play in three of the five matches and Edwards might be left kicking his heels. The coach, Roy Bish, had the perfect answer. After giving Edwards one outing in his normal position against North West Cape – inevitably he scored a try in the 23-12 win – he switched him to full back for two matches. This was by no means an eccentric decision because Edwards had played some schoolboy rugby there. The player himself was eternally grateful because in the number 15 jersey he had an armchair view of the most memorable match of a tour with many high points. His recollections are clear:

'It was a trip I'll never forget because our team was so strong, particularly in the backs. I was more than happy to get a couple of games at full back! When you've got guys like Howard Norris, Lyn Baxter and John Hickey with you on a tour there was never likely to be a shortage of what you might call memorable moments off the field as well as on it. I was privileged to be part of an incredible team performance against Eastern Province at Port Elizabeth.'

The cold facts of the game in question stand out. The Province, one of the strongest in South Africa, was beaten by 34 points to 9. Cardiff scored six tries to their opponents' one. More impressive than the stark score line, however, was the quality of the club's performance. Reporting the match in the *Cape Argus*, the doyen of South African rugby writers, AC Parker, wrote:

'This was the real Cardiff rugby magic at Port Elizabeth to crush Eastern Province with six glorious tries. The crowd of 11,000 gave the Welsh club a rousing standing ovation at the end of a spectacular match ... the most abiding memory for South Africans was the classical centre play of Gerald Davies and Ken Jones. Billy Hullin and Phil Morgan played their part by letting the ball flow and in midfield Davies was often devastating. He would jog along, feint and suddenly crack on the pace as the gap opened. Three times left wing Richards came on his inside to wrong-foot the defence for tries. Ken Jones was the perfect foil for Davies as they worked the dummy scissors and switched direction. The chant of 'Cardiff, Cardiff, Cardiff' from the Welsh club's small band of supporters helped create the atmosphere for a memorable victory.'

This, clearly was rugby played 'Cardiff fashion'. More importantly the sour taste left in the mouth by the events of 1960 had been washed away. The team of 1967 had regained the sense of ambition and style of 1907 and 1951 and the club was all the stronger for their tour. In the next 15 years they would be invited back twice to South Africa and would also undertake two tours to Rhodesia. The spirit of touring had been rekindled and now it was a two-way process.

To some extent, however, there was another blip in the feel-good factor in 1969 when the Springboks next came to Britain. Where the tour of 1960-61 had been too often downright ugly, its successor in 1969-70 was more a case of being uncomfortable. Wherever the touring team went they encountered anti-apartheid demonstrations. Venues were changed amidst a cloak of secrecy. The tour opener against Oxford University was switched to Twickenham, the match against Ulster in Belfast was called off altogether and a low-key fixture against a combined clubs' side was staged at New Brighton in its place. There were scenes of unparalleled violence on the terraces when they played at Swansea. The match with Cardiff escaped the worst of the disruption and should have been a special day. The first stage of the development of the new National Stadium at Cardiff Arms Park was nearing completion and Cardiff's match with the Springboks was the first to be staged there. Unfortunately the match, a mediocre affair, failed to live up to the occasion. The tourists lost five and drew four of their 25 games but Cardiff proved to be one of their 16 victories.

Twenty-five years on few of the Cardiff team on duty that day can recall anything of note in the game. The 17-3 final score speaks for itself. However, there was a personal achievement for one player. The prop, Howard Norris, was making his fourth appearance for the club against a major touring team. Several players over the years, including Bleddyn Williams, Cliff Morgan, Rex Willis, and CD Williams in the post-war period, had played three times against the All Blacks, Springboks and Wallabies. But Norris was the first to play four times against southern hemisphere countries. It was appropriate that this very popular former captain and future chairman should set this bit of history. During the four matches, as with his entire Cardiff career that stretched to a remarkable 413 first team games, he had experienced the full gamut of emotions.

Norris was another of the Rhondda-born players – in his case, Porth – who had gravitated towards the Arms Park in the 1950s because of the role models all around him:

'I make no bones about it, Cardiff was always going to be the only club for me,' he said. 'Two great Cardiff players, Gordon Wells and Kingsley Jones, were near-neighbours in Porth and they were my heroes as well as my friends. They gave me a goal to aim for. Even though I was away from South Wales for five years while I was gaining my teaching qualification in Exeter and then on national service in the RAF, I always knew I would try my best to make the grade at the club.'

Making the grade was not a problem when Norris returned to his roots in September 1958. Like so many before him he was prepared to play anywhere. He had won Wales Schools caps at lock but his natural position at first was in the back row. As a young number 8 he had the benefit of playing alongside John Nelson and CD Williams, two heroes of the All Blacks match of 1953. He was notably successful and good enough to play international trials in the position and be a reserve for Wales in Paris in 1961. He played in the torrid game against the 1960 Springboks and had the unenviable task of shoring up a depleted back row.

'Like the rest of the team I felt that game to have been incredibly over-physical. The Springboks had obviously targeted us up front and our front row was really taking the brunt of the pressure. Our hooker, Billy Thomas, couldn't even see the ball when Lloyd Williams was feeding the scrum. Once we were down to 14 men and Elwyn Williams was taken out of the back row to play on the wing I was left marking two men. To cap it all, their number 8, Doug Hopwood, was one of the first players in that position to pick the ball up and drive off the back of the scrum. How we held them to 13 points I'll never know.'

Then came the great conversion to the front row and within a season he was playing for Wales. He performed well on his debut against France and next came the 1963 All Blacks and their great prop, Ken Gray:

'It was my idea to move up to the front row. I was still only 28 and reckoned I had a few seasons left in the tank so decided to give it a go. I thoroughly enjoyed it though there was just that little doubt in my mind that we might struggle against the All Blacks. As things turned out, we didn't. I was at loose-head and up against Gray, who was a straight, good scrummager. Afterwards we became great friends. I gave him my Wales tie and a Cardiff jersey. A couple of years later a package arrived in the post. It contained a full All Blacks playing kit with the note, 'Respect our friendship – see you again some day.' I wrote back to say that, yes, we would meet again – in three months. I had been selected to tour New Zealand with the Lions.'

Howard Norris had advanced all the way from the club side to international honours and 17 games, including three test matches, for the Lions. He was also universally popular. His regular appearances for the Barbarians included the vice-captaincy against the next All Blacks at Twickenham in 1967. There were no matches against club sides on that tour but he had already completed a club hat-trick when he played against the Wallabies the year before. Then came the Springboks again and he was the first Cardiff player to represent the club four times in such matches. For him the wheel had turned full circle:

'I am immensely proud of every game I played for the club but obviously I cherish the fact that ten seasons after I first played against them I was still good enough to take on the Springboks again. The events of 1960 had long been forgotten and I had been part of the marvellous club tour to their country in 1967. Now I was playing them at the Arms Park again. My opposite number was Hannes Marais, who I had played against in Cape Town.

The 1969 match was a strange experience because of all that was going on with the politics. When we trained during the week at Sophia Gardens the anti-apartheid demonstrators were even there to make their point. I can still see Wilf Wooller yelling across the fence to their leader, Peter Hain. I knew what to expect in the game itself because I had been down to Swansea to watch their game there. As it happened we got off lightly in terms of disruption. Unfortunately, though, the match was utterly anonymous and forgettable.'

Norris' recollections of the 1969 match sum up the frustrations of all who saw it. Already the heady days of the early 1950s seemed a distant memory. South Africa's troubles in the political and human rights arenas would mean that the Springboks would not return to Wales to play rugby for 24 years. Few ordinary supporters or officials realised when they arrived in the autumn of 1994 that they might be watching the final chapter of one of the game's great traditions. For the previous decade or so the number of matches on such tours had been standardised at 13. This reduction in the number of games had obvious implications for the various clubs hoping for a fixture but was balanced by the fact that no more than three countries in Europe would be visited on any one tour. Thus, as the Springboks had played in France and England in 1992, and with a notable lack of success after their years of isolation, it was now the turn of Wales, Scotland and Ireland to play host to them. That allowed five Welsh clubs, Cardiff, Llanelli, Swansea, Neath and Pontypridd, to be allocated fixtures. Yet there was an air of unreality about the games. True, the nonsense at the Gnoll, when the Neath team was accused of brawling and the Springboks of 'sledging' became a candidate to put even the miserable Cardiff match of 1960 in the shade in terms of unpleasantness. But other things weren't quite right. The popular midweek matches, played on afternoons when an entire locality would down tools and close offices and schools to see a touring team, had given way to floodlit games in the evenings. Even the results looked strange. Llanelli conceded 30 points; Swansea, God forbid, an almost unbelievable 12 tries and 78 points in a game that was more like unopposed rugby for the Springboks.

A different form of misfortune befell Cardiff. The club again had the advantage of staging the tour opener at the National Stadium but the event failed to capture the public imagination. On a wet and miserable day less than 15,000 fans turned up to watch the game. It was a sad indictment of the apparent decline in popularity for spectator sport in Wales, not helped by inflated ticket prices set by the Welsh Rugby Union and live television coverage. A gallant Cardiff team deserved better. Two penalty goals established a 6-0 lead for them at half-time but an opportunist try by the Springboks' world-class scrum-half, Joost van der Westhuizen, set his team off to an 11-6 victory. At the end, the sparse crowd took only a couple of minutes to file out of the chasm of a stadium. Long gone were the days when seemingly endless queues snaked the length of Westgate Street in the hope of purchasing a ticket to see their local heroes taking on the men from the other side of the world. But those with equally long memories could at least think back to the days of Jack Matthews and Cliff Davies and, inspired by their deeds, read again about Percy Bush and his men at the beginning of the century.

PART THREE

AUSTRALIA

11

And Then There Were the Wallabies

The path to glory is still not complete. There remains one more essential piece of the touring team jigsaw to put in place – or, to be more precise, six pieces. The solitary wins over the All Blacks and the Springboks rightly shine like beacons in the Cardiff club's roll of honour. But single victories they remain. The saga of Cardiff against the Wallabies is on an even higher plane. Six matches played since 1908. Six wins for Cardiff. That is a record unequalled by any club, indeed any opponent, in the history of Australian rugby. Some might claim that, until recently, they have never dominated opponents like their southern hemisphere neighbours from New Zealand and South Africa, or that they have not played Cardiff during the two reigns as official world champions in the 1990s. Conversely, it can be pointed out that the club has beaten them consistently in the changing climate of the world game and when they have been strong as well as occasionally mediocre. Every one of the six Wallaby touring teams to Wales up to and including the renowned Grand Slammers of 1984 had major victories somewhere along the line. But not against Cardiff.

Australia entered the international rugby fraternity in 1899, four years before New Zealand. They made an immediate impression by beating the Great Britain touring team by 13 points to 3 in Sydney. Among their opponents was Gwyn Nicholls. They were less successful over the next few years but their last international before they prepared to tour Europe was a respectable 5-5 draw with New Zealand. That was again played in Sydney in August 1907. Exactly 12 months later they set sail from Circular Quay for England, Wales and North America where they would play 36 games. They were captained by a 23 year old back rower from Sydney University, Paddy Moran. After a seven-week voyage they landed in Plymouth and played their first three matches in the West Country, beating Devon, Gloucestershire and Cornwall in quick succession.

Then they moved into Wales. They were not due to play Cardiff until the last month of their tour. Before then, however, there would be two other appearances at Cardiff Arms Park – against Glamorgan County and then, on 12 December, Wales. Both sides would have Cardiff representatives. The county game, watched by a crowd of 20,000, was won comfortably by 16 points to 3, with the Wallabies receiving a standing ovation at the final whistle. One of the stars of the county side had been Cardiff's international full back, Bert Winfield, who, as always, kicked beautifully. Other blue and blacks in the side were the centre, Billy Spiller, and the forwards, Joe Pugsley, Jack Brown and Jim Casey. Only Winfield was selected for the international, where he was joined in the backs by Johnnie Williams. Percy Bush would have been a third Cardiffian in the team, and probably captain, but was ruled out by a bout of influenza.

After beating Glamorgan, the Wallabies had comfortably disposed of Penygraig and the combined Neath and Aberavon side but they had gone down 8-3 to Llanelli. In England, however, they had won 17 of their 18 matches before the international. They had also left their own mark in history by becoming the second Olympic rugby champions. This was not so significant as it might look. France had won the first Olympic competition in 1900 in Paris but only three teams competed – Germany, Great Britain and the hosts. In 1920 and again in 1924 the United States of America would be double champions, but without meriting any real status in the world game. They beat the only other entrant, France in the first, and retained the title four years later against France and Romania. It was much the same story for the Wallabies of 1908. Although the competition was held at Shepherd's Bush in London, Ireland, Scotland and Wales all declined invitations to participate and France withdrew at the eleventh hour. That left Australia and the Cornwall county team, masquerading initially as England and then, in line with Olympic requirements, re-invented as 'Great Britain'.

The Olympic final was staged on Monday 26 October in front of 5,000 spectators. The Wallabies had played and beaten London the previous Saturday and were due to play another game on the Wednesday against a combined Army and Navy team, but they slipped in the Olympic engagement and easily beat Great Britain by 32 points to 3. So they were Olympic champions but it was soon time for the real taste of international rugby against Wales. They had not lost a home international for nine years but some significant individuals were no longer part of the team. Gwyn Nicholls, Rhys Gabe, Teddy Morgan in the backs, and the likes of Cliff Pritchard, Boxer Harding and Jehoida Hodges in the pack, had all for a variety of reasons left huge gaps to fill in the national side. That was cause for optimism in the Australian camp. They, too, had their admirers, particularly among the English critics. The respected historian, EHD Sewell, was one of them. He wrote:

'Let us be fair to our guests and admit that they are a fine side. Without the brilliancy of the All Blacks or the sheer pace of the Springbok backs, they are a terribly difficult side to defeat ... The best points of their game are (1) straight running in which they are as a team superior to the Springboks, (2) the extraordinary way in which the man with the ball shakes himself free from would-be tacklers without actual handing-off or dodging, and (3) the all-round backing-up ability of the side, the man with the ball rarely being alone, however fast he may be going.'

Sewell's citation from nearly a century ago is eerily reminiscent of the familiar virtues of modern-day Australian test teams. Paddy Moran's Wallabies were not quite good enough to overcome a Wales team that, despite its own changes in personnel, was still unbeatable at home. The home victory by 9-6 was not, however, without controversy. The first try by the Pill Harriers' forward, George Travers, was the subject of endless speculation during and after the game as many eye-witnesses claimed he had knocked the ball on rather than touched it down over the goal line. The conversion of Australia's first try was ruled a miss after the touch judges failed to agree on its accuracy. These incidents may not have gone down in the folklore of the sport as much as Bob Deans' non-try for New Zealand against Wales in 1905 but they nevertheless hurt the touring team at the time. A month later they had the consolation of beating England in the only other international on the tour but in Wales the road continued to be a rocky one.

Immediately after the test defeat they recovered their winning habits against the Glamorgan League, in a match played at Taff Vale Park in Pontypridd, and then Newport. They also won an unofficial fixture against North Glamorganshire in Merthyr Tydfil but could only draw with Abertillery. Fixtures were now coming around thick and fast and there was another setback when they lost by six points to Swansea on Boxing Day. Their long-awaited game with Cardiff on 28 December would be their sixth in eleven days. Like Wales, the club side was in the throes of introducing several new players, and like Wales, also, they were continuing to be a successful side. Percy Bush was again club captain and by the end of the 1908-09 season only three matches out of the 33 played would have been lost. Nicholls and Gabe had gone from the centre but there were very useful replacements in the future internationals, Billy Spiller and Louis Dyke. With the conventional seven backs now instead of the eight used against the All Blacks and the Springboks, 'Rover' Reggie Gibbs reverted to the right wing with Johnnie Williams on the left. Both had recently returned from an Anglo-Welsh tour, a forerunner of the Lions, when they had played in two tests against New Zealand.

Bush, recovered from the sickness that had caused him to miss the international match, would be the controller at fly-half but his partner at half-back, Dickie David, was gone. Having belatedly won his only international cap against Ireland in March 1907, the Canton window-cleaner had thrown in his lot with Wigan rugby league club. The new scrum-half was William Morgan, brother of Teddy who had been the Wales try-scorer against New Zealand in 1905. The 24 year old from Aberdare had also toured Australasia with the Anglo-Welsh team and was destined for a future international cap. The club's pack had only three survivors from the famous victory over the Springboks nearly two years before. The two miners, Joe Alf Brown and Jack Powell, were still going strong as was Jim Casey. A fourth experienced campaigner, Fred Smith, was the season's vice-captain but had the misfortune to suffer a rheumatic attack on the eve of the match. His place went to Joe Daley. Another notable absentee was the redoubtable Billy Neill who had also gone north to Warrington three months earlier. The new faces in the pack were Dai Westacott, Frank Gaccon, and George Yewlett. Joe Pugsley, who had been injured before the Springboks' match, was now back in the side. One unexpected setback in the preparations for the Wallabies' match was a hand injury to Bert Winfield that rather took the gloss off another win over the Barbarians in the then traditional Boxing Day fixture. Winfield had hugely impressed the tourists in his appearances for Glamorgan and Wales against them but now his place was taken by Bobby Williams.

Cardiff's disruptions in anticipation of the big match almost paled into insignificance alongside an unforeseen development for the Wallabies. It snowed. Ernest Booth, a 1905 All Black who had played then against Cardiff and who was now covering the tour for the Sydney newspapers, reported:

'[At] Cardiff a real snowstorm greeted us … it was unique for the majority of the team who had never witnessed it before. One or two impromptu snow fights ensued. Thus on the morning of Monday, 28 December, the Cardiff Arms Ground was one white field of snow. Many of the unemployed with brooms and shovels soon cleared the playing area, and in the worst frozen parts lit up fires of straw to soften the ground. Thus, by 2.45 pm the ground was really quite playable, and presented a draughtboard appearance, with its burnt patches mixed with snow-coloured grass.'

The winter weather failed to deter the local fans because over 30,000 of them turned up for the latest chapter in the seemingly endless saga of Cardiff against 'the Colonials'. The All Blacks on Boxing Day 1905, the Springboks on New Year's Day 1907, and now this. Percy Bush, never one to miss a trick, contributed his own piece of theatre. The Wallabies had brought with them on tour a 'War Cry' but even as they performed it the mischievous fly-half responded by approaching them with a Zulu spear and shield that were apparently brought home from the battle of Rorke's Drift in the Boer War. Only Bush could get away with a stunt like that but this was only the beginning of the Wallabies' troubles.

Despite the snow there was no wind and both sides set out to play the game at a great pace with the half-backs, Chris McKivat and Fred 'Possum' Wood, probing for the Wallabies and Bush orchestrating many fine moves for the club. Typically, he conjured up a loop move with Billy Spiller to send Reggie Gibbs haring for the line, only for him to be caught near the corner flag by the full-back, Philip Carmichael. The first score was provided by the Cardiff forwards rather than their flying backs. Their much-used skills at dribbling the ball on the ground paid off as they rushed the ball into the Wallaby 25 and John Brown and Willie Morgan dived on the ball together with the scrum-half claiming the try.

Bush missed the conversion but soon made amends with a wide-angled penalty goal from the 25 after the Wallabies were caught offside at a scrum. The referee, incidentally, was again Gil Evans, the Welshman still operating out of England. At six points down the game was threatening to run away from the tourists. There was no shortage of hustle and bustle on their part as their centres, John 'Darb' Hickey and Eddie Mandible, were both stopped with the Cardiff line in sight. A try from the club's backs was long overdue and it eventually arrived. From a scrum Bush made the initial break and linked with Casey before Gibbs took full advantage of the overlap to cross near the corner. On the stroke of half-time the Wallabies hit back from a line-out when Wood and Hickey combined for the latter to score the try.

During the interval the Cardiff team retired to the warmth of the dressing room but, strangely, the Wallabies stayed on the pitch. This was reminiscent of the scene at the match with the Springboks in 1907 but then the weather was wet while now it was simply freezing. The break in proceedings might also have given both sides time to reflect on the increasing amount of niggle that was becoming an unwelcome feature of the play. Booth noted that, 'Both sides showed blemishes of football etiquette, Cardiffians on three occasions tripping, whilst the Australians resorted to hand-pushing Cardiff men with or without the ball.'

Cardiff's supremacy continued in the early stages of the second half. Bush missed with another penalty opportunity and Johnnie Williams, always alert to half-chances, chased the errant kick and almost claimed a try. Then the game erupted. At a maul near the Wallaby line their forward, Albert Burge, was spotted kneeing Dai Westacott and Gil Evans had no hesitation in sending him off. The crowd that was already out of sorts after jeering the awarding of Hickey's first-half try now broke out into a chorus of booing. Burge had been in trouble before during the Welsh international at the Arms Park. Then he appeared to kick the Swansea centre and Wales' captain, Billy Trew, in the head while he lay on the ground. On that occasion he had been given the benefit of the doubt by Gil Evans; this time he received his marching orders. He was the third Wallaby sent off during the tour.

Percy Bush's team quickly rammed home their advantage. Reggie Gibbs cross-kicked and Johnnie Williams seized on the ball for the try that was converted by the captain. The score was now 14-3 and there seemed every prospect of an avalanche of points from the blue and blacks. The pack had a real appetite for foot rushes that were clearly disconcerting the opposition. However, the visitors stemmed the tide momentarily when Syd Middleton burst from a line-out and Paddy Moran took the scoring pass. Carmichael's straightforward conversion gave his side a real hope of an upset but Cardiff were far from finished. Bush now took control of the game, instigating attacks from all quarters. In classic half-back play he was at a breaking Willie Morgan's elbow to carry on a move with Spiller and Gibbs that resulted in a brilliant try for Louis Dyke. Bush missed the conversion but soon made an amends with one of his speciality dropped goals in broken play.

A fifth try followed at the very end of the game as Westacott, his groin fully recovered from its painful contact with Burge's knee, gathered a loose ball and sent Johnnie Williams racing away for his second score of the day. Bush again sliced the conversion attempt but the game was long since won.

In the true traditions of touring team matches, the incident with Burge was forgotten, though he subsequently protested his innocence in a newspaper interview. He was only 19 years old at the time of the tour but the selectors didn't pick him for any of the remaining eight matches. Meanwhile, the two teams celebrated in style at the Queen's Hotel. The menu included sole, pheasant, turkey, and a queen's pudding with brandy sauce. Christmas had eventually arrived three days late.

The 24-8 score-line represented the Wallabies' heaviest defeat of their tour. In their next match, nearly a fortnight later because the games with Monmouthshire and France were cancelled because of the continuing bad weather, they beat England at Blackheath. After that they went on to win the final two games in the West Country and another six matches in North America on the way home. Their tour was over but Cardiff's stranglehold on the Wallabies was only just beginning.

12

Running and Running with Billy the Kick

After the first victory in 1908, nearly forty years passed by before the next Wallabies team arrived in Cardiff. Technically, they were the third Wallabies. The second Wallabies never played a game in Britain after landing in Devon 24 hours before war was declared on Germany in September 1939. A conference between British and Australian officials reached the only possible conclusion, that the tour would have to be abandoned. The young sportsmen busied themselves by filling sandbags to protect their hotel and its guests while awaiting their hazardous return voyage home.

Australian rugby was no stranger to such frustrations because there had been an earlier interruption to their development as a test-playing nation. The embryonic union game in Australia had always been based on the two states of Queensland and New South Wales but often under threat from the rival and popular league code. When the Queensland Rugby Union was disbanded in 1919 the game was effectively left without a national team. New South Wales soldiered on and their side, the Waratahs, did tour Europe and Canada in 1927-28. They were a strong team and beat Wales, Ireland and France in games that were designated internationals when caps were awarded. The Waratahs also played – and beat – Cardiff by 15 points to 9 despite, like their Wallaby predecessors, being reduced to 14 men after a forward, Jack Ford, was sent off for disputing a refereeing decision. Eventually, rugby union in Queensland was re-formed in 1929, allowing Australia to play full test matches again after a break of 15 years. They immediately made an impact, beating New Zealand three times in as many weeks and subsequently winning two out of five tests in South Africa. After that they hit a bad patch in the 1930s and in the years immediately after the war. But when they set foot in Britain again in 1947 they were full of hope for a successful tour.

Cardiff were set to play the Wallabies in their fifth match on 27 September. The background to the game was very similar to that of 1908 in that the club was once again enjoying a Golden Era. The groundwork done by Jack Matthews in the two immediate post-war seasons was reaching fruition under the captaincy of Haydn Tanner. The 1947-48 campaign is rightly regarded as among the greatest in the club's history on at least three fronts. Firstly, there were the results that are there for all to see: matches played 41, matches won 39. Secondly, there was the thrilling style in which all the games were played. And finally there was the recognition by the national selectors of the qualities of the individuals within the team. Eleven of them played for Wales during the season and in three internationals, against England, Scotland and France, blue and blacks made up two-thirds of the national side.

They are familiar names in the annals of the club. In the pack there were Cliff Davies and Maldwyn James in the front row, Gwyn Evans and Les Manfield at the back, and in between them was the powerful lock, Bill Tamplin. The backs were no less eminent with Frank Trott at full-back, Les Williams on the wing, Dr Jack Matthews and Bleddyn Williams in the centre, and Tanner at scrum-half. And completing the international quota was the fly-half-cum-utility back, Billy Cleaver. In many ways he was the most fascinating individual of them all.

At first glance there are many similarities between the playing career of Cleaver and those of Matthews and Bleddyn Williams. Like them he was dipping his toes into first-class rugby when the outbreak of war in 1939 put any international aspirations on hold for several years. Like them, too, he benefited from the experience of playing fleetingly with Wilf Wooller and then club and student rugby at the Arms Park during the war. Of course all three of them were also together throughout the five seasons that culminated in them touring with the 1950 Lions. But no one should ever be tempted to bracket them as something like the three musketeers. Each of them was their own man and none more so than the man who was misleadingly nicknamed 'Billy the Kick' There was much more to him than that.

William Benjamin Cleaver's family roots, like so many great backs that ended up at the Arms Park club, lay in the Rhondda. He was born in Treorchy in September 1921 and while he attended Pentre Secondary School he represented the Upper Rhondda Schools XV. Like so many of his contemporaries, the young Cleaver took care to keep a healthy balance between his sporting and professional ambitions. In his case the latter remained remarkably focused on a career in the industry that was all around him:

> 'I was very interested in all aspects of coal mining and set my sights on working in a management role within it,' he said. 'So when I left school I started a degree course in mining engineering at Cardiff University. There were plenty of sporting opportunities there so I played tennis and squash and captained the college rugby team. Also in existence was a combined University of Wales XV that I led in 1942. The unofficial wartime matches were a good time to start at the Cardiff club because I had the honour of playing in the same side as Wilfred Wooller and that was unforgettable. In one match he scored a try after a hundred yards' run from behind his own line. I was given the chance to captain the club in some of the matches in 1942-43.'

Cleaver is self-effacing about his many achievements at work and play but admits that sometimes it was a logistical challenge to fit everything in. Having obtained his honours degree he duly secured employment in the mining industry but the regulations required him to learn all aspects of the work before consideration for a management position at the age of 25 and with five years experience. As a graduate entrant he began as a deputy and then an overman and was appointed as an under-manager in 1944:

> 'I started work at Cwm Colliery in Beddau and, of course, everyone worked a six-day week. On Saturday mornings I would be needed underground where I had a specific responsibility to take the measurements. So I would walk one and a half miles to the coal face before returning to daylight. Once I had clocked off there would be a couple of bus journeys, changing at Pontypridd, and getting to Cardiff in time for an afternoon's rugby.'

In later years, when he was playing for Wales, Cleaver didn't work on Fridays but his new-found fame was never allowed to go to his head. His manager was known to tell him, 'You're playing for Wales on Saturday, Cleaver, so take Friday off – but be in first thing on Sunday morning!'

The resumption of official rugby in September 1945 saw him automatically selected for the Cardiff team where he formed a deadly midfield with Bleddyn Williams and Matthews. He also developed a particularly productive half-back partnership with Billy Darch. who he describes him as 'a good little scrum-half'. They were probably kindred spirits. The pint-sized Darch was from the Rhondda, in his case Trealaw and Porth Secondary School, and also a graduate of Cardiff University. In later years while Cleaver was advancing his career in coal mining Darch was appointed to a succession of senior posts in oil refining. Remarkably he eventually became president of the Alaska Pipeline Company that was responsible for pumping oil into the United States. Cleaver and Darch were good enough to be picked almost immediately for the Victory Internationals against the Kiwis and France in December 1945. The arrival of Tanner midway through the following season was to seriously curtail Darch's step up the representative ladder and he soon left the club and played for a while for Aberavon.

Tanner, like Les Manfield, played for Wales both before and after the war. Cleaver first teamed up with him before he joined Cardiff and was suitably impressed:

'I had played with Tanner for South Wales against the RAF during the war but in 1946 we were playing England at Twickenham in another of the Victory Internationals. We had a quick practice on the day before the match. He threw me a pass from eight or nine yards away at a perfect waist height but it almost knocked me off my feet. After that I knew that I could stand 15 yards away from him for the pass and be well out of reach of the English back row tacklers. His pass was often executed with a lovely flick of the wrists so he wasn't dive passing and taking himself out of the game. Tanner was a great player, the Gareth Edwards of his day, and one with all the skills.'

Others will assert that Billy Cleaver was himself a supremely skilled player, lending the lie to the 'Billy the Kick' label. Yes, he could undoubtedly put boot to the ball with both feet and to great effect but his play was far more rounded than being a mere kicker. A limited fly-half could not have orchestrated the gifted club back division as he did in 1947-48 when the team scored 182 tries, the vast majority from the outside backs. And he was no mean try scorer himself. Geoff Beckingham, who joined the team when Cleaver was already an established star, recalls one of his tries:

'We were playing Newport at Rodney Parade and our backs in those days always stood deep with the centres and open-side wing at an angle of 45 degrees so that they could run onto a pass at top speed. Billy never failed to get them moving onto the ball. Anyway, as we went down to a scrum on their 25 Billy shouted at me that he wanted a quick heel and no messing about. So I obliged. The next thing I knew was as I looked up from the scrum he was walking back after scoring under the posts. Some one-dimensional kicker he was!'

In fact Cleaver finished with 44 tries in his career with Cardiff. But the amassing of personal points was never a primary concern. For such a marvellous kicker out of the hand he had little interest in goal kicking – 'the ball was about 2lbs in weight and could be as heavy as lead when it rained.'

Any doubts remaining about his all round skills can be soon dispelled when his international appearances are analysed. In 14 official internationals he played in three different positions – full back, fly-half and centre. It was a versatility he didn't particularly welcome:

'Of course I was prepared to play for my country in any position, as I did for the Lions in New Zealand, but I make no secret of the fact that I much preferred to play at fly-half. When I played there I was in a position where I could control a game in a variety of ways. And that's what I enjoyed doing. For most of my time with the club that's where I played. There was a short period when Bleddyn wanted to play there so he was given a chance and I moved out to centre. It didn't last long – I think he was getting to much attention from the wing-forward.'

The experiment interested the national selectors and when Wales took the field for the first official international after the war Williams indeed partnered Tanner at half-back with Cleaver and Matthews in the centre. Wales catastrophically lost this home game against England. For the remaining three internationals of the season Williams returned to centre. Cleaver stayed there as his partner for the match at Murrayfield that Wales won, both centres scoring tries. Then for the victories over France and Ireland Cleaver was back in harness with Tanner at half-back. Normal business had been resumed – but the arrival of the Wallabies would bring with it further experiments with Billy Cleaver.

'I played against the Wallabies three times, for Cardiff, Wales and the Barbarians, in three different positions – and we won all three.' When Cleaver reminds the listener of that fact he does not in any way do so as a boast. More a case of being matter-of-fact with a philosophical streak of pride.

It would be tempting to conclude from Cleaver's 100 per cent record in three matches against them that the Wallabies of 1947-48 were no great shakes as a side but that would be entirely inaccurate. After Cardiff took their unbeaten record in the fifth match of the tour they did not lose again for another 15 matches. Scotland were beaten 16-7 at Murrayfield and later, after slipping to their second defeat against the North Western Counties in Manchester, in the last month of their trip they comfortably beat both Ireland and England.

The touring team was captained by a wing forward, Bill McLean, who was a Queensland state player before the war and had been with the second Wallabies on their fruitless voyage to Europe in 1939. Now he was back as captain but was again to find his British rugby experience cut unexpectedly short. Four days after the match with Cardiff he broke a leg playing against the Combined Services at Twickenham. He never played rugby again.

Injuries were to blight much of the Wallabies' tour, an ironic development considering they aimed to be the fittest side ever to tour Europe. Physical fitness became almost an obsession as every spare moment was devoted to training sessions. The dividend from this was an outstanding cover defence; so good that the four home countries all failed to score a try against Australia in the international matches. They were also no slouches in attack with several outstanding individuals. In the centre they had their 20 year old vice-captain, Trevor Allan, and outside him on the wings formidable opportunists in Charlie Eastes, until he also broke a leg, and the sprinter, Arthur Tonkin. There was a touch of real class from the full back, Brian Piper, and the half-back, Cyril Burke.

The Wallaby forwards, even after McLean's injury, were a good pack with Joe Kraeft, Doug Keller, Nick Shehadie, Col Windon and the hooker, Ken 'Killer' Kearney, all making a big impression. The number 8, Arthur Buchan, was one of the successes of the tour with an all-round game based on crash tackling that particularly confounded many of the opposing inside backs. Unfortunately, Windon was to be at the centre of one of the more unsavoury aspects of the tour when he was sent off against Llanelli for kicking an opponent. This led to a highly visible protest by the team management on the field of play at Stradey Park as they remonstrated with the referee, Ivor David. For some critics, this merely reflected the argumentative nature of several of the players throughout the tour. Refereeing interpretations were an issue with them from the very first game. Luckily the match with Cardiff passed without major incident.

While Cleaver and the Cardiff backs were the talk of the pubs and clubs in 1947, Cardiff's pack of forwards was by any standards a capable bunch of players. In the front row WG Jones, Maldwyn James and the future Lion, Cliff Davies, had been packing down together for three years. Billy Jones was a particularly useful club prop who, like his cousin Cliff Davies, was a miner from Kenfig Hill. He was also a fighter in the boxing booths but Bleddyn Williams remembers him for something even more unusual:

'When Wales were due to play France in one of the Victory Internationals in Paris on Easter Monday in 1946, Cliff Davies was named as one of the props. But he couldn't travel because he had been trapped under a seam of coal the previous Saturday when Cardiff were playing the Barbarians. So at the last minute Billy Jones went with the Welsh team. He didn't have a passport so he used Cliff's passport and no one spotted it. He played for Wales incognito without anyone realising and the record books still list 'C Davies' in the Wales' team!'

Maldwyn James, like Tanner and Manfield, might have played for Wales either side of the war. His international trial in 1937-38 took him to the verge of the national side before a serious foot injury sidelined him for two years. His burgeoning mining career meant that by 1946 he was a successful engineer at the Albion Colliery in his native Cilfynydd and he temporarily retired from rugby. Luckily he reconsidered the decision and was a crucial member of the celebrated 1947-48 team and would soon win his international cap. Davies, of course, was already an international and worked at the pit face of the Pentre Colliery in Kenfig Hill. His famed usefulness in loose play had reached new heights in 1945 when he raced away from the shell-shocked Kiwi coverers in the semi-final of the Middlesex Sevens at Twickenham to score a match-winning try.

There was also a special link-up in the second row where the cousins Roy Roberts and Bill Tamplin played alongside each other. Here Tamplin was the big name and would soon captain Wales against the Wallabies. Both were also related to Bleddyn Williams, with Roberts originally from Taff's Well and a Welsh Guardsman who had won a military medal during the war. With such a solid front five, the quality of the back row was a further bonus. Les Manfield was considered the finest number 8 of his generation, his seven caps for Wales interrupted by seven seasons when no internationals were played. Another valley man, in his case Mountain Ash, he had become a trained teacher, a squadron leader in the RAF, and by 1947 was teaching again at Cowbridge Grammar School. His game was based on an innate sense of being in the right place at the right time and an all-enveloping cover tackle.

On the blind-side of the back row was another Victory International representative, Elvet Jones, an impressively durable newcomer who had experience with Llanelli and Neath and who was to play 39 games for the first team by the end of the season. The open-sider, Gwyn Evans, had been an invaluable recruit to the ranks the previous season. Another product of the valleys in Treherbert, his formative years had been spent in West Wales and he had been an automatic choice for Wales in all the post-war internationals so far. He was a real tail-gunner of a flanker in the best traditions of a fly-half's nightmare. Cardiff's flowing and expensive play suited him down to the ground and he completed a pack that seemed to have a bit of everything from two cousins to three goal kickers (Tamplin, James and Roberts). It also would be far too good for the Wallabies.

Undeniably a key factor in Cardiff's forward supremacy in the match was based on a catalogue of injuries that befell their opponents. Once again in a touring team game a side was reduced to 14 men, though for the Wallabies the depletion was even worse as two more walking wounded left them with little more than a dozen competitive players long before the end. As early as the twelfth minute their hooker, Wally Dawson, was forced to leave the field with badly torn rib muscles. Fifteen minutes later, Nick Shehadie, playing at lock, damaged a shoulder and hobbled through the rest of the game packing down in the back row. In the second half a prop, Eric Tweedale, picked up another shoulder injury. Meanwhile Cardiff had not escaped unscathed. Jack Matthews was mildly concussed as he chased the kick-off and collided with Trevor Allan. In *The Daily Telegraph* JP Jordan reported that 'rarely have I seen a game more interrupted by injuries.'

The flow of the game inevitably suffered, the only points in the first period coming from a twentieth minute penalty goal kicked by Tamplin, awarded for an off-side against Windon bang in front of the posts. The Wallabies' best chances had come from the elusive running of Eastes on the wing but he was well marshalled by his opposite number, Doug Jones. Cardiff rammed home their numerical advantage in the second half. They were showing every inclination to run with the ball and when a loose Wallaby kick went to Bleddyn Williams he seized the opportunity to counter-attack. His clever cross-kick from the left was gathered by Manfield who swept the ball to the right wing for Doug Jones to cross at the corner. This was typical of the adventurous play that had won the team so many new admirers in the post-war seasons. Doug Jones never won an international cap but he scored 22 tries in 29 games in this one full season he had at the club.

The Wallabies eventually scored points when Trevor Allan kicked a magnificent penalty goal from inside his own half but Cardiff continued to seek tries. Ten minutes from the end the pack's supremacy finally told when Manfield and Roberts burst forward and the ever present Cliff Davies scampered over in the corner. Tamplin's excellent conversion from the edge of touch completed the well-deserved 11-3 victory. Cardiff's supremacy over the Wallabies was gathering momentum.

As if to rub salt in the wounds ten blue and blacks took the field for Wales against Australia three months later and won again. Tamplin was honoured with the captaincy and celebrated by kicking two long-range penalty goals in the first half-hour of the game. As a piece of sporting entertainment the international was rather better than the six-nil final score might suggest – but a truly classic spectacle was still to come in the final match of the tour with Cardiff players again in the limelight. In order to raise funds for the Australians' long journey home via Canada an extra match against the Barbarians was arranged. There was no question of the venue. It had to be at Cardiff Arms Park where another capacity crowd was guaranteed. Five blue and blacks were selected for the Barbarians on merit: Frank Trott, Bleddyn Williams, Billy Cleaver, Bill Tamplin and, as the captain, Haydn Tanner. Trott had missed out on the international match when Cleaver played at full back. Now Cleaver was moved forward – but to centre alongside Williams rather in partnership with Tanner.

The Barbarians scored three tries, a veritable feast by the standards of the 1940s, and the Wallabies replied with one of their own and a penalty goal in the 9-6 result. The glorious match was a personal triumph for Tanner. Williams, with his jinking and clean breaks, and Cleaver, with his cool appreciation of the ball moving faster than the man, each made their own contributions. Tanner played one more international season in 1949 but Williams, Cleaver, Matthews, Cliff Davies and Tanner's successor at scrum-half, Rex Willis, would get better and better in readiness for the career defining Lions' tour to New Zealand in 1950. For Cleaver it also turned out to be his swan song, but one he remembers with great affection:

'To tour with the Lions was a great experience. I played every match of the Grand Slam season for Wales in 1950 at half-back with Rex Willis but when the tour party was announced I was listed as one of the two full backs along with Ireland's George

Norton. The fly-halves were Jack Kyle and the Englishman, Ivor Preece. I was quite happy to be part of the squad and, of course, would be proud to be a Lion in any position.'

With 30 games in front of them in New Zealand, Australia and, on the way home, Ceylon, Cleaver might at least have anticipated the occasional game in his favourite position. Events, however, conspired against him when Norton broke an arm in the fifth game of the tour against Southland. From then on there was little doubt that Billy Cleaver's Lions' future was in the full back position:

'I was quite comfortable there and took the view that I would stay back and concentrate on the basics. When we reached the tests, of course, the All Blacks would have Bob Scott in the position but I saw no purpose in trying to be as attacking as he was. I would play my normal game.'

Cleaver is being unduly modest about his new role. The match programme profiles of the tour regularly described him as 'the complete footballer' and his consistently good performances in the games themselves justified the assessment. Norton's misfortune was a factor in him playing in nine of the first dozen games, all but one of them at full back, and the New Zealand newspapers found much to admire. After the first game at Nelson the *Weekly News* reported:

'Cleaver, at full back, impressed as a clever footballer. Things might have gone more kindly for the tourists had he slipped up to second five-eighths [inside centre] and sharpened things up a bit.'

Similar citations followed throughout the tour with the universal conclusion that he was proving to be a fine full back. Once again he had adapted to the needs of his team and there was no doubt that he would feature in the test side in that position. This he did for the first three tests against New Zealand. However, the realisation finally dawned on the team management that with Norton out of the tour even such a reliable team member as Cleaver required some rest from time to time. The richly talented Lewis Jones was sent for and eventually given his chance in the fourth test. Cleaver had no great problem with that, reflecting:

> 'Lewis was an exciting player who did well in the provincial matches he played in after he arrived. He also could look after the goal kicking that was the responsibility of one of our props, John Robins, in the earlier tests. When he played in the first test in Australia he ran through the card with a try and a dropped goal as well as kicking conversions and penalties.'

Jones was the headline grabber in the latter half of the tour but Billy Cleaver had been the Mr Dependable that marked him out as a real team man. By the end of the six-month trip he had played in a total of 15 games, including one in the centre but none at fly-half. The final irony was that when he came out of retirement to play for the Lions again in Cardiff's 75th anniversary match it was as a scrum-half. Again he was incredibly relaxed about the situation:

> 'I'd never played at scrum-half before but the prospect didn't particularly daunt me. I wouldn't be expected to run very far and my main task was to pass the ball out to Jackie Kyle. It was quite an enjoyable afternoon's rugby.'

Cleaver's retirement had been again determined by his level-headed evaluation of his professional and family responsibilities. He had already been invited to take over the captaincy of Cardiff on his return from Australasia but he was clear in his own mind what the immediate future held for him:

> 'Much as I enjoyed the Lions tour, and great honour as it would have been to be captain of Cardiff the following winter, I had to decide my priorities. I was already manager of North Celynen Colliery in Newbridge and being away for several months meant that I would have to give it up and be a supply manager on my return. There was also my family to consider so when I returned I told the club committee that I would have to stand down as captain and retire from playing.'

Life was never dull for Cleaver in the years that followed. He joined the club committee, took over the reins of the newly formed Welsh Youth Rugby Union 'because it seemed a natural extension of my work with young men in the mines', and further developed his interests in steam locomotives, art and fine wine. Needless to add, his mining career went from strength to strength culminating in his appointment as Deputy Director of the South Wales Coalfield. There he was regarded far and wide as a distinguished and authoritative figure. Fittingly, Cardiff Rugby Football Club also appreciated his true worth. When he made his last scheduled appearance in blue and black on 4 November 1950 the match programme paid an impressive tribute:

'Today's match marks the last appearance of that great clubman and footballer, Billy Cleaver, in the Cardiff colours … No player has ever enjoyed greater popularity on the Arms Park, and Billy has been something more than a mere bobby-soxers' hero, for through his play and likeable personality he has represented all that is best in the club. He has always played his hardest for Cardiff and Wales in all matches. Great success has come his way but he has always remained the same cheerful person. He has always been admired by his team mates, and invariably had a good word to say about everyone. Though he departs from the playing scene the memory of his ability and sportsmanship will remain, for he has set an example.'

13

Still Greater Glory

A one hundred per cent record after two matches against the Wallabies, spread, admittedly, over a period of 40 years, was a cause for quiet satisfaction at the Cardiff club. No one could have anticipated that the record would get better and better in each of the next four decades. Around the corner lay still greater glory.

Over the course of long tours Wallabies of successive generations may not have had the strength in depth of the All Blacks and Springboks to compile near-invincible playing records – a situation that would certainly change from the 1980s onwards. Yet they were always dangerous opponents on the big match occasions, capable of 15-man rugby that would defeat the strongest opposition. Throughout their test match history, even in their occasional periods of decline, they could still sneak well-merited victories over the might of New Zealand and South Africa – and on their own grounds. They did so in Christchurch and Wellington in 1952 and 1955 respectively and also in Cape Town in 1953. One of the recurring problems of Australian rugby at the time was the lack of regular matches on the international calendar. Between the departure of the Lions in August 1950 and the arrival of the Fourth Wallabies in Britain in the autumn of 1957, Australia played only 20 test matches. Four of them had been against Fiji and there had been no contact during the period with any side from Europe. This isolationism was in marked contrast to the international game in the modern professional era. Hence, a 34-match tour to the British Isles and France in 1957-58, with another couple of games in Canada and Japan on the way home, was something that the Australian rugby fraternity could cherish. Inevitably they would have to dig deep into their playing resources. Equally, and undeniably, a younger generation of Australian players could only benefit from the experience. It was a tour to look forward to with great enthusiasm.

Much the same applied to their hosts, remembering that such teams from the other side of the world were only seen every three or four years at best. And the Wallabies were certainly still an attraction in Cardiff. Two of the blue and black heroes from the victory over the All Blacks four years before even came out of retirement to play against them. Many observers assumed that Rex Willis and CD Williams had put the seal on their club careers by beating the All Blacks in 1953 but great players always set new targets, however belatedly. Williams, the speed merchant of a flanker, was certainly no exception. He had left the club in 1955 and eventually retired altogether to pursue his many business interests but, as he explained, a couple of factors combined to hasten a change of mind on his part:

'When I left Cardiff I had a season at Neath that I thoroughly enjoyed, not least because I won a second Welsh cap against France. By then I was well into my thirties and thought it was time to concentrate on my professional career. All went well until the Easter Saturday of 1957 when I was playing cricket at St Fagan's and the new president of the Welsh Rugby Union, Enoch Rees, was watching. He told me that I had scored almost as many runs as the Barbarians had scored points at the Arms Park that afternoon. I thought he was joking but when it was confirmed that the Baa-Baas had won by 40 points I was almost speechless.'

To be strictly accurate, the Barbarians' record breaking points haul was against a decidedly under-strength Cardiff side but that was no consolation to the club or its players. That certainly included CD Williams and he was still mulling it over when he met Rex Willis later:

'Rex was as flabbergasted as I was – but then we hatched a gentleman's agreement. I had played against the Kiwis, the All Blacks and the Springboks but never the Wallabies – and they were due in town the following December. I suggested to Rex that we should come out of retirement and give it a go and try to get back into the Cardiff team to play them. Rex had, of course, toured Australia with the Lions but never played for the club against a touring Wallaby side. So we shook hands on it there and then.'

Neither Williams nor Willis would have taken their places for granted and realised that they would quickly need to regain their form and match fitness. Williams didn't waste any time, turning out for the Athletic XV against Cardiff High School Old Boys 48 hours later on Easter Monday and setting himself a demanding summer training programme. The new season started in the best possible fashion for the team with a string of impressive victories. Winning a place in the first team was a challenge for everyone at the club. The Cardiff team of 1957 still had several influential players left from the glories of earlier seasons. One of them, Eddie Thomas, had taken over as captain at the start of the season and was making a particularly fine job of the role. The man himself had no doubts about his role:

> 'Being asked to captain Cardiff was the culmination of my playing career but I also realised it was a great responsibility. I enjoyed the challenge of all of that but when I looked down the captains' board at the club I decided I needed all the help I could get! I asked Cliff Morgan if he would be my vice-captain and, without a moment's hesitation, he said yes. I even felt that was another great honour for me personally to have one of the legends of the game as my right-hand man. I was looking forward to the season tremendously and the fact that we would be playing a major touring side again was the real icing on the cake.'

One of the idiosyncrasies of the club's history was that Cliff Morgan, like Gareth Edwards later, never captained Cardiff. Of course he did for the occasional match but never as the season's captain. Students of the game will find that strange for a man who captained Wales for a season, led the British Isles to a famous test victory over South Africa, and often was in charge of Barbarians' sides in high-profile fixtures at home and abroad. Part of the answer lies in the healthy balance between famous internationals and dependable clubmen who were invariably elected by their fellow players to take charge of the team for an entire season. In the two seasons before Eddie

Thomas, the captains had been Peter Goodfellow and Malcolm Collins and very good ones they proved to be. Cliff Morgan, with his boundless spirit and almost unmatched charisma, would have been a marvellous club captain in the mid-1950s but it was a period when he was often away from South Wales with a new business career in Dublin. Eddie Thomas' invitation to him to be his deputy was an inspired sense of timing because at the end of the season, at the tender age of 28, Morgan retired from rugby. Another club victory over a touring team would provide a fitting climax to a glittering career.

Other survivors from 1953 were the warriors of the front row, Geoff Beckingham and JD Evans, so that, along with the captain and the rejuvenated CD Williams, they would make up half the pack. The other half had a suitably hard edge. Into the front row berth previously occupied by Stanley Bowes came Colin Howe. Playing the Wallabies was an experience he found more comfortable than the horrors awaiting him with Piet du Toit and the Springboks three years later. Dai Hayward had joined the back row so that he and CD Williams, two natural open-side wing forwards, would play right and left. Two budding Lions occupied the lock positions. Kingsley Jones, like Howard Norris after him, would eventually move up to prop but in 1957 was a more than useful second rower, while Roddy Evans was the thoroughbred line-out jumper.

The back division looked to be in the best traditions of the club. Willis had fought his way back into contention and would once again form a celebrated half-back duo with Morgan. Alun Priday, at full back, would make his debut against a touring team and later complete a hat-trick against the Springboks and All Blacks. The three-quarter line was an interesting blend of skilful individuals. Howard Nicholls and Gordon Wells, like Gareth Griffiths and Alun Thomas previously, could play at centre or wing. For the Wallabies' match Nicholls stayed out on the left wing where he would win a cap in Dublin later in the season. Wells, already an international but an infrequent one, started at right centre and would turn in a virtuoso performance that secured his place in the national side for most of the season. Glyn John on the right wing had won a cap for Wales as a fly-half while the fourth member, Allan Barter from Cardiff High School and Cambridge University, was a tricky runner who would relish the rare opportunity of rugby on the big stage.

There was every reason to expect a big performance from this club team and the 50,000 crowd were not disappointed. The imponderable factor was whether the Wallabies, who started as clear second favourites, could raise their game at Cardiff Arms Park. Their eleven previous matches of the tour had sent mixed messages. A worrying first month had seen them lose to both Oxbridge universities, scrape a draw with London Counties at Twickenham, and succumb to Newport without scoring. On paper their team looked better than the actual results. They were well led by the prop, Bob Davidson, and had useful performers in most areas of the team. Terry Curley and Jim Lenehan were strapping full-backs whose abilities were to stand the test of time in the international arena. Two excellent wings, Ken Donald and Rod 'Phantom' Phelps, had a healthy appetite for try-scoring and there was little to choose between two capable fly-halves, Arthur Summons and Ron Harvey. The first choice scrum-half was Des Connor who gained the first of his 12 Australian test caps on the tour and later went to New Zealand and played another dozen tests for the All Blacks. In the pack the best players were John Thornett, Tony Miller, Norman Hughes and, a survivor from the previous tour ten years before, Nick Shehadie.

After the agonies of the early matches, the Wallabies had made a mini recovery by the time they reached Cardiff in mid-December. They had put together a sequence of five consecutive wins, starting with Leinster at Lansdowne Road, Dublin and, in the week of the Cardiff match, a significant victory over Llanelli. The latter result was a real morale booster that, if it could be repeated against Cardiff, would really put their tour back on the road. Realising the importance of the game they chose eleven of their shadow international side. They were to prove not quite good enough against an inspired Cardiff team in a flowing match.

On a fine winter's day the tourists did much of the early attacking with full-back Curley regularly involved but Cardiff, defending the river end of the ground, were well marshalled by Cliff Morgan. When the club gained possession Gordon Wells showed a real appetite for running, twice being stopped after half-breaks. The Wallabies might have taken the lead when centre John Potts was caught on the line. Once again it was Morgan who cleared and soon his side was at the other end and opening the scoring. Appropriately the try was claimed by Wells who collected a lobbed pass from Morgan, feinted to pass out to Glyn John outside him on the right wing, and crossed half way out on the right.

The Wallabies continued to be very competitive in the second quarter and gained their reward when Rex Willis was caught in possession by Allan Cameron and the veteran Shehadie took a scoring pass for the equalising try. The score remained at stalemate until half-time but the Wallabies could feel well pleased with their efforts. They had shaded the scrums, held their own in the line-outs and posed questions for Cardiff in the loose. But this was a good club side with a nucleus of players comfortable on the big occasions. Unfortunately for the Wallabies they were temporarily without Des Connor in the opening moments of the second half and while he was off the field the blue and blacks opened up a six-point gap. A penalty awarded for barging in a line-out was expertly goaled by Alun Priday from 45 yards and near touch. Then Curley was caught in possession for Wells and Hayward to combine and send Glyn John over for the second try.

Connor's return signalled another Wallaby comeback and Kenny Yanz pounced for a typical flanker's try as the ball bounced away from three Cardiff defenders over the goal-line. At 9-6 down the Wallabies scented the possibility of completing the comeback with a famous win and right wing, Otho Fox, was only stopped by a last-ditch defence. Realising that their lead was under threat, Eddie Thomas' men raised the already hectic pace of the game in the closing stages. It was Wells who again added the final touch, taking a long pass from Willis in a ploy known as the 'Elvidge move', after the 1953 All Black, to dive over near the right corner. Priday's magnificent conversion effectively sealed the result. A late penalty goal by Lenehan gave his team some hope at 14-11 but further late attacks were again covered by Cardiff's excellent backs.

Reaction afterwards centred on the high quality of the play. In the *Football Echo* Dave Phillips applauded 'a classic game' and particularly praised the back row of Williams, Thomas and Hayward. In *The Western Mail* JBG Thomas was more specific:

'The hero of the match was the Cardiff captain, Eddie Thomas, for he has not played a better game throughout his long career, and his tireless efforts inspired his pack to achieve the almost impossible task of holding the powerful Wallaby eight. In his greatest hour Thomas was the best forward on the field and a worthy captain. No praise can be too great for him.'

The report concluded:

'Rarely have I seen better rugby in such an important match, or two sides put as much, if not more, into attack than into defence. The spirit of both was tremendous and although the Wallabies lost, in defeat they proved themselves a fine side.'

The Cardiff players certainly realised they had achieved a major victory. At the final whistle Colin Howe, not one given to flamboyant displays of emotion, admits to jumping ten feet in the air with joy. On such days a slight exaggeration can be accommodated. As for Rex Willis and CD Williams, there was the satisfaction of knowing that they had come out of retirement and added another feather in their – and the club's – caps. Then there was the quiet man in charge who had joined the roll of honour of Cardiff captains that had beaten a touring team: Percy Bush, Haydn Tanner, Bleddyn Williams and, now, Eddie Thomas. And still there was more to come.

The next generation of Cardiff running backs and grizzled forwards were ready and waiting for the fifth Wallabies in 1966. This was the Cardiff team that at the end of the season would tour South Africa and dazzle the watching public with their six-try extravaganza against Eastern Province. First, though, was the domestic season and another major date with a touring team. John Thornett's Wallabies were no pushovers, a much more capable outfit than their forerunners of nine years before. Thornett had been part of that team, as had the lock-turned-prop, Tony Miller. They appreciated the task facing them at Cardiff but this time they had new stars to give them real hope of success. Top of the list were the exceptionally able half-backs, Phil Hawthorne and Ken Catchpole. Later in the tour, after beating Wales at the Arms Park, Hawthorne would contribute a hat-trick of dropped goals in the 23-11 triumph over England at Twickenham. He could pop over these improvised goals from seemingly anywhere, six in total in the five tests on tour, and another against Cardiff. He was also a brilliant runner, taking full advantage of one of the fastest passing scrum-halves the sport had ever seen. Catchpole's flick of the wrists propelled the ball to his partner so quickly that tacklers could rarely get close to Hawthorne before he inflicted further damage. Before they had arrived in Britain the two of them had already inspired Australian victories over South Africa and New Zealand. With Jim Lenehan back again outside them and another world class player, Greg Davis, at wing forward, these Wallabies were potentially a class act. For Cardiff to beat them would be a major achievement, indeed.

Though a subsequent injury would cruelly rob him of the chance to lead his team to South Africa six months later, Cardiff's captain was the giant lock, Keith Rowlands. Imposing in more ways than one, the red-headed powerhouse had made his reputation with the Lions in 1962. Since then, and infuriatingly, he had only made a miserly four further appearances for Wales in as many seasons. But for Cardiff he had been a successful captain, now in his second term. He had around him the vital components of any good side. Howard Norris and Billy Thomas had been joined in the front row by John O'Shea, a scrummager out of the top drawer who would also win caps and become a Lion in 1968. Packing down in the second row with the captain was Lyn Baxter, a fine ball-playing, all-action lock who gave several years unstinting service to the club. The blind-side flanker was John Hickey, the hard man who took no prisoners on the field, with the lighter Clive Evans at open-side and the Cambridge Blue, Tony Pender, at number eight. It was a good, no-frills, club pack – the sort that treated a match against a touring side as a major day in their playing careers and would not want to waste it.

The backs who later set South Africa alight were there in all their dazzling pomp: Ray Cheney at the back; the two Jones's, Keri and Ken, with Gerald Davies and Maurice Richards in the three-quarter line; the business-like Billy Hullin and Phil Morgan at half-back. No room there for the college student, Gareth Edwards – and this a mere three months before the first of his 53 consecutive caps for Wales. This could conservatively be described as a good back division.

The ace up the club's sleeve was Howard Norris who, with Ken Jones, had toured Australia earlier in the year with the Lions. The team was coached by Roy Bish, a deep thinker on the game who the committee had recruited from Cardiff College of Education with startling results. The new coach benefited from the input he received from several trained physical education teachers in the team, none more so for the Wallabies' match than the redoubtable Howard Norris. The prop was particularly looking forward to renewing acquaintances with his opposite number, Tony Miller:

'I had seen Tony and several of the rest of the team when I had been with the Lions. They were a team to be respected but the bottom line was that they were not the All Blacks or Springboks. I was confident we could handle them up front and I suggested to Roy Bish the best way of keeping Ken Catchpole under wraps. He liked to stand opposite the front of a line-out and then run along it to the catcher and take the ball when he was already moving. There was a simple way to stop that – get Hickey to flatten him. I'm pleased to say that he obliged and after that we didn't have too much to worry about.'

There was a rapier in the club's armoury as well. The backs, with Ken Jones in prime form, probed and tested the Wallabies' defence throughout the match. While all the talk before the game had been about the prowess of the world class Catchpole, it was his opposite number, Hullin, who became the star of the day. The 24-year-old bank official was never happier than when he was running with the ball but he also had a range of kicking skills. With his forwards well on top he opened the scoring by darting to the blindside for a try. Before half-time he picked up another ball at the back of a scrum and, under the shadow of the visitors' goalposts, nonchalantly swivelled around to chip the ball over the cross bar for the cheekiest of dropped goals. It was clearly going to be his day.

In the second period Cheney stretched Cardiff's lead to nine points with a penalty goal before the Wallabies threatened an upset. Lenehan appeared outside the left wing, Alan Cardy, to touchdown for a try that he converted himself. Then the prolific Hawthorne dropped a goal and there was only a one-point advantage to the club. But the pack was still on top and in the closing stages Ken Jones scored the try he richly deserved and Cheney's conversion completed a 14-8 victory. The true value of Cardiff's performance was seen in the light of the Australian's later victories over Wales and England. At the very end of the tour it was further underlined when they returned to the Arms Park and comfortably disposed of a powerful Barbarians' team containing eleven Lions. Cardiff's record against the might of Australia was now becoming seriously impressive.

By the time the Sixth Wallabies opened their campaign in October 1975 the need to break the blue and black bogey had become an urgent issue in Australian rugby. The occasional defeat against a particular club was digestible, but four losses in four outings was, to say the least, rather noticeable in the debit columns of the record books. Correcting that imbalance would have been one of the priorities of John Hipwell's team in 1975. For them the omens were reasonably promising. A two-nil home series win over England during the summer, followed by a rather less significant couple of victories over Japan, had left them in good heart. Hipwell, was emulating players such as Nick Shehadie, Jim Lenehan and John Thornett before him in returning to Britain for his second tour nearly ten years after the first. In 1966 he had been Catchpole's understudy; now he was the kingpin, a world-class player in his own right. His team was again strong in the back row of the pack where Ray Price was a worthy successor to Greg Davis on the flank and Tony Shaw was a useful foil. Their points machine on the tour would turn out to be the 22-year-old full back, Paul McLean. Originally pencilled in as a fly-half, team injuries forced him to move to the back but, wherever he played, his unerring goal-kicking would be a considerable threat to the opposition.

Cardiff's success rate in the previous matches was no help to the coaching staff at the club. A new partnership had taken over at the start of the season. John Evans had joined from the Penarth club and Chris Padfield from Newbridge. Evans makes no attempt to hide the great pressure he had felt under at the time:

'I had played for the club in the 1960s and after that coached the youth team for four seasons so I was well aware of the great traditions associated with touring team matches. But I have to admit that it didn't make my role as coach any easier to be told by a prominent member of the committee, 'Don't forget – we've never lost to them.' That's something I didn't want to hear as the date with the Wallabies drew ever closer. Thankfully, Chris Padfield and myself worked well together and we had the added advantage of a great captain to work with. Gerald Davies had taken over as captain at the start of the season and he was an absolute natural leader. He was no shouter and bawler – simply very articulate, a marvellous communicator and, of course, he wasn't a bad player either.'

Cardiff were again due to meet the Wallabies early in their tour, in this case the second match on Saturday 1 November. Three days earlier they made their first appearance against Oxford University and the captain and coaches travelled up to have a first sight of them. Oxbridge rugby in the mid-1970s was in the doldrums and Oxford were certainly a mediocre side. They had lost the last four Varsity matches at Twickenham and another defeat was on the cards. The Wallabies had little difficulty in disposing of them by six tries and 36 points to 3. Even allowing for the opposition against them, John Evans was impressed, Gerald Davies less so.

'I came away from Oxford thinking we had no chance against the touring team,' admitted Evans. 'We'd already lost half a dozen games, though all of them had been away from home, and Newport had put 16 points on us without reply. I kept my thoughts to myself but on the way back Gerald told me that he fancied our chances. The next evening we met again at my flat to talk things over. We did this quite a lot during the season and occasionally other senior players would have an input as well. In the case of the Wallabies' match, Gareth Edwards joined us so we had formulated a clear game plan 48 hours before our final team meeting. I remember that when we had that meeting one or two of the side felt that Gareth wasn't paying attention to what was being said – they hadn't realised that he was already a vital contributor to the talk being given to them!'

The match itself, however, could have been a nasty case of the best laid plans coming unstuck because before kick-off Edwards was forced to pull out with a bout of influenza. Luckily there was an able deputy standing by in Brynmor Williams. He would slot into the tactical plan very smoothly. Evans explained:

'The first I knew about Gareth's illness was on the Saturday morning but there was no cause for panic. Brynmor understood perfectly that what we wanted to do was put the ball up in the air as near the middle of the pitch as possible. Such was the size of the National Stadium that any catcher would have to kick the ball a long way to get to the safety of the nearest touchline. But we were also a skilful side. Throughout the season we had worked very hard to spread the ball wide and quickly. Sometimes we would take the ball to the narrow side first, suck in the defenders, and then move it back to the open side at pace. With wings like Gerald and the human tank, PL Jones, waiting for the ball tries would inevitably follow if we executed the plan well.'

With Gareth Davies in his first full season of senior rugby at fly-half and two workmanlike centres in Alex Finlayson and Paul Evans, every one of the 1975 backs could be relied on to play their part. They also had a very neat footballer at full back in John Davies. The team's other strength was that at least one of the pack had a score to settle. Loose-head prop Barry Nelmes had been to Australia with England earlier in the year and had experienced a torrid time. As what appeared to be a premeditated assault followed the kick-off, Australian boots went in on Nelmes as he lay helpless on the ground and within a minute his fellow prop, Mike Burton, was sent off. England played 78 minutes of that second test with 14 men and Bill Beaumont at tight-head prop. They had held the lead until the second half before Australia overpowered them to win by nine points. Nelmes was ready to wreak revenge in the colours of Cardiff. He had perfect allies in the front row in hooker Alan Phillips and iron-man, Mike Knill. Only the concurrent career of the exceptional Graham Price would prevent Knill winning more than a single international cap but he was widely regarded as the greatest scrummaging tight-head prop of his generation.

The back five of the scrum was again populated by some very reliable club men. Ian Robinson, at lock, played 384 first team games for the club, and would be completing a full house against touring teams after the Springboks of 1969 and the All Blacks three years later. He would look after his less experienced partner, Mark McJennett. The back row was another example how assembling a complementary trio can usually prove more effective than three brilliant individuals operating in isolation. Not that there was anything second rate about the vice-captain, Roger Lane. As Knill had to vie with Graham Price for international honours, so Lane had the misfortune to be Wales' reserve to Mervyn Davies, and without the consolation of a single cap in a long career that brought him every other honour.

His younger brother, Stuart, would at least break into the Wales team three years later and even become a Lion in South Africa in 1980. His particular misfortune was to damage cartilage in his right knee within 50 seconds of the start of the game against Eastern Province and his Lions career was over. In tandem for Cardiff, however, the two Lanes were a real handful and never more so than against the Wallabies. In 1975 they had been joined by the 21 year old flanker, Trevor Worgan, a former captain of Wales Youth and another considered to have a great future:

'Despite my moment of quiet pessimism in midweek, I was feeling more confident by the time the game was under way,' said John Evans. 'When we lined up for the team photograph there was a look of grim determination on everyone's face. They knew what to do and, my goodness, they certainly did it when the match started. We simply didn't give the Wallabies a chance to play. Up went the high kicks and the mistakes followed. At first we couldn't score but even when McLean kicked two penalty goals to put his side six points up I could see the way the game would go. Our front row was giving their opposite numbers a real going-over and it was only a matter of time before our backs cashed in.'

Evans was right. Before half-time Brynmor Williams, who was having an armchair ride behind the pack, cut away to the blindside and PL Jones powered over in the corner. Soon after the restart Gareth Davies kicked a penalty goal that put Cardiff ahead. The unfortunate Stuart Lane was stamped on in the 59th minute and replaced by Bob

Dudley-Jones but still Cardiff were in control. Davies had added a second penalty goal before he was at hand outside PL Jones to take the pass for the second try and an eight-point lead. McLean's third penalty goal had little bearing on the result. Cardiff had won by 14 points to nine and now it was five wins in five outings against the Wallabies.

As the final whistle was blown in 1975 it was hard to imagine that one hundred per cent record ever being more meaningful than it was then. Yet there was one way it could attain even more currency. What if an all-conquering Wallabies team came to Britain and Cardiff were to beat them? Given the staccato progress of Australian rugby up to then, that seemed a scenario built on fantasy. In 1984 it became reality. Suddenly Australia was a real force in the rugby world. The road to World Cup dominance in the 1990s began in Britain in 1984. On that tour Andrew Slack's team won the Grand Slam against the four home countries. They were a team of all the talents, with Gould, Campese, Burke, Lynagh, Farr-Jones and Mark Ella in the backs and a formidable pack built around Rodriguez, Lawton, Cutler, Poidevin and Tuynman. But in the first week of the tour Cardiff, once again, took their unbeaten record.

The game played on 24 October 1984 – for the first time since the days of Percy Bush not on a Saturday – was a true meeting of equals. The Wallabies were the up-and-coming form team of world rugby, not yet the finished article but a side of undoubted ability enhanced by moments of sheer inspiration. The Cardiff side of the early 1980s had already climbed the steep hill and from the peak of it were the lords of all around them. That is an assessment not born of arrogance or of 'The Greatest' tag hoisted on them by the local Member of Parliament, James Callaghan, and unfortunately repeated in the title of the club's centenary history. In the 1980s it was a position gained by consistent dominance of the only performance indicator of the game in Wales. They had won the Welsh Cup three times in four seasons. For good measure they had also completed a championship and cup double in 1982, though admittedly the so-called championship was still a flawed vehicle calculated on percentages of success in wildly different fixture lists from club to club.

The success rate of the team at that time, however, was a true reflection of the quality of the players within the side. For four seasons before 1984-85 they had been led by the England international number 8, John Scott. No player in the history of the club had ever led the team for four consecutive years. Scott was a worthy record breaker. For him, there should never be a hiding place on the field of play; he wanted to play with the best and against the best.

'I was already capped by England and nearly 24 years old when I came to Cardiff,' he said. 'In those pre-league days their fixture list was extraordinary and I knew that if I made the grade with the club I would be in a team where I would be tested nearly every week. I soon was because as well as the matches with the top English clubs and the derbies with Newport and the clubs from West Wales that had an agenda all of their own I arrived at a time when touring teams were arriving more often.'

Scott had played against the All Blacks in 1978 and 1980 and also led the team against the New Zealand Maoris in 1982 but the match with the Wallabies came at exactly the right time for the club.

'We had been getting better and better every season and by 1984 we really did have the complete club team. Everyone talks about the spine of the side, from Alan Phillips in the front row, Bobby Norster and myself at lock and number 8, Terry Holmes and Gareth Davies at half-back, and Mark Ring in midfield. Yes, we were a strong combination. But let's not forget the rest of the team. We had Pablo Rees at full back, Alun Donovan with Ringo in the centre, Adrian Hadley on one wing and Mike Carrington was having a good season on the other. It's hard to imagine a better club front row than Jeff Whitefoot and Ian Eidman propping Alan Phillips. 'Heavy Kev' Edwards was a perfect foil for Bobby Norster in the second row but we had a real selection headache at flanker. One of Bob Lakin, Owen Golding and Gareth Roberts would have to be left out and for the Wallabies' game Bob was the unlucky one.'

One unexpected twist in the preparations was the unavailability of the new club captain, Terry Holmes. The outstanding scrum-half had dislocated a shoulder the previous week. Once again, as in 1975 when Gareth Edwards had been sidelined with illness, or even way back in 1931 when the Lion and vice-captain, Howard Poole, couldn't play against the Springboks, the first choice scrum-half would have to watch from the stands. But as in the earlier games an able deputy was available, in this case Steve Cannon, a terrier at the base of the scrum with a fast pass and a good kicking game. Alan Phillips took over the captaincy though Scott maintains that with that particular team the planning was never left in the hands of one or two men:

'Roger Beard was a fine coach, well supported by Gary Samuel, but the senior players among us always had something to contribute. Our Thursday evening training sessions were more like a debating society with four or five of us – usually Gareth Davies, Holmesy, Alan Phillips and myself – chipping in. On a bad night Ringo would have something to say as well.'

As Scott also points out, such was the strength of the team that in planning for any one game there was at least three tactical options at their disposal. With the backs they had in the side spinning the ball wide was always an attraction. By the end of the season Hadley and Carrington would have scored 36 tries between them, and a third wing, Gerald Cordle, another 17. But the forwards, whether through text book eight-man control supported by kicking half-backs or a variety of moves off the back row, also wanted a leading role. The latter was particularly the case if the opposition's strength lay in its own pack.

'We never could resist the challenge of taking on a team at exactly the point they thought they were strongest,' added Scott. 'The classic case was Pontypool who had a frightening reputation at that time. Later in the season we demolished them in the cup semi-final by playing nine-man rugby. Our backs wanted to spread the ball and try to run them off their feet but, after one of our usual Thursday night arguments, common-sense prevailed – we did what the forwards wanted!'

The situation was much the same for the Wallabies' encounter. The tourists had selected only a handful of their likely international back line, with Mark Ella and Slack directing operations, but had gone for power up front with six of the first choice forwards. That was probably their undoing. Phillips and company relished the challenge posed by such a pack and wasted no time in taking them on. Unusually, John Scott, for one, was not aware of the club's one hundred per cent record against Wallaby sides of the past but that didn't take away the importance of the match. 'This was a touring team fixture and the highlight of any season and as with all big games we wanted to win it' was his view and, sure enough, the team went on to the pitch at the National Stadium with a single-minded determination.

'We absolutely smashed them in the first half-hour or so' said Scott and the scoreboard bears him out. Once again the Cardiff pack took control, with Norster dominating the line-outs and Gareth Davies in his element with the tactical kicking role behind. The fly-half was playing in his fourth club game against a major touring side, equalling the record of Howard Norris and, like Alan Phillips, was about to repeat the triumph of nine years earlier. It was a fitting climax to a magnificent club career that still had two years to run. By the time he retired in the summer of 1986 Gareth Davies had scored a phenomenal 3117 points, including 63 dropped goals, in 361 games for the blue and blacks. More than that he played throughout eleven seasons with a languid style that balanced a lethal kicking game with the priceless knack of conjuring decisive breaks against defences lulled into a false sense of security.

Davies' partnership with Terry Holmes was one of the great half-back pairings. Bush and David at the start of the century, then Cleaver and Tanner, followed by Morgan and Willis and in the 1970s Barry John and Edwards, all were of the highest quality and Davies and Holmes were no exception. Where the fly-half was all grace and stealth his magnificently built partner was the true powerhouse scrum-half. From five-metres' scrums Holmes was unstoppable but he was also the complete footballer. Both of them were Lions and captained their club and country at different times. It was Holmes' misfortune to miss the Wallabies' fixture but even in his absence Davies turned on a master class of the fly-half's arts.

The headlines, however, were made by the pack. Midway through the first half and attacking the river end of the ground a close range scrum proved to be the key moment of the match. With no Holmes behind them to charge over, Phillips' men simply kept the ball at the feet of the back row and walked the scrum forward, expertly controlled by Scott. Back went the Wallabies' near full-strength pack, in went an illegal hand to desperately steal the ball, and referee David Templeton had no hesitation in awarding the penalty try. It was a pushover try in all but name. The look on John Scott's face as he walked back to half-way was a picture. Exactly a month later the Wallabies would return to the ground and this time dish out the humiliation of a pushover try to Wales in an international they would win with embarrassing ease.

Against Cardiff it was a totally different story. Davies converted the penalty try and the club were well on the way to a 16-point lead. He also kicked a penalty goal and an almost inevitable dropped goal. Cardiff's second try by Adrian Hadley completed the team's scoring. The Wallabies never gave up, hitting back with 12 points of their own through two converted tries, but the blue and blacks' victory, by 16 points to 12, was never in real doubt. Later in their tour the Wallabies would also lose to Llanelli, Ulster and the South of Scotland but, yet again, it was Cardiff that had struck the first blow. Andrew Slack and his team might claim that the focal point of the tour was to win the four test matches, which they did in some style, but given the history of the rivalry a win over Cardiff would also have been a priority when they set out. They had failed.

For the Cardiff club, six wins in six outings spread over three-quarters of a century could be no fluke, more a case of sustained excellence. Alan Phillips had followed the earlier captains, Percy Bush, Haydn Tanner, Eddie Thomas, Keith Rowlands and Gerald Davies, into the record books. It is a record that is never likely to be beaten.

Alan Evans

Endpiece

Time Gentlemen, Please

Percy Bush didn't know what he was starting when he led the Cardiff team on to the pitch to play the All Blacks at Cardiff Arms Park on Boxing Day 1905. That first game with an international team from the southern hemisphere was the beginning of a historic tradition that survived for nearly 90 years. It continued, interrupted only by two world wars, until 1994. The club's game against the Springboks in that year was the twenty-second time that a major touring team had played the blue and blacks in the city. Sadly, all the indications are that it was also the last such fixture. A year after that rather undistinguished match the game of rugby union went professional. Many things in the sport would change.

  Long tours by international sides were already being shrunk. The 1950 Lions in New Zealand and Australia played 30 matches; their counterparts of 2001 went only to Australia and played ten. The pattern was repeated by the teams who came in the opposite direction. A typical visiting team to Europe before 1980 would play between 26 and 30 matches. The Lions now visit only one southern hemisphere country at a time. The idea of combining a trip to Australia and New Zealand, with a couple of games in Canada thrown in on the way home, would send the modern day professionals in search of sedatives to calm their nerves. Likewise the teams coming to Europe have long since visited only a couple of the Six Nations countries in any one visit. The last overseas team to undertake a full tour to Britain and France was the Wallabies in 1975-76. The writing has been on the wall for a long time. By the dawn of the new millennium, two or three games – all of them full-scale international matches – was all that could be contemplated. The top sides had neither the time in the crowded calendar or probably even the inclination to play more. The notion that the All Blacks might play

Cardiff or the Springboks take on Llanelli didn't even enter the planners' minds.

Obviously, significant changes in touring itineraries were already taking place long before 1995. As early as 1967 the All Blacks didn't play Cardiff but East Wales (with eight Cardiff players in the team) at the Arms Park. There were extenuating circumstances as it was a hastily arranged tour to replace an aborted trip to South Africa. In the 1970s and 1980s normal service was more or less resumed, though the tours were gradually shortening and new combinations were beginning to appear. The national unions, not least in Wales, were attracted to fielding a second-string international team against the tourists but even that development lacked any consistency or sense of identity. Within little more than a decade Wales B became Wales A, then Emerging Wales, and finally Wales A again. No one could seriously claim that the prospect of these matches could excite the fans as much as their own club side playing the All Blacks, Springboks or Wallabies.

Great clubs like Cardiff, however, have clung on to the hope that one day an old tradition might be revived. No one should blame them for that. One of the striking things about tracing the span of matches played by Cardiff against the tourists since 1905 is the clear pattern of eminent players continuing in administrative roles in later years. And without exception they have considered it an essential responsibility to foster old and new friendships through the medium of touring team games. These are not 'old blazers' living in the past without an appreciation of the modern professional game. They know from first-hand experience the benefits for clubs and individuals that accrue from such matches. They rightly believe, too, that Cardiff against the All Blacks, albeit the newly-created Cardiff Blues regional entity, would be an attraction not only for the die-hard supporters but also for the untapped thousands of rugby fans that the modern game is desperately trying to attract.

As the Cardiff club began planning the celebrations for its 125th Anniversary season in 2001, the first suggestion for a special fixture to mark the occasion was a game against the Wallabies who were scheduled to play internationals matches against England, France and Wales that autumn. They were also due to play Oxford University as a warm-up to the Twickenham test. The eight days between the

French and Welsh internationals were given over to training. A suitable time, perhaps, for a game against Cardiff. The idea lasted about ten seconds. Modern touring teams simply didn't play games of that nature – not even when it provided the Wallabies with an opportunity to beat the club for the first time and put the record straight. Factors like that don't loom large in the professional's priorities.

Concomitantly, the current generation of players may never play for their club (or region) against a major touring team. The equally worrying question is whether they would feel they have missed out on a vital part of their rugby education. The sad suspicion is that they would not. If he was around today, Percy Bush, that ace fly-half, career diplomat, and man of the world, might be scratching his head and trying to work it all out. Thankfully, along with the ghosts of Bush, Gabe, Nicholls and Willis, we have the enduring presence of Bleddyn Williams, Dr Jack Matthews, Cliff Morgan and, from more recent generations, Howard Norris, John Scott and many others.

All of them were better players for having encountered the All Blacks, Springboks or Wallabies at Cardiff Arms Park. And, of course, they tamed the tourists.

Appendix

Cardiff v New Zealand

Match 1: 26 December 1905
Cardiff 8 All Blacks 10

Cardiff: HB Winfield; JL Williams, EG Nicholls, RT Gabe,
RC Thomas; RA Gibbs *[rover];* PF Bush (captain), RJ David;
W Neill, G Northmore, JA Powell, F Smith, JA Brown, LM George,
E Rumbelow
Scorers – Tries: Nicholls and Thomas; Conversion: Winfield

All Blacks: WJ Wallace; HD Thompson, RG Deans, EE Booth;
JW Stead, J Hunter; F Roberts; ST Casey, F Newton, D Gallaher
(captain), FT Glasgow, A McDonald, GW Nicholson, JJ O'Sullivan,
CE Seeling
Scorers – Tries: Thompson and Nicholson; Conversions: Wallace (2)

Referee: Gil Evans (Birmingham)
Attendance: 40,000

Match 2: 28 November 1924
Cardiff 8 All Blacks 16

Cardiff: TH Wallace; TA Johnson (captain), RA Cornish, J Powell,
P Rayer; DE Davies, WJ Delahay; I Richards, F Stephens,
S Hinam, W Ireson, TW Lewis, J Brown, C O'Leary, WJ Ould
Scorers – Try: Delahay; Conversion: Wallace; Penalty goal: Wallace

All Blacks: G Nepia; KS Svenson, HW Brown, FW Lucas;
MF Nicholls, AE Cooke; J Mill, CG Porter (captain); Q Donald,
WR Irvine, MJ Brownlie, RR Masters, J Richardson, AJ White,
JH Parker
Scorers – Tries: Lucas, White and Porter; Conversions: Nicholls (2);
Penalty goal: Nicholls

Referee: Capt AS Burge (Penarth)
Attendance: 40,000

Match 3: 26 October 1935
Cardiff 5 All Blacks 20

Cardiff: T Stone (capt); AH Jones, HO Edwards, RW Boon,
A Bassett; HM Bowcott, JE Bowcott; VR Osmond, J Regan,
JR Bale, HT Rees, LM Spence, EN Rees, EV Watkins, G Williams
Scorers – Try: Osmond; Conversion: Boon

All Blacks: G Gilbert; NA Mitchell, CJ Oliver, NJ Ball;
THC Caughey, JL Griffiths; BS Sadler; GD Adkins, WE Hadley,
A Lambourn, RR King, JE Manchester (capt), ST Reid,
HF McLean, A Mahoney
Scorers – Tries: Caughey (2), Mitchell and Reid; Conversions:
Gilbert (2); Dropped goal: Gilbert

Referee: G Goldsworthy (Newport)
Attendance: 35,000

Match 4: 21 November 1953
Cardiff 8 All Blacks 3

Cardiff: JEL Llewellyn; G Rowlands, AG Thomas, BL Williams
(capt), GM Griffiths; CI Morgan, WR Willis; JD Evans,
GT Beckingham, ADS Bowes, E Thomas, ML Collins, JD Nelson,
S Judd, CD Williams
Scorers – Tries: Judd and Rowlands; Conversion: Rowlands

All Blacks: RWH Scott; AEG Elsom, JT Fitzgerald, RA Jarden;
DD Wilson, LS Haig (captain); VD Bevan; HL White, RC Hemi,
KL Skinner, GN Dalzell, RA White, WH Clark, WA McCaw,
DO Oliver
Scorer – Penalty goal: Jarden

Referee: VS Llewellyn (Llansamlet)
Attendance: 56,000

Match 5: 23 November 1963
Cardiff 5 All Blacks 6

Cardiff: AJ Priday; S Hughes, HM Roberts, MCR Richards,
RA Wills; C Ashton, LH Williams; CH Norris, WJ Thomas,
KD Jones, W Graham Davies, KA Rowlands, ER Williams,
C Howe, DJ Hayward (capt)
Scorers – Try: Howe; Conversion : Priday

All Blacks: DB Clarke; MJ Dick, PF Little, RW Caulton; BA Watt,
MA Herewini; CR Laidlaw; WJ Whineray (capt), D Young,
KF Gray, CE Meads, AJ Stewart, DJ Graham, KR Tremain,
WJ Nathan
Scorers – Penalty goal: Clarke; Dropped goal: Herewini

Referee: DM Hughes (Llanelli)
Attendance: 50,000

Match 6: 4 November 1972
Cardiff 4 All Blacks 20

Cardiff: J Davies; JW Lewis, N Williams, AAJ Finlayson, JC Bevan;
KM James, GO Edwards; FMD Knill, W Gary Davies, RJ Beard,
IR Robinson, LD Baxter, R Lane, C Smith, M John (capt)
Scorer – Try: Edwards

All Blacks: JF Karam; BG Williams, BJ Robertson, GB Batty;

M Sayers, RE Burgess; SM Going; JD Matheson (rep: GJ Whiting),
RW Norton, K Murdoch, HH Macdonald, PJ Whiting, AJ Wyllie,
B Holmes, IA Kirkpatrick (capt)
Scorers – Tries: Kirkpatrick, Sayers, Batty; Conversion: Karam;
Penalty goals: Karam (2)

Referee: J Young (Scotland)
Attendance: 45,000

Match 7: 21 October 1978
Cardiff 7 All Blacks 17

Cardiff: P Rees; DW Thomas, MJP Murphy, PCT Daniels,
C Camilleri; W Gareth Davies, TD Holmes; BG Nelmes (capt),
MJ Watkins, FMD Knill, RL Norster, H de Goede,
RDL Dudley-Jones, JP Scott, C Smith
Scorers – Try: Smith; Dropped goal: Davies

All Blacks: CJ Currie; BG Williams, WM Osborne, SS Wilson;
JL Jaffray, EJ Dunn; DS Loveridge; BR Johnstone, AG Dalton,
GA Knight, AM Haden, FJ Oliver, LM Rutledge, GA Seear,
GNK Mourie (capt)
Scorers – Tries – Wilson (2) and Osborne; Conversion: Currie;
Penalty goal: Currie

Referee: RC Quittenton (England)
Attendance: 43,000

Match 8: 8 October 1980
Cardiff 9 All Blacks 16

Cardiff: G Davies; D Preece, DH Burcher, RN Hutchings,
PCT Daniels; W Gareth Davies, TD Holmes; J Whitefoot,
MJ Watkins, IH Eidman, A Mogridge, RL Norster (rep: P Souto),
OM Golding, JP Scott (capt), JR Lewis
Scorer – Penalty goal: WG Davies; Dropped goals: WG Davies (2)

All Blacks: BW Codlin; FA Woodman, BJ Robertson, BG Fraser; WM Osborne, NH Allen; DS Loveridge; JC Ashworth, AG Dalton, GA Knight, AM Haden, G Higginson, MW Shaw, MG Mexted, GNK Mourie (capt)
Scorers – Tries: Fraser and Woodman; Conversion: Codlin; Penalty goal: Codlin; Dropped goal: Allen

Referee: F Palmade (France)
Attendance: 33,000

Match 9: 14 October 1989
Cardiff 15 All Blacks 25

Cardiff: MA Rayer; C Thomas, MG Ring, GW John, SP Ford; DW Evans, AH Booth; J Whitefoot, IJ Watkins, D Young, MA Rowley, HE Stone, T Crothers (capt), MW Edwards, RG Collins
Scorers – Try: Edwards; Conversion: Rayer; Penalty goals: Evans (2) and Rayer

All Blacks: MJ Ridge; JJ Kirwan, CF Innes, TJ Wright; NJ Schuster, GJ Fox; GTM Bachop; RO Williams, SBT Fitzpatrick, RW Loe, MJ Pierce, ID Jones, AJ Whetton, WT Shelford (capt), MR Brewer
Scorers – Tries: Loe, Whetton and Brewer; Conversions: Fox (2); Penalty goals: Fox (3)

Referee: RJ Megson (Scotland)
Attendance: 28,000

Cardiff v South Africa

Match 1: 1 January 1907
Cardiff 17 Springboks 0

Cardiff: HB Winfield; JL Williams, EG Nicholls, RT Gabe, CF Biggs; RA Gibbs *[rover]*; PF Bush (capt), RJ David; W Neill, G Northmore, JA Brown, JA Powell, AB Brice, JP Casey, F Smith

Scorers – Tries: Nicholls, Gibbs, Williams, Gabe; Conversion: Winfield; Penalty goal: Winfield

Springboks: AFW Marsberg; JA Loubser, HA de Villiers, JG Hirsch, AC Stegmann; DC Jackson, FJ Dobbin; JWE Raaff, DS Mare, DFT Morkel, PA le Roux, HJ Daneel, DJ Brink, PJ Roos (capt), WA Millar

Referee: Gil Evans (Birmingham)
Attendance: 28,000

Match 2: 21 December 1912
Cardiff 6 Springboks 7

Cardiff: RF Williams; W Bowen, WJ Spiller (capt), T Evans, WT Gransmore; J Rogers, JMC Lewis; WJ Jenkins, JS Michael, J Birch, F Gaccon, A Baker, A Green, E Mithan, C Palmer
Scorers – Try: Spiller; Penalty goal: Rogers

Springboks: PG Morkel; JA Stegmann, RR Luyt, JWH Morkel, EE McHardy; FP Luyt, JH Immelman; DFT Morkel, TF van Vuuren, GW Thompson, JD Luyt, AS Knight, JS Braine, JAJ Francis, WA Millar (capt)
Scorers – Penalty goal: DFT Morkel; Dropped goal: JWH Morkel

Referee: J H Miles (Leicester)
Attendance: 20,000

Match 3: 21 November 1931
Cardiff 5 Springboks 13

Cardiff: T Stone; RW Boon, GG Jones, BR Turnbull, J Roberts; HM Bowcott (capt), MJ Turnbull; TW Lewis, DJ Tarr, RJ Barrell, T Gadd, VR Osmond, A Skym, C Ross, I Isaac
Scorers – Try: Boon; Conversion: Stone

Springboks: GH Brand; DO Williams, BG Gray,
JC van der Westhuizen, M Zimmerman; BL Osler (capt),
P du P de Villiers; MM Louw, PJ Mostert, SR du Toit,
AJ van der Merwe, WF Bergh, V Geere, JN Bierman,
JAJ McDonald
Scorers – Tries: Zimmerman, Gray and McDonald; Conversions:
Brand (2)

Referee: WH Harries (Risca)
Attendance: 34,000

Match 4: 20 October 1951
Cardiff 9 Springboks 11

Cardiff: RF Trott; AG Thomas, J Matthews (capt), BL Williams,
HT Morris; CI Morgan, WR Willis; C Davies, GT Beckingham,
A Hull, WE Tamplin, ML Collins, S Judd, DJ O'Brien, CD Williams
Scorers – Try: BL Williams; Penalty goals: Tamplin (2)

Springboks: JU Buchler; MJ Saunders, MT Lategan,
RAM van Schoor, JK Ochse; JD Brewis, JSA Oelofse; HPJ Bekker,
PW Wessels, AC Koch, WHM Barnard, EE Dinkelmann, SP Fry,
HSV Muller (capt), CJ van Wyk
Scorers – Tries: Ochse (2) and Oelofse; Conversion: Buchler

Referee: DC Joynson (Caerleon)
Attendance: 53,000

Match 5: 29 October 29 1960
Cardiff 0 Springboks 13

Cardiff: AJ Priday; R Glastonbury, CAH Davies, HM Roberts,
GT Wells; TJ McCarthy, LH Williams (capt); CT Howe,
WJ Thomas, KD Jones, DJE Harris, W Graham Davies,
ER Williams, CH Norris, DJ Hayward

Springboks: LG Wilson; MJG Antelme, JL Gainsford,
AI Kirkpatrick, F du T Roux; CF Nimb, RJ Lockyear; SP Kuhn,
GF Malan, PS du Toit, JT Claassen, AS Malan (capt), GH van Zyl,
DJ Hopwood, HJM Pelser
Scorers – Tries: Pelser and one penalty try; Conversions: Lockyear
(2); Penalty goal: Lockyear

Referee: DG Walters (Gowerton)
Attendance: 50,000

Match 6: 13 December 1969
Cardiff 3 Springboks 17

Cardiff: D Gethin; SJ Watkins (rep: PL Jones), AD Williams,
DK Jones, AAJ Finlayson; B Davies, GO Edwards; CH Norris,
W Gary Davies, JP O'Shea (capt), LD Baxter, IR Robinson,
J Hickey, JHH James, M John
Scorer – Penalty goal: Gethin

Springboks: OA Roux; SH Nomis, E Olivier, JP van der Merwe,
AE van der Watt; MJ Lawless, DJ de Villiers (capt); JFK Marais,
DC Walton, JL Myburgh, IJ de Klerk, AE de Wet, AJ Bates,
TP Bedford, PJF Greyling
Scorers – Tries: Nomis, van der Merwe and Roux; Conversion:
de Villiers; Penalty goal: Lawless; Dropped goal: Lawless

Referee: Air Commodore GC Lamb (England)
Attendance: 28,000

Match 7: 22 October 1994
Cardiff 6 Springboks 11

Cardiff: C John; SP Ford, MR Hall (capt), C Laity, NK Walker;
A Davies, AP Moore (temp rep: AH Booth); M Griffiths,
JM Humphreys, LC Mustoe, WS Roy, D Jones, HT Taylor,
EW Lewis, OL Williams

Scorers – Penalty goals: Davies and John

Springboks: AJ Joubert; CM Williams, BVenter, PG Muller,
C Badenhorst; JT Stransky, JH van der Westhuizen; IS Swart,
UL Schmidt, SJ Hattingh, MG Andrews, H Hattingh, RJ Kruger,
RAW Straeuli (capt), GH Teichmann
Scorers – Try: van der Westhuizen; Penalty goals: Stransky (2)

Referee: JM Fleming (Scotland)
Attendance: 14,329

Cardiff v Australia

Match 1: 28 December 1908
Cardiff 24 Wallabies 8

Cardiff: RF Williams; RA Gibbs, WJ Spiller, LM Dyke, JL Williams;
PF Bush (capt), WL Morgan; J Daley, JA Brown, JA Powell,
JP Casey, D Westacott, F Gaccon, G Yewlett, J Pugsley
Scorers – Tries: JL Williams (2), Morgan, Gibbs, Dyke; Conversion:
Bush; Penalty goal: Bush; Dropped goal: Bush

Wallabies: PP Carmichael; CJ Russell, JJ Hickey, EF Mandilbe,
F Bede Smith; CH McKivat, F Wood; M McArthur, CA Hammand,
JT Barnett, PA McCue, AB Burge, SA Middleton, NE Row,
HM Moran (capt)
Scorers – Tries: Hickey and Moran; Conversion: Carmichael

Referee: Gil Evans (Leeds)
Attendance: 30,000

Match 2: 27 September 1947
Cardiff 11 Wallabies 3

Cardiff: RF Trott; DH Jones, J Matthews, BL Williams,
WLT Williams; WB Cleaver, H Tanner (capt); C Davies, DM James,

WG Jones, R Roberts, WE Tamplin, E Jones, L Manfield, G Evans
Scorers – Tries: DH Jones and Davies; Conversion: Tamplin;
Penalty goal: Tamplin

Wallabies: CJ Windsor; JWT McBride, ML Howell, T Allan,
CC Eastes; NA Emery, RM Cawsey; E Tweedale, WL Dawson,
RE McMaster, GM Cooke, NM Shehadie, CJ Windon, AJ Buchan,
WM McLean (capt)
Scorer – Penalty goal: Allan

Referee: G Goldsworthy (Penarth)
Attendance: 44,000

Match 3: 14 December 1957
Cardiff 14 Wallabies 11

Cardiff: AJ Priday; DG John, GT Wells, AF Barter, HCW Nicholls;
CI Morgan, WR Willis; JD Evans, GT Beckingham, CT Howe,
WR Evans, KD Jones, CD Williams, E Thomas (captain),
DJ Hayward
Scorers – Tries: Wells (2) and John; Conversion: Priday; Penalty
goal: Priday

Wallabies: TGP Curley; OG Fox, JKM Lenehan, JM Potts,
R Phelps; RM Harvey, DM Connor; RAL Davidson (capt),
JV Brown, NM Shehadie, AS Cameron, AR Miller, PT Fenwicke,
NM Hughes, K Yanz
Scorers – Tries: Shehadie and Yanz; Conversion: Harvey; Penalty
goal: Kenehan

Referee: L Griffin (Abertillery)
Attendance: 50,000

Match 4: 5 November 1966
Cardiff 14 Wallabies 8

Cardiff: RFH Cheney; WK Jones, DK Jones, TGR Davies,
MCR Richards; PJ Morgan, WG Hullin; CH Norris, WJ Thomas,
JP O'Shea, KA Rowlands (captain), LD Baxter, J Hickey,
AR Pender, WC Evans
Scorers – Tries: Hullin and DK Jones; Conversion: Cheney; Penalty
goal: Cheney; Dropped goal: Hullin

Wallabies: JKM Lenehan; ES Boyce, JE Brass, PV Smith,
AM Cardy; PF Hawthorne, KW Catchpole (capt); JM Miller,
PG Johnson, AR Miller, CP Crittle, RJ Heming, DA O'Callaghan,
DA Taylor, GV Davis
Scorers – Try: Lenehan; Conversion: Lenehan; Dropped goal:
Hawthorne

Referee: R Lewis (Maesteg)
Attendance: 35,000

Match 5: 1 November 1975
Cardiff 14 Wallabies 9

Cardiff: J Davies; TGR Davies (capt), P Evans, AAJ Finlayson,
PL Jones; W Gareth Davies, DB Williams; BG Nelmes, AJ Phillips,
FMD Knill, IR Robinson, M McJennett, T Worgan, R Lane,
SM Lane (rep: RDL Dudley-Jones)
Scorers – Tries: PL Jones and WG Davies; Penalty goals:
WG Davies (2)

Wallabies: PE McLean; PG Batch, LJ Weatherstone, GA Shaw,
LE Monaghan; KJ Wright, JNB Hipwell (capt); SC Finnane,
PA Horton, SG MacDougall, GS Eisenhauer (rep: DW Hillhouse),
RA Smith, AA Shaw, JK Lambie, RA Price
Scorer – Penalty goals: McLean (3)

Referee: JR West (Ireland)
Attendance: 30,000

Match 6: 24 October 1984
Cardiff 16 Wallabies 12

Cardiff: P Rees; M Carrington, MG Ring, AJ Donovan, AM Hadley;
W Gareth Davies, SN Cannon; J Whitefoot, AJ Phillips (capt),
IH Eidman, K Edwards, RL Norster, OM Golding, JP Scott,
GJ Roberts (rep: R Lakin)
Scorers – Tries: Hadley and one penalty try; Conversion: Davies;
Penalty goal: Davies; Dropped goal: Davies

Wallabies: JW Black; RG Hanley, AG Slack (capt), TA Lane (rep:
MP Lynagh), BJ Moon; MG Ella, PA Cox; EE Rodriguez,
TA Lawton, AJ McIntyre, SAG Cutler, SA Williams, WJ Calcraft,
SN Tuynman, SP Poidevin
Scorers – Tries: Black and Slack; Conversions: Black (2)

Referee: DN Templeton (Ireland)
Attendance: 20,000

Summary of Results against Other International Touring Teams

28 December 1888: NZ Maoris: W 8-3
29 March 1919: NZ Army: D 0-0
6 November 1926: NZ Maoris: L 8-18
28 December 1926: NZ Maoris: L 3-5
3 December 1927: NSW Waratahs: L 9-16
15 September 1945: Australian Air Force: W 28-3
3 November 1945: NZ Services: W 14-3
26 December 1945: NZ Kiwis: L 0-3
22 September 1951: British Isles: L 12-14
7 September 1955: Romania: W 6-3
5 May 1956: NZ Navy: W 40-10
1 September 1956: Germany: W 25-0
3 October 1956: Italy: W 8-3
3 September 1966: West Germany: W 41-3
2 October 1976: Argentina: L 25-29

30 October 1976: Italy: W 54-22
19 September 1979: Canada: W19-8
23 October 1982: NZ Maoris: L 10-17
12 October 1985: Fiji: W 31-15
28 October 1995: Fiji: W 22-21
26 November 1996: Western Samoa: L 29-53

Designated 'International Touring Teams' excludes New South Wales in 1997 and Rugby Canada in the 1998 WRU Challenge Trophy match

On tours overseas Cardiff beat Rhodesia 24-6 on 27 May 1972, Zimbabwe 34-17 on 6 June 1981 and Zimbabwe again by 35-23 on 13 June 1981

Subscribers

*Names of supporters who placed an advance order for this book
with Cardiff Rugby Supporters Club*

Alan Barnett
Noel Bater
Brian Bennett
Margaret Billing
Craig Bishop
Graham Bishop
Joan Brewer
Gareth G Brown
Jonathan Brown
Jill Burgess
Cardiff Athletic Club
Trish & Neil Collingwood
Ian Cox
Ieuan Christopher
Howard Cross
Martin R Davies
Simon Down
Andrew Emery
Alf & Rita Evans
Carole Evans
Paul Roger Evans
David George
Alan Gilbert
Peter Goodfellow
Rhys Goodfellow
William TT Griffiths
Douglas Hall
Daphne Harrison
Edward CC Harry
Gareth Hart
David Hellyar
Mervyn J Henderson
Brian Isaacs

Ceri James
Rhys James
Ernest V Jones
Kenneth Arthur Jones
Wynford Jones
BR Kelly
Jeffrey Kirby
Benjamin Thomas Lafford
Cliff Lewis
John Loaring
Marian & Ray Lowe
John & Marion Manfield
Mr Nicholas James Moore
C Murphy
Peter Nash
Gareth Oram
Ken Osment
Jill & Stephen Parker
Roy Bapp Pearce
Gwyn Pritchard
Neville Rees
Jeremiah Regan
Mr Brian John Robins
Carl & Ruth Rogers
Mr Miles Sainsbury
Raymond Simmonds
Michael Stephenson
Ken FG Thomas
Anne Waddicor
Anthony Westlake
David Williams
Eric Williams
Vaughan Williams

Other Publications by...

No Pain, No Gain; the Kevin Ward Story
Authors: Dave Sampson and Kevin Ward
ISBN: 1-904091-08-3
Price: £10.99. Softback
The biography of one of the all time greats of rugby league. A
Castleford, Manly and St Helens legend who's career was cruelly
ended by a horrific on-the-field injury.

Fast Lane to Shangri-La; The Story of a Rugby League Family
Author: Dave Sampson
ISBN: 1-904091-00-8
Price: £9.99. Softback
Dave Sampson's autobiography captures the essence of rugby league
and mixes it with a good dose of northern humour.

Dean Sampson; My Shangri-La
Authors: Dave Sampson and Dean Sampson
ISBN: 1-904091-04-0
Price: £10.99. Softback
Dean's story of growing up amongst other stars of rugby league in
the Sampson household and of his high profile and often
controversial playing career with Castleford Tigers, England and
Great Britain.

Just Champion!
Yorkshire's 33-Year Fight for their Cricketing Birthright
Author: David Bond
ISBN: 1-904091-03-2
Price: 14.99. Hardback
David Bond tells the story of the internal power struggle and
internecine warfare as Yorkshire County Cricket Club battled to
regain the County Championship.

...Vertical Editions

Salford City Reds; A Willows Century
Author: Graham Morris
ISBN: 1-904091-02-4
Price: £18.99. Hardback, large format
Author Graham Morris has compiled the definitive illustrated
history of Salford City Reds and their famous stadium. A critically
acclaimed publication.

Who Let the Dogs Out; The Revival of Newport Rugby
Author: Steve Lewis
ISBN: 1-904091-01-6
Price: £15.99. Hardback
Steve Lewis tells the story of how Newport Rugby fought back from
the brink of obscurity to win the Principality Cup in 2001 and just
miss out on the league title in 2002.

COMING SPRING 2004

Glory of their Times,
Crossing the Colour Line in Rugby League
Editors: Tony Collins and Phil Melling
ISBN: 1-904091-07-5
Price: £15.99. Hardback
Rugby league is one sport in Britain that has never adopted a colour
bar and actively welcomed coloured players into its ranks. Glory of
their Times tells that story, not only through its icons but a whole
range of players – indigenous and immigrant – and journalists, fans,
historians and academics.

Vertical Editions